A Territorial Army Chaplain in Peace and War

Canon J.E. GETHYN-JONES

M.B.E. T.D. M.A. F.S.A.

A Country Cleric in Khaki

1938–1961

Gooday Publishers

First Published in 1988 by Gooday Publishers
P.O. Box 60, East Wittering, West Sussex PO20 8RA

The author, at his own request, has decided not to receive royalties for this work.

British Library Cataloguing in Publication Data

Gethyn-Jones, Eric, *1909*
A Territorial Army chaplain during peace and war : a country cleric in khaki, 1938–1961
1. Great Britain. Army. Territorial Army, chaplains. Gethyn-Jones, Eric, 1909–
I. Title
355.3'47'0924

ISBN 1-870568-20-6

Typeset in Times by Woodfield Graphics, Fontwell, West Sussex.
Printed in Great Britain by Hollen Street Press, Slough, Berks.

Contents

Acknowledgements

The author wishes gratefully to acknowledge assistance and permission to use items from the following: Bodleian Library, Gloucester Citizen and Journal, Dursley Gazette, Cheltenham Newsletter, Shooting Times, Illustrated London News, Picture Library, Picture Post, D.J. Gethyn-Jones, Gloucestershire Regimental Museum, 43rd Recce Regt., H.M. Bateman, Salisbury Journal, R.A.Ch.D. (Bagshot), The Keystone Collection, The Ven. I.D. Neill.

Foreword

by The Very Reverend I.D. Neill CB, OBE, MA
(onetime Chaplain General)

In writing these memoirs, Canon Eric Gethyn-Jones has captured something of the quality of Gloucestershire life prior to the Second World War. The country folk who were his parishoners and friends accompany him down the laneways of memory, sometimes in sport and high spirits, sometimes in the deeper fellowship of suffering. He identifies himself with officers and wartime soldiers alike; he shares the weight of Army discipline on civilian shoulders; he cares for them whoever they are with such a care as sometimes himself to face censure and misunderstanding.

More than half the regiment he chaplained were to face death in a burnt and sinking ship, and he was the one to go back to that sinking part of the ship, regardless of the extreme danger, to rescue more than one. For this he received the award M.B.E. because, the regiment not having yet joined the battle, he was not eligible for the gallantry award of high degree for which he was admittedly deserving. Thus what he did was recognised by an 'Order' trimmed to the equivalent rank he then carried.

We met in 1943 when, as newly joined senior chaplain of the 43rd Wessex Division, I found in him a lasting friend and gallant companion. I owed him much for his friendship, wisdom and loyalty when I became S.C.F. to a number of excellent but not very happy chaplains.

Canon Gethyn-Jones was then essentially a Unit Padré whose love for his men was no love born of duty. He knew the heartbreak of bereavement when so many were lost off the coast of Normandy, and he went wild with distress when, later in the battle, they had to assume an infantry rôle for which they were not trained, and suffer the consequent casualties. Infantry officers could not agree with him that his men were superior to infanteers and were being squandered as foot-soldiers! Yet all the staff respected and loved him in his fearless and generous impetuousity.

To take up these memoirs will not be easy to put them down again; for here grandeur is found in ordinary country folk who prove not so ordinary after all, and the Church is found caring for its sons in complete unselfishness, and without thought of dignity or safety.

Dedication

In 1949, General Sir Ivor Thomas, wartime commander of the 43rd (Wessex) Division, wrote of the 5th Glosters/43rd Recce Regiment in the Introduction of 'A History of the 43rd Reconnaissance Regiment (The Gloucester Regiment):'

> Only a regiment trained to the high pitch, and with magnificent ésprit-de-corps of the old 5th Glosters, could have taken advantage of the organisation and done what this story tells. The tragedy off the Normandy beaches is an incident I shall personally never forget. It would have broken any ordinary unit; it acted as a spur to them. I am grateful for this opportunity to pay my tribute to the 43rd Recce Regiment who never demurred at any task, and who were always brilliantly successful.

These men had inherited a regimental tradition of Service, Courage, Resolution and Sacrifice, and upheld it to the full. And, like F.W. Harvey, the Gloucestershire poet-soldier of the 1914-1918 conflict, I feel:

> Lucky to live, lucky again
> To have met and marched
> With the finest men...
> Earth ever bred

To those men of the 5th Battalion The Gloucestershire Regiment, later the 43rd Reconnaissance Regiment (The Gloucestershire Regiment), with whom I had the great privilege to serve, I dedicate these memoirs.

Preface

This project was suggested to me in 1956 when I became D.A.C.G. (TA) Southern Command, and the bulk of the work, very much in the rough, was written before the end of 1959. Suddenly, parochial affairs, and the establishment of the Roman status of ancient Dymock, caused it to be laid aside. My appointment as Rural Dean of the large deanery of the North Forest in 1960 effectively 'buried' the exercise. Now, in the eventide of my ministry, it has been hinted by members of the Regiment that it is time to complete the task begun so long ago.

This is in no sense an attempt to write a Regimental history, although much that is recorded took place within the 'family' of one unit.

Neither is it intended that it shall be a complete catalogue of events that took place during the service of a single individual.

It is instead a setting down of incidents, minor as well as major, which made a deep impression upon the mind and memory. These are told chronologically and so, in a sense, they record the life of a T.A. chaplain in the days of peace and in times less pleasant.

The first concern of an Army Chaplain, as of any minister or priest, must be the well-being, spiritual and physical, of the men or women under his care.

The church services (with the possible exception of the Sacrament of the Holy Communion), padré's hours, confirmation classes, and what may be termed the 'clerical routine,' important though they may be, I conceive to be less vital than the task of getting to know your men, giving them the opportunity to get to know you and, if possible, building up with them a feeling of trust and confidence. The method of approach to this daunting task naturally varied with the individual cleric. Personally, I believed that 'identification' of oneself constituted the first faltering steps along that road. All this may sound high-falutin', sanctimonious piety and cant of the first order. I am certain, however, that this is the ideal; an ideal which none of us who were chaplains, I believe, fully attained. If, however, even a modicum of understanding, or a measure of acceptance of the chaplain, was achieved, then the beginnings of true pastoral work were possible.

This getting to know, and to be known, involved weeks, indeed months, of patient and methodical 'work' of a type which was far from easy, and often downright difficult. One had to be with them on route marches, at their games and in the canteen, and generally to be around and accessible. One had to be amongst them, almost of them, but one was not expected to be like them. This attempt at friendliness, almost identification, was a difficult, indeed terrifying, tightrope along which to walk; one slip could, and often did, ruin any hope of useful work within the unit for weeks, perhaps for ever.

This building up of confidence, trust, or call it what you will was, for a T.A. chaplain during peacetime, a long process due to the infrequency of contact, though the situation changed. One lived with the unit and identification was possible and quicker.

It was only when this process had begun to mature that the chaplain's really useful work could be done. It was then, and usually only then, that the men (the word 'men' is used here and throughout as embracing all ranks) would open up and discuss their problems, fears and difficulties. When that point had been reached the chaplain was indeed lucky and he could begin to feel that at last, perhaps at long last, he might be able to fulfil in some measure his real task, and to exercise the ministry for which he had been ordained and commissioned.

The most frightening aspect of work as a minister or priest, whether in a parish or the Army, was the feeling that *I am in a manner God's agent of Eternal Life*. I have always been horribly aware of that declaration which must surely be constantly in the minds of all who minister God's word and sacraments that *Their blood (Spiritual Life or Life Eternal) will I require at thine hands*, in other words, I hold you responsible for their salvation.

In the memoirs which follow, the constant daily routine of services, prayers, interviews, visits to cook-houses, company areas and so on, are rarely mentioned. To do more would be to produce a boring daily diary of interest to nobody and at times might constitute a violation of the confessional. It must however be remembered that they were all there, taking place every day, and formed the very foundation of the chaplain's work and daily life; a life which could only be maintained and made useful by his own personal programme of prayer, reading and personal devotion. And how difficult, how desperately difficult, at times well nigh impossible, it was on active service to fit in those times of withdrawal (often only metaphorical withdrawal) for a vital spiritual recharging without which it would frequently have been impossible to carry on. All chaplains, at least all I have ever met and with whom I have discussed this problem, were aware that through lack of this recharging we have at times failed (some of us have felt that we have failed lamentably) to give out because we had not struggled hard enough to take in.

All this must be borne in mind.

None of this must be lost sight of as the pages are read. Day by day, often night by night, the basic work of the chaplain went on yet, because of its very repetitiveness, it is rarely recorded.

J E Gethyn-Jones
Dymock Rectory, Gloucs. 1937–1967
The Chantry, Berkeley, Gloucs. 1967–1976
Canonbury House, Berkeley, Gloucs. 1976–present.

CHAPTER ONE

The Early Days

I come from a family with a strong clerical bias, having a grandfather, father, two uncles and four cousins in the priesthood.

In my teens, a conflict of conscience developed. It was generally assumed that I would follow the family tradition and enter the ministry. I, however, secretly wished for an army career. This, no doubt, was partly due to the glowing accounts of life in the Services which I had heard from regular members of His Majesty's Forces. The opportunity to travel, the importance placed on sport and the carefree life, and the cameraderie were obviously the main attractions. Mother, a parson's daughter, was my confidante, and in our discussions she made it quite clear that if, after very careful thought and prayer, I decided in favour of the Services, she would be quite happy. Not so my father!

The mental struggle, which for a time was considerable, finally ended in a victory for the Church, and I was ordained in 1934 and went as a curate to St Catherine's Parish in Gloucester.

The vicar, Canon H J Hensman, was an ex-chaplain who gave me adequate opportunity to continue my games. He was Chairman of the Gloucester Rugby-Football Club, and through his influence the Committee willingly extended me facilities at Kingsholm; an advantage which no doubt helped materially in the winning of international recognition in the hockey world.

The district of this large parish allotted to me for visiting had, close to its eastern boundary the Battalion Headquarters of the 5th Battalion of the Goucestershire Regiment, and I found that many of the parishioners were members of the HQ Company.

For several years I had disliked the trend of international affairs, and by 1935 had become convinced that war lay in the foreseeable future.

Late in the latter year, Canon G F Helm, the vicar of Berkeley and D.A.C.G. (T.A.) Southern Command, suggested the possibility of a chaplaincy in the Territorial Army, and hinted that a vacancy might occur at any moment. I welcomed the idea, provided that the attachment could be to a local unit. I would naturally be expected, as one of the youngest diocesan clergy, to volunteer for active service if war should come. Commonsense dictated that it would be far more sensible to be mobilised with men one knew, and with whom one had worked, than be posted (unfamiliar with Army routine) to a unit of complete strangers. Perhaps too, there was an almost unconscious revival of the earlier desire for an Army career: an attempt, maybe, to satisfy both conscience and ambition? Who knows! I honestly was not aware of this aspect at the time, but in retrospect is seems possible that the alacrity of my acceptance of the invitation could have been prompted by the earlier sublimated longing.

Alas! There were two difficulties: firstly, the anticipated vacancy did not materialise and secondly, I had not reached the minimum age (28) required for a commission in the R.A.Ch.D..

In 1938, by which time I had moved to Dymock, both conditions had been satisfied. The vacancy (with the 5th Battalion The Gloucestershire Regiment) was ideal, since many of my recent parishioners were members of the Battalion. Canon Helm had been Chaplain to the 5th from 1911 to 1915, and was high in his praise of the Unit. Incidentally, he assured my father (who was a great friend of his) at a diocesan conference, that there was no need to fear for my safety. "For" said the Canon, "war will never come in our time".

I had already been interviewed some months earlier by the A.G.C. of Southern Command. The next step was a call on the Commanding Officer of the Unit. The latter interrogation (it was no less!) had its humourous side: on being ushered into the 'presence' (and only those who have experienced the rigid pre-1939 oligarchal regimental system can appreciate fully this ordeal), I found the august gentlemen, Lt. Col. G.A.H. Buxton and Captain F.W. Priestly, momentarily hesitant and uncertain of themselves. Rapidly recovering their composure and determined to put me off they commenced a verbal assault. Perhaps they had a candidate of their own behind the scenes?

"We understood", they said, "that you had served in the War, but it is obvious that you are too young to have done so."

It was clearly a case of mistaken identity. They had, in their talk with Canon Helm, confused my father with myself. The adjutant continued:

"Do you realise that if you're commissioned you might be called up and even, perhaps, sent overseas?"

They pointed out that war could be dangerous at times, and asked whether I had faced up to the possibility of being killed. On being assured that these points had indeed been considered they agreed (reluctantly, it seemed) to accept me as their chaplain.

The Bishop of Gloucester, Dr A.C. Headlam, sanctioned my application for a commission, but persistently avoided using the precise phraseology required by the War Office, who demanded his written declaration that in the event of an emergency I, as with all T.A. chaplains, could be mobilised and sent abroad.

"I give my permission for Mr Gethyn-Jones to join the Territorial Army as a chaplain, and agree to the conditions laid down" and "I appreciate the obligations of service, and have already granted permission for Mr Gethyn-Jones to join the Territorial Army" were two of his replies. But it was not until a typed form of consent was sent to the Bishop for his signature that a commission was forthcoming. The Bishop, a much travelled prelate, had been attending conferences in Greece and Norway during this interchange of letters, and so it was November 23rd 1938 before the commission was granted.

How much more exacting in 1938 were the duties required of a T.A. chaplain from those expected in the post-war years! The Adjutant was explicit: one Drill Hall visit per week would be the very minimum, but it was hoped that more frequent attendances might be possible. The full period of the annual camp would, of course, be considered obligatory. On drill nights, one met the men during their free time, listened in to the lectures and watched the drills. When all this was over, the chaplain could (and often did) take evening prayers, and during the subsequent recreational period or in the canteen, pastoral work was sometimes possible.

Early in 1939, a Chaplains' Conference was held at Salisbury. We were addressed (inter alios) by General Wavell. This great man, small of stature, whose unblinking, hawklike, piercing single eye bored through to one's very heart and mind, possessed a dynamic personality:

he was the principle lecturer, and took as his subject for the first period, Allenby's campaign in Palestine. What a graphic and gripping tale he told! All through the narrative ran a parallel account of the biblical history brought to mind as that army had swept through the Land of Israel. The accounts of those Old and New Testament events, Wavell had studied afresh on the ground in the Greek text, as the army had campaigned through the Holy Land. The General was indeed an able scholar as well as an outstanding military leader. At the end of the first lecture, an eminent chaplain said, as the General left the room:

"There goes one of the greatest Christians in the British Army!" One felt that was no idle statement.

In the afternoon, Wavell talked of the work of the chaplain in War. We realised that here was a firm reminder that we as chaplains must prepare ourselves for the grim ordeal of battle. The General repeatedly stressed the fact that much would be expected of us. He pointed out that a chaplain whose foundations were solid was of inestimable value both to individual and unit, but that one who was found wanting as a man of God was depriving the men of their right to spiritual strength, support and guidance. It was a clear directive to remember our Lord's warning that *to whom much has been committed; of that person much would be required.* I have on many occasions heard bishops and inferior clergy speak on this subject at theological lectures, diocesan synods and chaplains' conferences, but never have I experienced so great an impact and such manifest sincerity. Perhaps after all it was natural, for here was one who had passed through the fiery trial, and whose shrewd perception had probed the strength and weakness in many a chaplain. It was a humbling and salutary experience.

The 5th Glosters, with their newly formed 2nd line Battalion (7th), went to their annual camp at Windmill Hill near Luggeshall, on August 9th. Memories of that first camp under canvas remain vivid even today. I drove down in pouring rain from Dymock after Evensong, and found the task of moving into a bleak bell tent a little depressing; it was an unkind baptism!

The following day, initiation began. The Reverend Ben Isaac, the other Church of England chaplain in the 144 Brigade, and a most experienced padré, had invited me to his Kidderminster vicarage in early July to discuss the coming camp, and to check my kit and general preparations. Now on that Monday morning, he took me in hand.

The NAAFI was visited, and permission granted for prayers to be taken nightly, and a popular sing-song and service on the Sunday evening. A tour of the whole battalion area was made, all cook-houses, Company offices and Quartermaster's stores were visited. Ben Isaac pointed out, quite rightly, that the men of the administrative and catering staff and those employed on routine maintenance duties had not the same excitement and thrills of Camp that the main body experienced, so should receive special attention. The Brigade Field Ambulance was located and booked as a daily obligation.

Later that week came the Battalion's first experience of gas. Each man passed through a tent filled with tear-gas, first without a respirator, and then (after the eyes had ceased to run and smart) with his mask fitted. During the remainder of the camp there were regular respirator drills.

On the middle Sunday, Drum-Head Parade Services were arranged for all three Battalions (5th Glosters and 7th & 8th Worcesters), each with their second line units. Canon Helm came on Saturday and stayed over until the following day when he, as their ex-chaplain, took the Glosters' service. I was detailed to take that of the 8th Worcesters. It is a fearsome ordeal, facing for the first time some 1100 men formed up in a hollow square in the open; and mainly strangers at that!

Later in the morning, buses brought families and friends down from the home areas, and sports and a general get-together followed. Battalion and Brigade exercises took place during the second week when, fortunately, the weather was fine; but one incident will forever remain in my memory.

A night exercise was in progress, and at about midnight I arrived at Battalion H.Q. to find the C.O. and the 2.I.C. studying new Brigade orders. Almost at once, the C.O. called for his runner and handed him a message for one of the Companies, adding as the lad turned to go: "report back to me here." Half an hour later, Battalion H.Q. moved 500 yards to a new location. At 2.30 a.m. the exercise ended, and the entire unit returned to Camp a mile distant; all, that is, except the C.O.'s runner. The roll-call was made a second time, the camp searched, and a party sent back to the last exercise location, but there was still no trace of the missing private. At 4.30, in desperation and knowing the lad to be one who took things very literally, I suggested to the Colonel that we might try the area where he had given the runner the midnight message. It was a shot in the dark, but it came off: the runner was found curled up asleep under the trees where the C.O. had issued the order "report back to me here!"— the runner had done just that!

A cavalry unit (the Queen's Bays, I believe) were encamped less than a mile away. What a fine sight it was to see the mounted squadrons moving out in column in the early morn! Shortly afterwards, the unit was mechanised. This, I fully realise, was necessary; but oh, how very much less attractive! War had become, for the soldier at least, a grim impersonal conflict increasingly dominated by robotry and other Machiavellian inventions of the scientists.

One of the frequent topics of conversation towards the end of the camp was "how long will it be before we're back in khaki?" or "will general mobilisation come before Camp ends?" In fact, only the rear party, who stayed behind to strike camp, received their call-up papers while still on Windmill Hill.

I found, on returning to Dymock, that the County Civil Defence authorities were rapidly speeding up their organisations, and that parties of volunteers from outlying hamlets, villages and market towns were going into Gloucester nightly to assemble respirators for young and old. In Dymock, between twenty and thirty men, women and children met on Wintour's Green at about seven in the evening, and then drove into the city, where certain factories and warehouses had been placed at the disposal of the civil defence officials. These nightly sessions lasted from two-and-a-half to three hours and, it appeared, were enjoyed by the majority of the helpers. The number and composition of the parties varied, of course, from night to night, but there was a solid core of "regulars" who quickly became the group leaders and assistants to the qualified instructors.

And all the time, War became more imminent...

CHAPTER TWO

War

German troops crossed the Polish border during the early hours of September 1st, and most people must have felt that the rising sun had swept aside not only the September mists but also the last faint hope of peace.

Britain's treaty with the invaded country made general mobilisation inevitable, and the summons to arms went out through the modern medium of radio as well as by the more conventional methods of the telephone, telegraph and letter.

That morning I motored to Gloucester and visited the diocesan authorities before going to Battalion H.Q. to ask for instructions. The latter said my official call-up would be independent of them. They suggested, furthermore, that even if the embodiment notice came before Sunday, I need not in fact join the Battalion until the Monday. They rightly pointed out that they were busy beyond words, and that my time on Sunday would be wasted at the Drill Hall. In addition, there was sleeping accommodation for only a few of the Battalion's officers. This was a welcome reprieve, giving further vital time to complete the handing over of parochial affairs to my father. On leaving the Drill Hall, I drove to Cheltenham to confirm with a retired clergyman, the Revd. W. Turner Long, the tentative arrangements made earlier. He agreed to be ready to take up residence on the Monday. He and his wife were to have my study, the lounge, and the largest of our spare bedrooms, and Mr Turner Long agreed to work under the direction of my father, whose parish, Kempley, marched with Dymock.

The same day, news arrived that large numbers of school-children were being evacuated from London and numerous other major cities, and that Dymock must be ready to billet Lozell's School, Birmingham, immediately.

The Saturday (September 2nd) was spent entirely within the two parishes of Dymock and Kempley, visiting the sick and trying in vain to prepare and legislate for parish life under conditions that, for the moment could only be vaguely conjectured. An emergency session of the Cabinet had been called, and an ultimatum had been sent to Germany. The tension of waiting for the (apparently) inevitable explosion was unpleasant.

At 11.00 p.m. that evening, while talking on the telephone to my father, the operator broke into the conversation and said:

"There is an important telegram for Dymock 70 from Salisbury. Will you take it, please?"

I naturally accepted. The message ran:

> Prepare to join 144 (Gloucs. & Worcs.) Infantry Brigade. Instructions following. Commander Salisbury.

I telephoned the Battalion and was told again that there was no need to report until Monday. I was grateful, feeling that I would be of greater service remaining in the parish over the weekend, rather than 'hanging around' at the Drill Hall in Gloucester.

Who, having lived through them, will ever forget the events of the following morning? In Dymock, Matins began at 11.00 a.m.; the hour at which the British ultimatum was due to expire. My wife, anticipating some special bulletin, remained at home listening to the wireless.

At 11.15, the Prime Minister spoke to the Country—indeed to the world. He announced that no undertaking of any withdrawal of any troops had been received from Germany, and that in consequence, we were now in a state of war with that country.

Soon after 11.20, when I was in the pulpit leading intercessions, my wife entered the church and handed up a slip of paper on which the fateful words were written. It was a grim moment but, in a strange way, there was a sense of relief; for the tension, which had borne heavily on most people, was finally broken.

I reported to Battalion H.Q. on Monday morning and was promptly sent for my 'medical.' This supposedly exacting examination turned out to be a friendly (and farcical!) affair. The M.O. (whom I knew and liked both on and off the tennis courts) said:

"Well Padré, you're looking fit! How has the tennis been going?" Turning aside he ordered, "Smith! Bring another cup of tea and collect the Padré's papers from the Orderly Room."

The events of the last few days were then discussed, the tea was drunk, my papers were filled in, and one more chaplain was passed fit for foreign service without so much as the sight of a stethoscope, spatula or any other tool of the medical trade, let alone the removal of a single garment!

Most officers and other ranks who lived within easy reach of the Company or Battalion H.Q.s were allowed to sleep at home during the short period we remained in Gloucestershire. We aimed to arrive at our unit soon after 8.00 a.m. and tried to be back with our families in time to enjoy a late tea. During the daytime, I visited various Drill Halls, accompanied the men to the ranges and on minor exercises, and generally began to shake down into the strange new life.

It was during this period that I first drove a Bren Gun Carrier. The instructor, a friendly P.S.I., gave me my head at Sneedham's Green; but he grabbed the controls pretty quickly when I ventured onto the road and began to grub up a hedge and went on to flatten a fence!

Major Vigrass (known as 'Old Ben'), the king of the Quartermasters, checked that all the chaplain's G1098 items were in store and ready for use. Ben was a tower of strength and knew all the answers. And well he might, for had he not, at the age of twelve, as son of a Sergeant-Major, gate-crashed into one of the Local Defence volunteer companies that were formed in parts of India when certain units of the Regular Army embarked for the South African War, and left areas denuded of troops? From that time until he finally retired from civilian employ at the Regimental Depot in 1955, Ben lived for the army and latterly, especially for the Gloucestershire Regiment.

Early in the week, the arrangements for the Laying Up of the Battalion Colours in Gloucester Cathedral on September 10th were worked out with the Dean and Chapter. They were kind, and agreed to almost every request, only suggesting modifications when they felt these were absolutely necessary. The service was beautifully taken and sung, and the ceremony of the Laying Up of the Colours was impressive. The Dean, however, in his otherwise excellent address, stressed rather too much the grimness of the future for us and our families. Most mothers, wives and sweethearts wiped an eye that afternoon, while *we* felt that we were bidding farewell forever to Colours, Cathedral and families, and that the only future for us was 'some corner of a foreign field that would be forever England.'

Three days of final stock-taking and packing followed, and at noon on Thursday 14th September, the Mayor, the Sheriff and the Dean of Gloucester came to Drill Hall to bid us 'Farewell and God's Speed' (the Mayor gamely mounted a large packing case to make his speech), and so we left Gloucester for the 48th Divisional concentration area, which for us meant Marlborough.

The road discipline was good, but the map-reading of a certain convoy guide was a trifle uncertain. Coming twice, on the same run, to the same crossroads within half an hour is a little unusual!

Marlborough was a period of settling down and final preparation for a move overseas. The whole Brigade was centred on the town, and units were thus able to get to know each other and build up that esprit-de-corps so essential in a fighting formation.

The Marlborough people were kind, and efforts were made to integrate members of our unit into the local community and church circle. This resulted in many lasting friendships. A large canteen, with reading and rest rooms attached, was set up in the Town Hall, and an enthusiastic team of ladies made this an attractive and popular centre.

Shortly after the canteen was opened, a certain Mr Johnnie Johnstone made his appearance. Mr Johnstone, a veteran of the 1914–18 conflict, had a weak heart and so had been rejected by the recruiting authorities. This 'old war horse,' anxious not to be left out, voluntarily devoted his whole time to the welfare of the Brigade. His stay with us was a record of devoted Christian service which was appreciated by all ranks. The association with the Brigade became very close.

At the canteen, short evening prayers were held nightly, and a somewhat longer service took place on Sunday evenings. These prayers and services were taken by the Brigade Chaplains or by Mr Johnstone. The Roman Catholic Padré of the 8th Worcesters (the Revd. Brian Withers) was most co-operative. He helped in the canteen and took his turn on the prayers roster until his ecclesiastical superiors forbade the practice. In addition, he encouraged unconfirmed Anglicans in his unit to enrol for the confirmation classes that were being held.

Seventeen came forward of whom, to my surprise, nearly half had not been baptized. The local incumbants placed their churches at our disposal, and church life became more normal. Families and friends frequently came on visits at weekends, and this too helped the illusion of normality. The majority of Glosters used the Church of St Peter and St Paul, which was literally on their doorstep, as their parish church. There we held the weekly Parade Services and confirmation classes, and occasionally banns of marriage were read. On the evening before the Confirmation Service, a multiple baptism took place. The candidates included young militia lads and older reservists; over thirty in all.

Two companies of the Glosters were billeted at Manton Stables where Mr J. Lawson had his training establishment. There in the private chapel of the stables, our men and the stable lads knelt side by side and received the Blessed Sacrament, and joined in the singing of their favourite hymns.

Soon after our arrival in Marlborough, changes began to take place within the unit. Those too young or unfit to serve abroad were posted to the 7th and other Battalions, and a large number of reservists (drawn from many Regiments), and a considerable militia draft, joined the unit. Some of these reservists disliked, naturally enough, being posted to a strange Regiment, and on their first night (fortified by various beverages) were very vocal in their protestations and, for some strange reason, selected the Mayor of Marlborough as the principle target of their abuse. Fortunately, this outbreak of ill-temper died with dawn; several new officers, including some recently commissioned, arrived, and the unit began to assume its operational form. The new subalterns were at first not as respectful in Mess to senior officers as tradition required. Both sides, however, moderated their ideas and a *modus vivendi* was soon established.

I wrote to the celebrated cartoonist H.M. Bateman, and he drew an excellent cartoon on this theme for the *Fifth Gloster Gazette*. This periodical had first seen light of day in the trenches during the 1914–18 war. It had been intended in those far off days both as a medium of information and also, through its humour, as a possible agent for the alleviation of boredom, and to help take the minds of its readers away from the grimness, discomfort and realities of the war in the mud and stench of those Flanders fields. The frequency of its appearance had been dictated by the exigencies of the war, and also by the availability of material, both literary and printing-wise. That early editor was fortunate in that he had within the Battalion several able contributors, including such men as F.W. Harvey and Ivor Gurney, who later made their names in literature, especially in the world of poetry.

The first two issues of the revived publication came out in November and December 1939.

F.W. Harvey contributed several short poems, for which we were grateful. These include part of F.W.H.'s '*Rogues Gallery*', published in the first issue of the *Fifth Gloster Gazette* (Nov 1939).

GOEBBELS
Limerick Sequence
or
(Pick up your Goebbels)

'Magna est veritas,' Goebbels!
But that's not the end of your troubles.
A liar should be
An artist, you see -
Not a blower of venomous bubbles.

Such bubbles are pricked and soon broken
So hold you thereby for a token:
Propaganda must fail
when the lies one can nail
Which were very much better unspoken!

HITLER
Objection sustained?
(all in favour hiss assent!)

I'm told (and I devoutly hope it's true)
They're killing off the reptiles at the Zoo,
In case a German bomb should let 'em loose,
(I never thought the beggars any use!)
'But wait a minute!'
One wise old viper hisses, 'What's the fuss?
You ought to stifle Hitler (gasp) 'not us!'
(dies)
And maybe reasons' in it!

The Bishop of Gloucester and others also outside the Battalion sent in items; but it was intended that the bulk of the material should come from within the unit itself. It was hard work at first, trying to persuade members to make a contribution, and secondly (equally difficult!) to meet a publication deadline! So it was a great relief to me when Lieut. J. Taylor, a professional journalist, joined the Battalion in France and, with Lieut. Michael Shepherd (who had been on the *Citizen* in Gloucester), took over the duties of joint editors!

Organised games were quickly established, and the Battalions speedily began to build up that vital 'family feeling.' Hockey, which was my particular responsibility, was run on a Brigade basis, and the School, Marlborough College, with its great hockey traditions, were most kind. They lent us all the 'gear,' and placed their 2nd XI ground at our disposal. When ultimately we went overseas, they presented us with twenty-four sticks and several balls—a pleasing gesture. They invited me to play for their Senior Common Room, and I had several enjoyable games playing alongside my old opponents of happier and more peaceful days, David Milford and John Maples.

The Transport Platoon had its H.Q. at the Cricketers' Arms, and they kept the place alive! The lads were mainly cheery Cotswold boys well versed in country lore and skilled in the ways of wildlife. The use of snares, sticks and catapults was second nature to them. Often, when passing the cook-house, appetizing aromas would be wafted to one's nostrils, as well as the pungent smell of burning fur and feathers to be detected coming from the incinerator. They worked hard, but they lived jolly well!

Early in November, Canon Helm, D.A.C.G. Southern Command, visited the Brigade and invited me to a meal in Salisbury. He added:

"I should put on a collar and black tie; you won't feel so conspicuous."

I duly arrived at his H.Q. and was directed to his office. On the stairs, a tall, austere and be-ribboned figure confronted me and said:

"Are you a chaplain? If so what is your name?"

Receiving my reply, the A.C.G. (for it was the great man himself) motioned me to his office and gave me one of the severest verbal flayings I have ever had the misfortune to receive. I was improperly dressed (black tie) and ought to know better. There was no defence—Helm, obviously could not be involved—so I just had to take it. It was a biting but totally unjustified 'carpeting,' resulting from the autocratic attitude, almost despotic at times, which was adopted and favoured by some of the very senior pre-war regular chaplains.

A number of marriages took place during the Marlborough period. This was understandable, but the Dean's powerful but lugubrious sermon at Gloucester Cathedral on September 10th may well have been a contributory factor; the feeling being, in some cases, "if I am not coming back, Betty (or Jane or Mary) may as well have my pension!" It was clear that with the heavy casualty figures of 1914–18 as our obvious yardstick, many were conscious of the possibility of never coming back. Few, however, admitted this fact. Despite all this, and the realisation that our move overseas was imminent, the morale of the unit, and the whole Brigade, was very high.

In December, embarkation leave commenced. The key parties began the roster and then, over Christmas, came the turn of the main bodies.

On our return, the tempo of life at Marlborough increased, and despite the snow and ice, training was intensified. Who will forget that grim forty-eight hours spent digging trenches on the frozen Downs above Ogbourne St George? The exercise was designed as a fitness test, and nature's co-operation made it so!

Marlborough was by this time full of wives, mothers and sweethearts staying over to have the last precious few days with their loved ones. Rumours were rife, one of these emanating, it was said, from a certain barmaid, who gave correctly the date of our departure.

The highlight of this period was the inspection by H.M. The King in Savernake Forest. It was an open secret and the units (and their 'camp followers' who unofficially watched from the cover of bushes and bracken) were thrilled.

Early in January, our transport was entrained at Pewsey, and we knew that the reunion was scheduled for 'somewhere in France.' Reveille sounded at 3.00 a.m. on Sunday 14th January, and by 5.30 a.m. the Glosters (the first contingent of the 144 Brigade) marched to Marlborough station with drums and bugles playing and waking the whole town. The 7th and 8th Worcesters followed, and by midday the entire Brigade had entrained.

At Southampton, we embarked on our respective ships. The Glosters' trooper, *The Tynwald*, an Isle of Man ferry, moved out in a convoy headed by *H.M.S. Royal Sovereign* and flanked by destroyers. Those next to us were the H.40, H.42, H.85 and H.89. A thick fog suddenly descended, causing the convoy to anchor for several hours, and it was not until late on the 15th that the shores of France were sited. We docked at Le Havre early on the following morning, and were the first Territorial Division to land in France in the war.

F.W. Harvey sent his good wishes for 1940 thus:

'TO 1939'

Old Year, farewell!
Much have you given which was ill to bear:
Much have taken which was dear, so dear:
Much have you spoken which was ill to hear:
Echoes of speech first uttered deep in hell.

Pass now like some grey harlot to the tomb!
Yet die in child-birth and from out your womb
Leap the young year unsullied! He perchance
Shall bring to man his lost inheritance.

F.W.H.

And God bless every one of you.

CHAPTER THREE

France

Landing in France, to most of the Battalion, was an exciting occasion; for some, however, the thrill was tempered by the realisation that ahead lay 'War,' their second war on French soil in a little over twenty years. These veterans, mainly among the officers and senior N.C.O.s, were quiet and kept their thoughts largely to themselves.

Breakfast, the usual black coffee and hard rolls, followed on the quay. The first roll broke a front tooth which I had had repaired at Marlborough only three days before—a bad beginning! Later that morning, the Brigade entrained for Yvetot, leaving behind in Le Havre Hospital several who had succumbed to the 'flu which had hit the units just prior to departure from Marlborough, and which continued to take its toll for several days.

I expected to collect my Morris 8 at Yvetot. Alas! A harassed Brigade Transport Officer (the road conditions were appalling) broke the news that my precious new car, run in so carefully at Marlborough, had seized up; the temporary driver, when he and the car had disembarked, had put in petrol and oil, but forgotten the water!

The journey to Caudebec was, from the scenic point of view, exquisite; the trees laden with a silver film, the hedgerows sparkling in the pale sunshine of a winter's afternoon and the roads, glistening ribbons of packed ice, made a picture that, if seen on a Christmas card, would have evoked admiration. The *Seine* at Caudebec was a mass of ice-floes moving noisily downstream. The cold was intense, and the condition of much of the billeting, to raw T.A. personnel drawn mainly from the mild-climated West Country, was horrifying.

Later, these same billets would be looked on as palaces of comfort, but as a baptism into foreign service it was unpleasant. But these Cotswold and West Country lads were resourceful and soon created a modicum of comfort. They were, however, somewhat regardless of the consequences.

Driving on the right-hand side of the road for the first time is a little awesome, especially when the vehicle has right-hand drive. When, in addition, the roads are covered with a sheet of ice and there are hills in plenty, one's nerves and ability to control the car are taxed to the full. It was surprising, however, how quickly (mercifully!) one became acclimatised to the conditions.

My diary records deep snow on the 17th, and visits to Companies at St Arnault, Villequier (so closely associated with Victor Hugo) and Caudebec. The following day was spent visiting the Companies and also chasing straw with Bérenge (*Caporal Chef*, our French Liaison Officer). Sickness figures frequently in the entries of this period, and derelict vehicles are often recorded.

The move to the Lille area, which was to be our 'home' for two months, began on the 19th. The road party left at 9.00 a.m., while the main body entrained at Yvetot and left at about 11.00 p.m.. That day had been hectic: a trip to Division to try and sort out the conflicting orders and times had occupied much of the morning; in the afternoon Bérenge and I went round to settle the damage claims. These were far less than expected, due to the kindness of Mlle. J. Wergaine, the châteleine of two large houses or *châteaux* where our men had done much damage. The young lady would not hear of making a claim (the estimated damage was approximately £300!) because a certain Lieut. S. of 'B' Company had been 'so charming'! That young officer, who later won the Military Cross and Bar, was quite a Romeo! By a million-to-one chance, I met the young lady again during the withdrawal, and her first question was: "How is Lieut. S.?" But for the collapse of France, there might well have been a romantic sequel to the table and chair burnings at Caudebec in mid-January 1940.

When all the damage claims had been settled, Bérenge and I ate a good meal at the *Hôtel de la Marine* in Caudebec, to fortify ourselves for what we knew would be a long and cold night. During our meal, a number of the 51st Scottish Division advance party came in, and amongst them were two old friends. One, Carmichael, had been with me at Pembroke College, Oxford, and the other was Kinsey, with whom

I had played hockey at Cardiff in the mid 1930s. After the meal, we ferried returned sick personnel to the trains at Yvetot. The water pump froze several times, and a Royal Army Medical Corps ambulance on a similar task to ours had like trouble and had to be abandoned. It was well after midnight before we returned to St Arnault.

Both the road and rail parties, so we heard later, suffered greatly from the cold, the former finding conditions much worse than expected. My diary reads:

> Road party had awful time—night in Lateines. Next morning, starting was terrible—men lighting fires under engines to thaw them—even shirts soaked in petrol. Train party even worse, perhaps. Heat pipe burst—cold intense. 28°C frost at one place, 40°F at another.

The road party commander found a billet in Lateines, but was nearly thrown out. He was frozen, and in his best French, asked Madame for (as he thought) a hot water bottle or bed warmer. His request in dictionary French seems to have been unfortunately phrased, for he appeared to indicate to Madame that he desired something rather more cuddlesome for his bed. The good lady blew up, saying that if he wanted that sort of thing he wouldn't find it here and had better get out! 'Daddy' H. was badly shaken!

The following morning, the 20th, we ran into more trouble at Caudebec and did not leave until 11.45. We had a comparatively good run, in spite of the icy road, to Corcelles. Eventually we arrived at Thumèries around midnight, and found the Battalion H.Q. in the Château Blanc. A thoughtful member of the Mess Staff had left our supper on the table: a tin of salmon, frozen solid, and a loaf of bread. Mercifully, he had also left three-quarters of a bottle of whisky. We finished the whisky before unrolling our fleabags, and slept on the floor.

Thumèries was situated about ten miles south-west of Lille, in the heart of that mining district. It was an unattractive village, and some of its inhabitants were rabidly anti-British. One of the more prominent ladies, so I was told, spat at the Brigadier when the unit marched in. This hostility may be attributed partly to the forcible billeting of our troops upon them, and partly to the propaganda leaflet raids by German planes. The more important points made in these leaflets (there were several varieties of them) were:

a) The French and Germans should be good friends. There was no need for Frenchmen to be separated from their families and to man the distant Maginot forts.

b) The French Government had lost contact with the people of France, and were indifferent to their real interests, being more concerned with power politics.

c) The British troops were luxury-loving libertines whose lives were centred around wine and women, and especially the wives of the brave but absent Poilu. They, the British, would fight to the last Frenchman.

Some training was carried out in the Thuméries district, but much more time seemed to be devoted to the digging of a sector of an anti-tank ditch and defence (known to us as the Gort line) which passed through the 48th Divisional area. These defences were never operationally used, because when the 'hot war' began, the British Expeditionary Force were ordered up into Belgium and the Gort line was left deep in the rear, never again to be seen.

Living conditions at first were generally rough. Slowly, however, and thanks mainly to the ingenuity of the men themselves, conditions improved. The primitive sanitary arrangements in my own billet, for example, beggar description and quickly caused psychological constipation. After three days of acute discomfort, pills compelled an acceptance of the situation.

On the 25th January, the Press descended upon us *en masse*. This honour was accorded because the 48th was the first T.A. Division to join the B.E.F., and because we had the first contingent of conscripts to be drafted overseas.

The weather for the first few weeks was severe. A number of casualties in the early days were caused by carbon monoxide fumes given off by the coke or coal braziers which the men, contrary to orders, brought into their billets to combat the intense cold. In addition, cerebro-spinal meningitis (C.S.M.) was brought on, it was said, by the crowded conditions of the billets.

There were no fatalities among the Glosters, but the 8th Worcesters and 2nd Warwicks (the other Battalions in the Brigade) were less fortunate. Cases of C.S.M. were first suspected on 1st February. These were isolated at once and later that day, the earlier diagnosis was confirmed, causing a considerable scare. The eight cases within the Brigade were sent to the C.C.S. at Rovroy where, at first, the medical staff refused me permission to see the patients. The A.D.M.S. finally gave consent on condition that I wore a white coat and mask, and washed in some preparation when I left the tented ward. A lance-corporal of the 8th Worcesters died on the 2nd, and was buried in the 1914–18 War Cemetary of Orchard Dump (Plot 3, Row 7) on Sunday 4th February. This was my first Active Service burial.

A few days after our arrival at Thuméries, we (the 5th Glosters in conjunction with the 144 Field Ambulance) opened a canteen in the disused local cinema. On Sunday mornings the large room became our church. We had no piano, so a mouth organ band was formed. The men were enthusiastic; they practiced regularly and were a great help. The canteen turnover was enormous and often compelled two or three trips a week to the NAAFI for fresh supplies. We bought cigarettes in crates of 10,000 or 25,000, and vast quantities of chocolate. My diary entry for the 29th records that twice on my return trip from the NAAFI in a heavy snowstorm, I missed the road and finished up in the ditch. On both occasions, passing troops lifted the car bodily back on to the road.

The Battalion pay was drawn each week from the Army Paymaster in Douai. This duty, and that of collecting the Battalion mail, not infrequently fell to the Padré. The journey to collect the pay was made in a 15 cwt truck with an armed guard composed of an N.C.O. with a revolver, and a private with a rifle. The task of counting the francs (the number ran into six figures) was tedious, and an over-payment of just ten francs once caused the cashier and myself to spend two hours cross-checking!

The mail in those early days was irregular; on one occasion the train was derailed! The accident was caused by frozen points.

The Battalions were allowed the use of the pit-head baths once a week. These were well appointed, and the water always hot. This weekly visit, in view of billeting conditions, was very necessary and was also much appreciated by all ranks. Officer in Command of the bathing party was yet another duty which often fell to the Padré.

Entertainment was not forgotten. Boxing, soccer, rugby and hockey were quickly organised, and inter-unit games and representative matches against civilian sides soon followed. This helped somewhat in the establishment of a better relationship between the B.E.F. and the local population. Our first E.N.S.A. party, billed for 6th February, did not arrive, but unit concerts caused amusement and revealed some unexpected talant.

Soon after our arrival in Thuméries, the War Office replaced one T.A. Battalion in each Brigade with a regular Battalion. In the 144 Brigade, the 2nd Warwicks were substituted for the 7th Worcesters. We had hoped that the 2nd Glosters would come to us, but they were sent instead to 145 Brigade. Likewise the 2nd Warwicks would naturally have preferred to go to the 143 (Warwick) Brigade. The official explanation why these desired postings did not take place was that should a particular Brigade suffer very heavy casualties, it would be better that these should be spread over the Battalions of three counties.

On one of my visits (on February 9th) to my Senior Chaplain, I noticed two cameras on his desk. I asked, knowing that B.E.F. personnel were forbidden to carry these, to whom they belonged and pressed the question until an answer was forthcoming. It turned out they were owned by the Divisional Commander and the Senior Chaplain. I informed the latter that there would soon be a third member of the 'camera club;' a Kodak Bantam was bought that afternoon which became almost my constant companion until June 1944,[1] when it, and all my kit, went down with our ship when it was sunk off the Normandy Coast. Unfortunately I lost two spools of the Saar period when going on leave in May 1940.

Two of our officers, Major D. Over and Lieut. G. Scott-Plumber, had a narrow escape on 14th February when their truck was nearly hit on a level-crossing near Thuméries during a blinding snowstorm.

I accompanied Majors Hind and Over on 22nd February on a recce of the ranges at Le Touquet, in preparation for the Battalion's training period which was scheduled for the end of the month.

The following day, a chaplains' conference took place at G.H.Q.. On the way back, we visited the 1914–18 Canadian War Memorial at Vimy Ridge. This was beautifully kept but was a grim reminder of what the future might hold for the British Expeditionary Force.

On the 27th February, Mr Johnstone, who had done so much for our units in Marlborough, arrived unexpectedly in Thuméries. I took him to see the 8th Worcesters, and later found him a temporary billet. The following day was largely devoted to making a recce for Mr Johnstone and the Y.M.C.A., who appeared (in some strange and roundabout way) to have been his sponsors. The whole affair was completely unofficial, but welcomed by the whole Brigade, for Mr Johnstone was a great man and a friend to all.

February 29th and 1st March were spent on the Le Touquet ranges. These two days passed without any serious accident, although one young soldier slipped when throwing a Mills grenade and dropped it in the bay! The instructor picked it up and flung it out before it exploded, but it was a very near thing. I had a turn with the anti-tank rifle aimed at a moving tank two hundred yards distant, and scored three hits out of four. The diary also records that I had shot the bren with some success at the local range a few days earlier; five single shots and a burst of five resulted in six bulls and a group of four just below. The overall group was two-and-a-half inches.

During this period, opportunities occurred enabling me to visit several Dymock men in their various units; for example, Donald Wood, Donald Wilsden and Ron Bayliss. We talked, naturally, of our families at home, and exchanged news of the Leadon Vale we knew so well and loved so dearly. For those few minutes we were, in spirit and mind far away and the discomfort of the local situation and the grim potential of the future were forgotten.

> In northern France we may have been,
> But for the time it was unseen.
> Our thoughts were in a distant land,
> A garden, house, familiar hand.
> And then we came right down to earth,
> But still, thank God!, retained our mirth.

Early in March, 'Spy Fever' broke out, and we were told to watch 'the blondes in the Café de Tabac near the Post Office, and the Café with a wireless shop'.

The Chaplains' leave roster was drawn up and was due to begin on the 15th April, with one chaplain going on leave every other Sunday. I was first out of the hat. Later, I exchanged with Number 2 in view of the Saar operation. This would also enable me to be home on my wife's birthday.

I was told, confidentially, on the 7th March that we were to have battle inoculation in the Saar. The 144 Brigade would (in a fortnight's time, so the grape-vine declared) be coming under French command, and would take over Battalion positions, by rota, both ahead of and behind the line of the Maginot forts. Another rumour suggested that the whole 48th Division would shortly be withdrawn from France and sent out East, by which it was assumed was meant the Middle East.

Sunday Services, with two Battalions and a Field Ambulance dispersed over a wide area, were a rush. An Armourer Sergeant in the 8th Worcesters, who used to prepare the room and Altar in his Company Office whenever a Service of Holy Communion was scheduled there, suddenly announced that he was an Anglican priest and that his 'orders' were valid. Sgt. Jones, before the war, had been in a Devon parish and had suffered a type of mental breakdown. The doctors advised, after convalescence, that he should for a year or two take up some sort of manual or mechanical job; he became an engineer with a motor firm. Now, he offered his assistance. This must have been a tough decision, for it automatically necessitated revealing his true background to the C.O. and to the whole unit. His Diocesan, Bishop Curzen of Exeter, confirmed these facts and sent his episcopal blessing to Sgt. Jones. The C.O. was informed and agreed, when he saw the Bishop's letter, that Sgt. Jones should, when available, exercise his priestly office. Sgt. Jones, having declared himself, was thereafter a great help, especially so during the withdrawal to Dunkirk. Later, a fully fit Sgt. Jones returned to an active ministry in the Church.

An air-raid alert (these were becoming more frequent by this time) occurred on the 10th March as we were filing into the cinema for Church Parade. The troops at once put on their respirators and we carried on. This, for some reason, caused great amusement in the unit and district: it turned out to be another leaflet raid!

A Brigade exercise took place on the 13th, and the rôle alloted to me was that of an old, battle-shocked Pole (white-haired) who ran around shouting his head off. The torrent of Welsh, some of it abusive, *mea culpa*, caused much speculation among the troops and onlookers as to the identity of the old man, and of the language spoken.

On March 19th, the Deputy Chaplain General again called in all chaplains to a conference. This began with a service of Holy Communion celebrated by the Moderator of the Church of Scotland. Although the printed form of service indicated that reception was optional, the pressure was considerable—my diary records that it was almost a case of 'having to participate.'

The following day, by which time the Maginot Line rumour had been confirmed, was spent largely in final preparations for our five weeks' trip to the Saar. At the briefing, the unit had been told that in the two lines of outpost positions forward of the Maginot forts, infiltration by enemy patrols must be expected, and therefore arms would, at all times, be carried. Knowing that positions in the *ligne de contact* were often hundreds of yards apart, and that there was much scrub and woodland around and between the posts, I went out and bought a small .25 revolver as a means of personal protection when moving from one post to another. This, of course, was a breach of the Geneva Convention and most reprehensible. Had it been discovered would, quite rightly, have resulted in a Court Martial. Its use never became necessary, but its presence in the trouser pocket gave some measure of confidence despite its tiny calibre and consequent limited effectiveness. That night of March 20th/21st was, though we did not know it, the last we were to spend in Thumériès.

Notes

1. I was on leave when the 'hot war' began, and decided not to take the camera back to France at that stage.

CHAPTER FOUR

The Saar—A Trial Run

Early in March 1940, as mentioned above, the unit had been told that 144 Brigade was to take over the British sector in the Saar. Few British Battalions had yet had experience of the War as represented by the minor activities ahead of the Maginot Line. The 144 was the first Territorial Brigade to be selected—no wonder excitement was at fever pitch when we entrained at Le Forest on March 21st.

The following evening (Good Friday) we reached Metz, and were billeted in the smelly but delightful village of La Maxe. The sun shone, and the hilly Lorraine countryside was a welcome change after the bleak winter months spent in the flat mining district near Lille.

Soon after de-training, the Colonel commanding the Field Ambulance made contact and suggested that the distances between units would make if difficult on Easter Day for a complete C of E chaplaincy coverage for the two Battalions and the Field Ambulance under my care. He offered to take the Parade Service for his command and asked for a Communion Service at any time that could be fitted in, but preferably between 6.30 and 7.30 a.m.. There were very few C.O.s who would have made such an offer, and fewer still who would have acted so ably *in loco capellani*.

The Glosters' Church Parade on Easter morning was held in a barn at the centre of the village with the farm stock well represented. It was a warm, sunny morning, and there seemed a strangely relaxed, almost holiday, atmosphere; it was as though both past and future were forgotten, and the present alone mattered. This amazing feeling was probably engendered by a combination of circumstances; the glorious weather, the friendliness of the people, the smell of hay, and the completely rural surroundings. One unrehearsed incident caused much amusement: half-way through the sermon, a large rat, perhaps disturbed by the troops, appeared out of the hay and, seeing no movement, walked calmly over the feet of a somnolent subaltern, whose startled reactions were much enjoyed by the rest of the Battalion, and perhaps made up a little for the dullness of the address!

After two further days of soccer and swimming (the *Moselle* flowed nearby), the Brigade moved up some twenty miles and took over the British Sector. The actual Maginot Line was supported by a series of three defensive systems. The first two, the *Ligne de Contact* (the outposts) and the *Ligne de Soutien* (the reserve), were ahead of the Maginot Line proper, while the *Ligne de Réceuil* was sited behind the Maginot forts and was intended for active use only if disaster befell the actual forts. The Battalions spent a period in each of these three positions in turn. The cycle was repeated, giving the three Battalions approximately ten days in each line.

The 5th Glosters (my Battalion) began in the *Ligne de Réceuil* at Kédange, where life was pleasant and quiet, and war seemed an impossibility.

On April 1st, we passed through the Maginot Line of forts with its anti-tank ditches and obstacles, and took over the *Ligne de Contact*.

The forward companies held a series of posts, mainly in the forward edges of two woods (the *Grossenwald* and *Hartbusch*), which were supposed to command the valley between the Allied lines and those of the Germans on the opposite slope. These positions had been hastily constructed months before, and were poor. The arcs of fire were too restricted and the earthworks were mainly above-ground contraptions of corrugated iron sheets, wooden stakes and earth. Had there been a Bairnsfather in the Unit, what a magnificent set of cartoons could have been inspired, possibly to enliven the pages of *Punch* and arouse anger, no doubt, in the hearts of some of the high-ranking generals who might have had the misfortune to read such an issue.

The Company H.Qs were sited along a road running in dead ground a quarter of a mile to the rear of the crest, and Battalion H.Q. was in a village called Walweistroff a short distance behind them. The French artillery occupied the narrow wood between Company and Battalion H.Q.s, and an International Post marked the lateral limits of the British Sector. It was, from a military point of view, a most untidy set-up, breeding a certain amount of uncertainty as to responsibility and freedom of action. In addition, the Maginot-mindedness of the French High Command worried some of the senior British officers from the beginning, and most of us before the end of our tour of duty.

During the day, limited movement was allowed behind the outposts, but from dusk to dawn, all units were wired in, and only the recce and fighting patrols left the enclosures.

Life back in Thumériés, as far as the padré was concerned, had broadly followed the pattern of the Marlborough days. Now, in the *Ligne de Contact*, conditions had changed.

On the second day of our first tour in the *Ligne de Contact* came an incident which, for me, had personal and painful consequences. The C.O., returning from his early morning round of the units' positions, met me on my way forward to one of the outposts.

"Good morning, sir!" My cheery greeting met a cold response:

"What are you doing in the forward area, Padré?"

"Going to see 'A' Company, Sir." I answered.

"You cannot go forward; I cannot be responsible for your safety." His crisp retort prompted my first mistake, for I replied:

"Colonel; I, and I alone, am responsible for my life. It is my duty to go forward. My father was a chaplain in the last war, so I know what is expected."

"Padré, I forbid you to go forward!"

"Very well, Sir. You must see, however, that feeling as I do, I have no alternative but to go back and put my case to the Brigadier."

I went to see the Brigadier. He was silent for what seemed an age, and then he said:

"Well Padré, please give my compliments to Colonel Buxton, and say that chaplains are officially on Brigade strength, so I have to bear responsibility for their safety. If you feel strongly that you must go forward, then go forward, but for Heaven's sake be sensible. And don't endanger the lives of the men either."

At lunchtime, the Brigadier's message was delivered. The C.O. was understandably furious, and life for the chaplain became extremely difficult, although it must be admitted that chaplaincy services were given normal facilities as far as operational conditions allowed. No reference was ever made to the daily rounds of the *Hartbusch* and *Grossenwald* positions, even when, as occasionally happened, we met en route or at one of the outpost positions.

On April 6th, the Glosters handed over to the 8th Worcesters and returned to the *Ligne de Soutien* where life was quiet, and thence on the 9th to the *Réceuil*. The programme was then repeated.

The memories of those five weeks which stand out are mainly concerned with the two periods in the *Ligne de Contact*. There it was that one came to realise that war could be grim, and death (as this world counts it) final. All this built up gradually, and the summer-like weather and recreational and bath trips to Metz when in the reserve, helped to prolong the initial, almost charade-like, illusions of warfare during this final period of battle initiation.

During our second rest period, we were shown over the largest of the Maginot forts. This much-boosted defence line was the brainchild of Marshal Pétain and General Debèny, and was named after the French War Minister, André Maginot. While the 144 Brigade, under French command, formed part of the forward defence force, the *Picture Post* published a feature article on this gigantic system by Charles Morice, the leading French military journalist. He described the Maginot Line as 'the greatest defensive fortification of all time'. The line of forts, stretching for sixty-five miles, was built between 1929 and 1936, and had cost £100 Million.

The tour of the Hattenburg, one of these mole-like fortress cities, for they were no less, was an experience which few will forget, and was enjoyed by most units of the 144 Brigade.

The great underground galleries which honeycombed the mountain-side, some wide, others narrow, and along which men marched and trains and other vehicles drove, extended for miles, linking cavernous rooms, larger than many a town hall and some of smaller size, some of which bristled with weapons of varied calibre. Lifts linked the different levels. One of those used during our tour linked seven levels in its three-hundred-foot descent, and may well have been part of an even greater system. The periscopic vision and sighting system, the ventilation and thermostatically-controlled temperature systems, and other refinements of unbelievable sophistication (bearing in mind the date of construction), were very impressive. The Maginot motto too, '*On ne passe pas*', conveyed the confidence of the French in their magnificent creation but, to the British, seemed unnecessarily ostentatious, and perhaps a little too confident.

Outside, the detailed planning was obvious also. The arcs of fire for the many gun turrets ensured that the entire front was covered while on the lower reaches, stretching as far as the eye could see below the guns, but covering them, were wide ribbons of steel stakes set in concrete, except on the roads, where they fitted into slots for easy removal for the passage of vehicles. These were the forward anti-tank defences, commonly termed 'dragon's teeth'. They also protected the flanks and rear of each fortress.

Hundreds of thousands of troops lived in these vast blockhouses which were linked by smaller fortresses built on similar lines. They were, for the German army of 1940, impenetrable by direct assault and it was assumed that the Belgian water line defences and other natural obstacles, extensions as it were of the Maginot Line, would hold. History, however, records that this failed to happen, and thus the immobile Maginot Line was outflanked and left useless in the rear - probably the most costly defensive miscalculation of all time.

We in April 1940, not being gifted with foresight, felt proud that we had, for a brief period of five weeks, been privileged to take our place in this grandiose system, even if our responsibilities were minimal and on the periphery.

I remember going with Major Biddle at stand down one morning to visit his Company in the *Hartbusch* and receiving quite a shock. I recognised amongst the men sleeping in the mud a lad from near my home. Two hours later, on our return, we found the lad shaving. I put to him a question I had asked of several others that morning:

"What do you think of this? "—it was their second day in the line. He replied:

"We're not paid to think, Sir! We're paid to fight!"

What a complete and withering answer! There was, I am certain, no malice in that comment. I had known the lad since his birth and appreciated that he was a very factual young man, and had just said what he felt.

During the Glosters' first period in the *Ligne de Contact*, a senior French Protestant padré, Pasteur Jean Dautheville Guibal, paid a friendly visit to Walweistroff when several photographs were taken. He was a charming man. Three weeks later he wrote a most friendly letter and enclosed some photographs as souvenirs of our meeting, and asked that one should be passed to the Colonel.

The leisurely tenor of the war during daytime (apart from the regular patrols into Grindorff village) may well be illustrated by the daily visit of a horsed battery of French 75s to Bizing (a Company H.Q.). They trotted up with a jingle of harness, positioned their guns, then brewed coffee. After a suitable rest, they loosed off about a dozen rounds per gun. Another quick brew of coffee followed then, their day's work done, they limbered up the guns and galloped off. It may have helped French morale but, strange to relate, it rarely stung the Germans into reciprocal action, for which we, the 'residents', were grateful. From the forward positions, German working parties could occasionally be seen across the valley, but orders from French Command forbade action being taken.

At night-time, things were different. Both sides patrolled through eacth other's lines, and occasionally clashes resulted.

On April 3rd, the Battalion experienced its real baptism of aggressive warfare. 12 Platoon of 'B' Company suffered a prolonged and very heavy artillery and mortar attack upon its two outpost positions at the edge of the village of Grindorff. At 8.00 p.m., the Platoon Commander, Lieut. Michael Shepherd, led an observation patrol to lie up at the far end of the village. A little later came the first assault on the two posts. For almost nine hours, wave after wave of the enemy stormed the positions, and it was several hours before Lieut. Shepherd and his patrol could fight their way back and so reinforce the posts. During an early attack, the Germans knocked out the bren gunner in the barn, and the precious (and only) automatic weapon fell over the parapet. Sgt. W.G.H. Adlam, realising the danger, recovered the gun and, standing on the parapet, forced the enemy back. This outstanding act of bravery won for Sgt. Adlam the Military Medal, the first awarded to a Territorial in the War. Several hours later, to support the harassed platoon, the French Command ordered the first 'Grand Barrage' of the hostilities. The foiled, beaten, enemy retreated before the dawning of day, undoubtedly feeling that a postponement of their withdrawal to that point might well result in heavy casualties. This engagement considerably boosted the men's morale.

Another night, the Germans attempted a repeat of an action they had used successfully, weeks before, against a Company post of a regular Battalion. A box barrage was put down on 'D' Company forward positions which cut all communications. Nos. 16 and 17 Platoons were then attacked by a large force (estimated at four hundred) accompanied by dogs. Bangalore torpedos were used to blow the barbed-wire, and fierce fighting followed. The enemy finally withdrew in some haste and, for the first time in the War, left their six dead behind. Our casualties were three dead, four missing (P.O.W.s), and more than twenty wounded. Charles Graves, writing in *Sphere* (22nd May 1943, page 248) on the work of the Imperial War Graves Commission, mentioned these casualties. He wrote:

> When I was out in France in April 1940, I saw... the first purely British Military Cemetery. This included Lancashire Fusiliers and men from the Glosters... another hundred yards along were the graves of half a dozen Germans, over whom a Church of England burial service had been read.

I will never forget that burial. After the battle had ended, a digging party was arranged by Brigade. Our three boys were brought down in a 15 cwt. truck, and the French Army Commander and several 'Top Brass' attended the Service. A second 15 cwt. truck, containing the German dead, was timed to arrive half-an-hour after the internment had been completed. The generals would thus have ample time to fraternize and disperse. The driver of this second truck, one Private Lionel Cuss, was a professional boxer and his mate, Private Greenburg, an all-in wrestler. Reverently, they lifted each blanketed corpse from the truck, and placed it on the ground. At least, they did this for Nos. 1 to 4, but as they lifted No. 5 off No. 6, the chest of the latter, deflated by the previous weight of his comrades, expanded with a prolonged moan. My pugilistic wrestling assistants dropped their burden and fled, and it was some time before I could persuade them to return and help me place the bodies in their graves before taking the burial service!

In 1947 I returned to France on a pilgrimage to photograph the graves of my men from the 1940 and 1944–45 periods. At La Maxe, when I was photographing one of the billets of Easter 1940, my wife, who was sharing the driving, and who speaks French fluently, remained in the car. In the May sunshine, two old crones were sitting on chairs outside their homes, opposite the car. They discussed us, and concluded rightly that I must have been there in 1940. They then speculated about my wife thus:

"She is not his sister, it is clear. He is a priest, so he cannot have a wife. She must be his mistress!"

Eavesdroppers hear nothing good of themselves!

Another incident of April 1940 had its repercussions in later years. On a midden heap just outside Battalion H.Q. in Walweistroff, I noticed a parchment book written, in German, in an early hand. It was in fair condition considering it had probably been lying there for some time. I could not read German anyway, and this 15th century German was completely beyond me. I took it to my billet, but could make little of it. I realised, however, that it might be of some importance and so, after the Saar period was over and I went on leave, I took it with me, intending to consult our local Archivist. Then the 'balloon went up' and I was recalled. I put the book in Dymock Church safe and forgot it. Years after the War I found it again and took it to the County Archivist. It's 'home' was ultimately traced, and it was returned to its rightful place. The *Archiviste en Chef* of the Moselle at Metz wrote to the Gloucestershire Archivist saying:

> Je vous prie de vouloir bien être mon interprête de Révérend J.E. Gethyn-Jones pour lui dire combien je lui saie gré d'avoir sauvé ce préieux document.[1]

The Glosters handed over the *Ligne de Contact* positions to the 8th Worcesters on the 19th, and moved back to La Maxe. On the next day, when visiting the Worcesters for normal chaplaincy rounds and prayers, I found at a platoon post near Grindorff a patrol on the point of setting out to search that straggling village where parties of British and German troops sometimes 'laid-up' and observed the position. What followed, most people today would, perhaps rightly, classify as an act of crass folly, while some might denounce it as a disgrace to the Cloth. Extenuating circumstances is the only plea.

I had visited regularly the forward positions in the Hartbusch and Grossenwald, and those near Grindorff. Despite those activities, I realised that I could not fully appreciate the mental strain of going on patrol in no-man's land beyond the forward positions—a routine operation at both Brigade and Battalion levels. The realisation came that this would be my last opportunity in the Maginot Line to undergo this occupational hazard, and experience the daily tension of my companions. It may of course have been an attempt to 'prove myself to myself' though I was not conscious of such a motive.

The Lieutenant agreed that I should accompany his party and be treated as a Private in all respects. Off came the clerical collar and battledress jacket with its tell-tale insignia, and equipped with a revolver instead of a stick, the 'rookie' passed through the wire into the lane leading to the village street. The searching of each house was carried out methodically and by strict rota.

My feelings, as I took my turn to kick a door open and enter the passage or room behind, were a mixture of excitement, fear and, let it be said, guilt. This last reaction was engendered no doubt by the knowledge that I was breaking the Geneva Convention that a chaplain should not be armed, and that I had placed the young officer in an embarrassing position, particularly if I should be killed or wounded.

By the Grace of God, no Germans were laying up that day, and the patrol returned without incident. What would have happened, had a German faced me in one of those rooms, I now dread to think, more for the officer's sake than my own. That I would have pulled the trigger (had there been time) there is no doubt. I had used the revolver and rifle on the ranges both in England and at Le Touquet before the Brigade came up to the Maginot Line, and had shown some proficiency in the use of both weapons.

Had Colonel Buxton heard of the incident at the time, or had the matter been reported to the Brigadier, a court martial would inevitably have followed. Thank Goodness, nothing happened. During the reformation at Kington in Herefordshire I believe the secret came out, but a firm policy of ignorance was followed.

In retrospect, I frankly admit that in theory the action was culpable—extremely so—but it helped considerably in the appreciation of the stresses and problems faced by many other members of the Battalion. I hoped it helped me to be more understanding and sympathetic in my relations with them. Maybe this was my guilty conscience attempting to justify my actions – I cannot tell.

I took Sunday Services in La Maxe area on the 21st, and on the Monday drove up to take Holy Communion for the Worcesters in the *Ligne de Contact* and for the R.A.M.C. 'set-up' at Bizing. At this hospital I met Captain Eric Dunster, the ex-radio commentator who had covered the funeral of King George V and the coronation of King George VI.

The return to the Glosters that afternoon was made in full anticipation of a pleasant road trip on the next day, in my own car (authorised by the Brigadier), back to Le Forest. The Brigade route lay through Rheims, which suggested there might be an opportunity to see that magnificent Cathedral.

Petrol for the journey was drawn at 5.45 a.m. the following morning and at 7.45 I said good-bye to the wounded in the Château

Longe. The day promised well. Alas! at 8.45 the C.O. forbade the trip and ordered me to travel on the train and hand over the car to the Quartermaster. He had no right to do this because both the car and I were on Brigade establishment, and furthermore, he and many others of the Battalion were going by road. All this was disappointing, but it was expedient to accept the train situation rather than precipitate a second crisis by appealing to the Brigadier as had been done previously. In the earlier dispute with the C.O., it had been a question of plain duty and obligation which was at issue—the padré just had to be with his men in the outposts—but on the 23rd, it was more a matter of personal pleasure and convenience, so the car was at once returned to Brigade H.Q. for their use.

Later that morning, the Medical Officer and I borrowed bicycles and rode into Metz to visit the hospital and have a good meal. I bought two bottles of Champagne (they cost 2/6d each!), two of Benedictine, and various souvenirs in preparation for my leave, which was due to begin in about ten days' time. My diary for the 23rd records:

> I fancy I will apply for a transfer. The C.O. has now thoroughly got his knife into me. I would go tomorrow to Boultbee (S.C.F.) and ask for a transfer if I thought the C.O. would be with the Battalion long—but will he?

We entrained at 6.30 p.m.. The journey has for me one vivid and pleasant memory. At 1.00 a.m., we were shunted into a siding a few miles outside Rheims. It was a warm night, and the nightingales were in full song in every bush and tree. It was a glorious finale to an interesting five weeks of battle inoculation, which had shown that the morale of the Brigade was high. Living with the Glosters, one realised that 'B' Company were cock-a-hoop by reason of their testing Grindorff action, in which Lieut. Shepherd, and Sgt. W.G.M. Adlam in particular, had distinguished themselves. 'D' Company were equally pleased that during that early morning battle in the Grossenwald they had beaten off a greatly outnumbering German fighting patrol bent on repeating their highly successful foray some weeks earlier against outposts of another British Battalion in the Hartbusch. On this occasion, the tables had been turned, and the enemy retired with a very bloody nose, and for the first time in War, they had been forced to leave some of their dead behind. 17 and 18 Platoons, led by Lieut. M.F. Carter, had performed well,

British Battalion in the Hartbusch. On this occasion, the tables had been turned, and the enemy retired with a very bloody nose, and for the first time in War, they had been forced to leave some of their dead behind. 17 and 18 Platoons, led by Lieut. M.F. Carter, had performed well, though I have never understood why their gallantry was not officially recognised.

The morale of the men throughout those five weeks was magnificent; they felt that at last they were beginning to justify the hours of training in camps and drill halls. They were grateful too that they were being eased into war conditions by means of patrol exploits and the occasional major engagement, and the whole Battalion, indeed the entire Brigade, felt they had come through the initial trials of warfare not without honour.

There are two other personal incidents which I should record.

The first was a midnight 'alert' during the *Ligne de Contact* period. We had received from the French Command a message to load all trucks and stand-to, and await a possible order to move back within the cover of the Maginot forts. Major Frank Priestly and I were walking along the lines of parked trucks and chatting to the men when he stopped, listened, and then said:

"Padré, it sounds as though the French are moving back already."

When dawn came, the British front, held by the Glosters, was isolated; for the French had withdrawn on both flanks, either without having waited for the second order or because they had forgotten to pass that order on to 144 Brigade. Luckily, the Germans did not mount the anticipated attack.

The other incident was when the Glosters were handing over the *Ligne de Contact* for the last time. The Colonel, the bravest man I have ever met, came up and, in a voice more friendly than usual, asked what I thought the morale of the men had been like. I replied that I thought it had been excellent, to which he shot the question:

"Were you ever frightened, Padré?"

"Yes," I replied, "indeed I was!"

"Good God, Padré!" he exploded, "Did you not expect to be? I'm always frightened in action. All we have to do is see that it does not take control"—he had fought in the First World War.

Thinking back on the Saar period, I have occasionally wondered whether Colonel Buxton had (a) heard of my illegal patrol with the Worcesters, had privately not taken too dim a view of it and, because it had not involved his unit, had taken no action, or (b) shot that question about fear to warn me that he had heard of the incident and that it must not be repeated. I still wonder, because when he had recovered from his wounds sustained during the evacuation, and had returned to command the Glosters, his attitude towards me had completely changed.

Notes

1. In 1982 I bought for the Jenner Museum in Berkeley a plate decorated with a scene portraying Dr Jenner vaccinating in a French farmhouse with a cow feeding in the background. The stamp on the reverse revealed that it had been fabricated in Lorraine. Enquiries to certain museums produced nothing of value. Frustrated, I made photocopies of the above letter and the plate, and sent them to the Archivist at Metz and suggested that in return for saving his precious terrier in 1940, he might care to do a little research on the plate for me. The response was most generous—does not the 'Good Book' say: "Cast your bread upon the water"?

CHAPTER FIVE

May 1940

The 144 Brigade detrained at Le Forest in mid-afternoon of the 24th to learn that another Brigade had taken over our billets in the Thuméries area and that we had been allocated to Auby.

This village, five miles south of Thuméries and three miles north of Douai, was, like our previous centre, a mining community, but a rather more friendly one. The first two days were spent settling in and companies had the additional task of integrating the new officers and militia draft (mainly from Cheshire) who had been awaiting our return in Auby. These reinforcements brought the Battalion up to full strength. Training began in earnest, and now had behind it some experience of the realities of war.

I called in on the S.C.F., Revd. H. Boultbee, because of the tension between the C.O. and myself, and obtained the promise of a transfer if, after leave, things remained difficult.

On the 29th, the Colonel-in-Chief, the Duke of Gloucester, visited the Battalion and spent part of the day in the training area.

Leave was at hand, and in the evening of May 3rd, I joined the leave train at Le Forest, taking with me the souvenirs of the Saar and other presents for the family. Because of these, several treasured possessions had to be left behind including my bulky Bible, which had been a constant companion since theological college days and which contained a mass of notes written in margins and on pages stuck in. It was a veritable mine of information, and invaluable when it came to sermon-making. How foolish, in retrospect, it was not to take it, despite its bulk! On the other hand, one could not have been expected to anticipate that the balloon would go up during leave and that it would be impossible to rejoin the Glosters until after the greatest and most miraculous military evacuation of all time, and that a Mills grenade and a can of petrol outside Dunkirk would ensure that neither my car nor my kit would be of any use to the enemy—or anyone else for that matter!

The rail journey to Boulogne was slow but uneventful. The long wait from 5.30 a.m., when we detrained, until the boat actually sailed (the delay was caused, it was said, by mines dropped that night in the Channel) was passed in wandering around the market and shops. The last few francs were spent in buying more wine, perfume and cigarettes. Late in the afternoon, the ship docked in Dover, and leave had begun.

The Customs Officer was magnificent. Though he must have been able to see bottles sticking out of every pocket, he asked routinely:

"Anything to declare, Padré?"

"Yes, two bottles of champagne, two of Cherry Brandy, two of Benedictine and two of Cognac; three bottles of perfume, two hundred cigarettes, some butter and a lobster. But don't worry, my wife's birthday is at the end of the week, and they will all be dead men by the end of leave."

He did not bat an eyelid, and merely said:

"Well, good luck, Padré; but keep sober!"

Vivienne and the dogs met me at the dock gates, and we drove home through the gathering dark.

Leave began well, with a round of visits, the birthday party and a picnic in brilliant sunshine on the bank of the *Severn*. All this was too good to last—and it did not!

The wireless news on the 10th made it clear that the phoney war was over. I telephoned my S.C.F., who was also on leave, and learned from him on the Monday that we were to report to the R.T.O. on Victoria Station by 6.00 p.m. on the Wednesday.

The R.T.O. was a little harassed, and we were told to report back the following morning. That evening several of us went to the theatre and saw Emlyn Williams in *How Green was my Valley*. The following morning, we reported to Victoria and, to everyone's surprise, were entrained for Southampton en route for Cherbourg.

What a collection we were; and almost all had but one thought, namely "When shall we rejoin our unit?" On board, I met another Pembroke College man of my period—Holland, who was in the Welsh Guards. It was, of course, as it had been in the case of Carmichael at Caudebec, simply *Salute et Vale*. We did, however, meet once more. That final meeting took place during the Normandy campaign in 1944 when, one evening, the 43rd Recce Regiment (the Goucestershire Regiment) laagered for the night near the Welsh Guards. I walked over and saw both Holland and Maurice Turnbull, another old acquaintance of pre-war days. Their greeting that evening could well have been *nos moritori te salutant*, for they were both killed soon afterwards.

On disembarkation, we were billeted in villages eastward towards Barfleur, and speculation was rife. The following day, leave personnel were formed into composite Battalions, and what a mixture we were! In the company to which I was attached, there were over thirty Battalions represented. There were several 2nd Glosters, including Major John Biddulph, in our original group, but personnel changed almost daily. The Argyll and Sutherland Highlanders and several other Battalions from the 51st Highland Division were well represented at first, but soon left to rejoin their respective units when that Division moved back to the Seine and on to their gallant but ill-fated stand at St Valéry. Uncertainty was the key-note and, understandably, there was little cohesion or ésprit-de-corps. We did some training and defensive preparation, and the talk was all of a move to the line of the Seine. Events moved too rapidly, however, for this to be completed.

Some of us volunteered to drive lorries to help in the evacuation of Rouen, but this plan too was abortive.

I saw our 2.I.C. of Marlborough days, Colonel Dennis Over, now at G.H.Q. in Le Mans, by accident, and asked him whether he could get me back to the Glosters or, failing that, to any real unit. When he suggested a posting to a Battalion of 51st Division, I jumped at the idea. Later that day, a message came through that the vacancy had been filled.

Further unit activity followed, and on one occasion I had difficulty in persuading a bucolic Norman farmer, armed with a pike, that I was not a German paratrooper disguised as a padré.

Finally, a withdrawal towards Cherbourg began. We were a bewildered and frustrated body of men as we embarked for England on the 1st June. We had, metaphorically speaking, like the Duke of York's men, marched up the hill and down again, not knowing what we were supposed to be doing. Furthermore, the news of our units and comrades, confused and rumour-riddled as it was, portended serious trouble for them, the magnitude of which we mercifully could not at that moment fully appreciate.

CHAPTER SIX

England—Reformation

The ship docked at Southampton soon after midnight (2nd/3rd June) and it was learned from the R.T.O. that we were to be sent to the North of England. This news was disturbing and I reasoned that if I went North, there would be little hope of rejoining the Glosters. Consequently, I insisted to the R.T.O., harassed man that he was, that I had to report direct to the War Office, and then to the unit's depot in Gloucester. In desperation (and maybe to be rid of a pestering priest) he issued a chit. If the required destination had been the North Pole, the chit would probably still have been signed! I telephoned Vivienne before boarding the London train.

We reached Victoria at 5.30 a.m. and, after a wash and shave, a registered letter was sent to the Chaplains' Branch of the War Office, stating that I was proceeding to the Drill Hall, Gloucester, in an attempt to trace the 5th Battalion so that I could rejoin them. The Drill Hall knew nothing of the 5th Battalion beyond the fact that they had seen several members of the unit, and that evacuation had taken place. The Drill Hall suggested that I found accommodation for the night and contacted them next morning. It was late on the 5th June that they telephoned the news that the 5th Battalion were reforming somewhere near Kington in Herefordshire.

I left Dymock early on the 6th and found Hereford a centre of much coming and going. It was a great relief to see the blue parrot, the 48th Division H.Q., and officially reported in—scores of others were doing the same—and learned the location of the 144 Brigade. They occupied, or were scheduled to occupy, a group of fields just outside

Kington where tents were being made available. How fortunate it was that the fine weather, which had played so vital a part in the successful evacuation from the beaches, continued.

And so, on the sunny afternoon of 6th June, I at last rejoined the unit. A month earlier it had been about 750 strong; now, on my return barely four weeks later only a handful were present. During that time they had taken part in a world-shaking campaign that had left the British Army mentally undefeated, though greatly depleted in numbers and desperately short of equipment.

What a sorry sight we must have looked to the passer-by in those first weeks, and how pathetically unprepared to resist an immediate 'follow-up' invasion, if that had been possible to Hitler. Most of the rifles, for example, had been taken from the men at the ports of disembarkation for, overhaul and re-issue. It was indeed some weeks before the first consignment of a hundred fresh rifles arrived, in the meantime almost our only weapons were pick-handles.

There were, that afternoon, some hundred-and-fifty Glosters already in Camp, including Major F.W. Priestly (now acting C.O.) and Major Hauting (Adjutant). Further parties and individuals continued to arrive over the next three weeks, bringing up the number of old faces to nearly four hundred. In the withdrawal, certain companies had been detached on a separate rôle, and in the final night march to the beaches, parties had been split up. On the beaches, the loading of the boats (not all going to the same port) had further fragmented the unit. What a gigantic task it must have been, sorting out those mixed parties all over England, and returning them to their respective reforming locations!

It is little wonder, in view of the confusion which prevailed, that the Chaplains Branch of the War Office made repeated requests for chaplains to report their whereabouts. Having reported to official quarters on June 3rd, 5th, 6th, and 7th (three days before receiving the first order to notify them of my return to England, and of my location), I was somewhat peeved when, on the 27th, a telegram arrived with yet another appeal for information as to whether or not I was in the U.K., and if I was, my unit and location. The following reply was sent:

5th Battalion the Gloucestershire Regt
The Camp
Kington
Herefordshire

27th June, 1940

SUBJECT: *Telegram re Reporting to 48 Divn HQ*:
June 3rd: Reported by letter to War Office that I was in England.
June 5th: Reported by telegram that I had traced unit and was rejoining.
June 6th: Reported at Hereford and rejoined unit at Kington.
June 7th: Reported to 144 Brigade and asked them to report me to 48th Division H.Q..

Since that date I have been over to Divisional H.Q. (Chaplains' Dept.) on several occasions to see the acting S.C.F. and later the new S.C.F..

J.E. Gethyn-Jones. C.F.

No Acknowledgement was received, but no further requests for locational reports were made either!

Almost at once was begun the harrowing task of interrogating all survivors about the dead, wounded and missing. The acting C.O. (the Colonel, in spite of wounds in the ankle, thigh and shoulder, had led the main part of the Battalion to the beaches before collapsing—"I marched my b..... Battalion into France, and I'll b..... well march them out!" was the retort to the M.O. when the latter suggested a stretcher!), the Adjutant and I questioned and took statements from every officer and other rank; I still have one of my notebooks. By this cross-questioning, it was hoped to obtain a fair idea of the possible fate of those who had not returned. When one remembers the conditions during the withdrawal, it is amazing how clear a picture was built up and how accurate, generally, was the information relating to the missing. The only major mistakes, fortunately, were pleasing ones.

One of the two was on a list of four reported buried in one particular action; the writer of the message died later so it was not possible to check the accuracy of his statement. The second 'dead' was reported to (and according to several said to) have had "half his head blown off". Both these supposed casualties turned up later as prisoners of war, one wounded, the other intact. This latter information, by way of the Red Cross, of course took many months to come through, and by that time the 'widow' of one had drawn the insurance benefit. The Company, when full details were explained, very graciously allowed retention of the benefit as a 'Thank Offering' for the safety of the husband.

This necessary interrogation, though delicately conducted, was at times very distressing, for many were reluctant to relive their traumatic experiences during the withdrawal to the beaches. Others frankly looked back on those last few days in France with amazement and gratitude that they had survived. A number, but by no means the majority at that time, in retrospect felt proud that they had played a part in a remarkable moment in history—defeat though it had been. Several even put pen to paper. The following example was ultimately published in the Regimental Gazette:

On Dunkirk Beach

On Dunkirk Beach a soldier lay,
Thinking of home so far away;
Wounded, footsore, tired and worn,
One of the heroes, British born.
He lay for hours on the golden sands
Which filtered slowly through his hands;
His thoughts were of the folks at home,
Of the English vales he used to roam;
When from the sky a Heinkel came,
Spitting death at this chap so lame.
He did not shout or cry aloud,
He was but one of a suffering crowd
Who on a blood-bespattered shore
Thought of the friends they'd see no more.
The daylight faded fast away,
With it this hero, sad to say;
He was but young—just twenty-one—
But he died just like a British son.
So when this mighty struggle is O'er,
And Dunkirk beach knows peace once more,
Think, my friends, of the soldiers brave
Who died in France, Britain to save.

(L/Cpl. V.S.)

During the Kington period, about 450 reinforcements arrived; over a hundred from the Glosters depot, and a much larger contingent from the Welsh Regiment. In spite of this outnumbering, the unit retained its T.A. character.

A local curate caused a great deal of trouble at this time. It is not clear whether he was a rabid pacifist or merely an out-and-out defeatist. His talks with the men, however, were certainly calculated to lower morale and sap the determination of the Army personnel to resist invasion if and when it came (and to most people, now that France had capitulated, invasion within a few months seemed a near certainty). The offender was picked up by the C.M.P.s, arrested, and arreigned before the local Magistrates. His case, reported in the *Hereford Times* on 13th July 1940, was widely discussed. The charge was that 'on 17th June at Kington, he had unlawfully endeavoured to seduce from their duty certain persons in H.M. Services, or to cause among such persons disaffection likely to lead to a breach of their duty'. He was alleged to have said:

"Now that France has capitulated we might as well lay down our arms and give up the fight" to which our men replied:

"So long as the British Government give the orders to fight, we shall fight to the last man."

"But it wouldn't be much good if we carried on; we'd only get bombed, and then they would come over and finish us. There would be no Government to give the order; Churchill would be shot, and Moseley, Hitler's representative, would be dictator of the Country" he was alleged to have continued.

The offender was sent to prison for three months. He was lucky, for had he been in most countries, he would have been shot. Indeed, many of our own men would, had they been allowed, willingly have dealt with him in such a manner.

Many families came to see the Battalion; some to visit relations, others to make enquiries about those who had not returned. It was indeed a sad, sad period. One felt so helpless when faced by a relation who asked "Can you tell me something about Tom (or Dick, or Harry)?" when in so many instances there was little or nothing that could be said except, perhaps, that 'X' had reported seeing him in a slit trench, or on the march back, at 'Y' hours on 'Z' day. Most relations, though terribly worried, were very understanding and appreciative of the efforts being made to trace the movement of all those who had not returned.

The wives of some of those who were in Camp found accommodation in or near Kington for short periods. My wife was one of those who stayed at weekends at the Oxford Arms.

Here too, an official request was made that all private cars that could be spared should be loaned to the units to replace transport lost in France.

We left Kington early in July on what was, virtually, a 'Cook's Tour' of the South West and South East coasts of England. The first stop, almost a staging camp, was at Midsomer Norton in Somerset where again, the weather made the operation easy. During the first week, a chit came through from Division saying I would be granted a few days' leave in lieu of the foreshortened one in May. This was unexpected, but most welcome.

I arrived back at my billet in Midsomer Norton on the appointed afternoon to find that the unit, indeed the whole Division, had moved. The position was extraordinary, for no instructions had been left for me. All I could find out from local inquiry was that the Glosters had gone, it was thought, to Cornwall; there was a suggestion, but no more than that, that they were in the Bodmin area. I packed up my kit in the billet and set out at about 4.00 p.m.. This major move was unexpected, and money and petrol presented a serious problem, so I drove with extreme care.

Enquiries in Exeter and Okehampton confirmed that the Glosters were indeed in Bodmin, and the former place even produced a little petrol. All went well until about 10.00 p.m.; I came to Altarnum, the last village before Bodmin Moor, and it was evident that my petrol was too low for safety. Fortunately, a trusting local lent me half a gallon for the last lap of the journey. It was nearly midnight when I located Battalion H.Q. in the Royal Hotel, Bodmin, and was profoundly thankful to turn in after such a long and, at times, worrying day.

CHAPTER SEVEN

Bodmin

The ten months the Battalion spent in Bodmin, from July 1940 to May 1941, were so full of incident and interest that they could constitute a book on their own. Consequently, it will be necessary during this period, as also of the time in the Dover area, to focus attention on a few incidents which were representative of the general pattern.

Billets, from the start, were good, and even the disused prison, which had been taken over, possessed some distinct merit. The people of Bodmin, both individually and corporately, were kind. The Rector placed the church at our disposal and later part of the Town Hall became a social centre. This latter was run along the lines of the set-up which had worked so successfully at Marlborough in 1939. The local clergy, of various denominations, were a great help.

Soon after we arrived in Bodmin, I selected for one of our Parade Services (because of the large Welsh contingent) the hymn *Guide me, Oh Thou Great Redeemer*. Unfortunately, the church organist could not find *Cwm Rhondda*, so set the hymn to another well-known tune. Nobody sang, and afterwards a delegation of Welshmen, headed by Sgt. Bevan (the large Cardiff and International Rugby trialist) lodged an official protest. The following Sunday, led by Sgt. Bevan's private choir, *Cwm Rhondda* was sung unaccompanied, and the walls of that ancient church echoed with a volume and harmony they could rarely have experienced.

Almost as soon as we arrived in Bodmin, orders came through that selected beaches on the south and north coasts should be mined in view of possible invasion. This work was carried out mainly by sapper units.

One morning, when part of the Battalion were on a short route march, a perspiring R.S.M. arrived on a bicycle with a message that there had been an accident on a certain beach, and that a chaplain was urgently needed. The R.S.M. handed over his bicycle and took my place in the marching column. After hard peddling, I reached the Barracks, but alas! there was no four-wheeled transport in the camp. A dispatch rider quickly demonstrated the clutch, gears, brakes and twist-grip throttle controls of his *Norton 500*, and five minutes later, a rather apprehensive padré was wobbling his way through the lanes towards the main road to Plymouth via Liskeard. In remarkably short time, having spread alarm and confusion in Liskeard and the small villages en route, Norton and padré, *mirable dictu*, arrived safely at the casualty beach. Two hours later, a rather more confident (perhaps too much so) padré roared homeward, but failed to negotiate a sharp bend in the lane near Camp. Parson and bike shot through the hedge and ended up in a stubble field. Luckily, neither man nor machine were much the worse for their rustic frolic.

Much later in the war, the issue of motorcycles for chaplains was considered and approved, but acceptance was optional. This chaplain declined with thanks preferring, if his car was not available, to walk, or else beg, borrow or steal a lift when occasion demanded.

September 1940 was a period of extreme tension; our counter-attack rôle, in the event of an invasion, was an ever present possibility, and each Battalion in the Division had its containing or counter-attack rôle in specific areas. On Saturday the 7th, an 'O' Group was held in the D.C.L.I. Depot in Bodmin, and the Brigadier ended something like this:

"Well, gentlemen, it seems probable that we shall meet next time in the heat of battle. Good luck, and God bless you!".

Nothing transpired that weekend, but the following Sunday morning, the flap was really on. Holy Communion had been fixed for 6.00 a.m. at the 144 Field Ambulance, who were in Trebartha Hall on the Launceston side of Bodmin Moor. (Trebartha Hall, incidentally, had been selected some years earlier as the location for the filming of *The Hound of the Baskervilles*) I arrived at the Field Ambulance H.Q. and found it almost deserted. The unit, I was told, had moved out half an hour earlier, and were en route for their battle station. I returned quickly to Bodmin and found that my unit, too, had moved out. I joined them but, as the world knows, the German 'Operation Sea-Lion' never developed. Whether the alert on September 15th was a genuine one, or a hush-hush exercise to test Divisional mobility, we never heard.

Certain flying personnel from the Coastal Command stations of St Morgan and St Eval (we played them at rugby, soccer and hockey) stoutly maintained that barges had been bombed inside and outside certain ports on the north coast of France. They had seen it, so they said, with their own eyes!

Late in the month, an occasion of horse-play very nearly had unpleasant repercussions for the Battalion. A rather highly-strung lad who had been through Dunkirk with (apparently) no ill effects, reported to the M.I. Room with tummy ache. The foolish medical orderly, after the M.O. had seen the lad, took the boy into the waiting room and announced (with a wink to the others) that he would have to have an emergency appendectomy. With the help of the others, the poor chap was placed on the table, his trousers lowered, and the steely-cold *back* of a knife run across his stomach. The lad fainted in shock, and became quite ill. The M.O. blew up, but the matter did not end there; the unfortunate victim went on leave a little later and, on hearing of the event, his mother set out on the warpath. Her brother, a titled gentleman, was a prominent lawyer, and legal proceedings and questions in The House were threatened. At the C.O.'s request, I went to see 'Mama', and eventually the affair was smoothed over.

Training was a serious affair, and strenuously undertaken both on the beacon and all over the Moor. Fitness, in view of the experience in France and the possibility of German invasion and the consequent war of movement which might ensue, was a top priority. Route marches or forced marches took place about twice a week in the early days. Normally the Wednesday march was a minor affair of some twelve to fifteen miles, while the Saturday one was twenty-plus, reaching in time twenty-five to thirty miles. Exercises, too, were tough; especially when the hard weather set in. I remember two in particular.

The first was a forced march which ended with an assault crossing of the Fowey River in quite adverse conditions. I heard a young private say, in between gasps, to his mates, referring to his platoon officer:

"That there Mr Shepherd will kill the b..... lot of us before the end!"

Mr Shepherd didn't kill any of them in the end, but he hardened all of them up considerably!

The second exercise I remember, was a twenty-four hours Divisional scheme on the Moor in, literally, a blizzard, when for the first time in my life I developed chilblains. This, however, was not the remarkable event, but the fact that three times only in the whole twenty-four hours did I return to Battalion H.Q. for periods of twenty or thirty minutes to get a bite to eat and a drink; and *mirabile dictu*, on each occasion my Senior Chaplain (a charming Methodist, but a rabid teetotaller) arrived when I was either drinking neat rum, or enjoying it in my tea! I was taken on one side and warned of the dangers of alcohol!

Recreation, in spite of training pressure, was not forgotten; in August and September, exercises were often arranged so they ended on or near a safe beach to enable those who so wished to bathe. Later, field sports, soccer, rugby and hockey, were played regularly. A Punjabi Mule Battalion was stationed near Bodmin for a time, and two hockey matches were arranged. These were played on a tarmac pitch at terrific pace. The results, 3-3 and 4-4, were an indication of the evenness of play. Eight of our Battalion team had had county experience, while the Punjabi centre-forward was an Indian Olympic player. Several Battalion rugby players, including Sgt. Bevan and Lieut. Douglas Scarr, were selected for the Division and played in other representative games.

The late autumn and early winter (by which time the immediate threat of invasion was over) brought a number of changes in personnel. Several drafts had to be found for sister Battalions in India and the East, and the departure of old friends who had passed successfully through the fiery trial of battle was much regretted, for one realised that the break could be final.

With these went others who had not fitted into the unit. The M.O. left, and was replaced by Lieut. Kulkhany whose posting was, however, of a temporary nature while we awaited the arrival of a Doctor John Ellis, who soon settled in and stayed with the unit until the end of hostilities in Europe.

One change caused me considerable apprehension; Major Priestly had reformed the Battalion after Dunkirk (Colonel Buxton, it will be recalled, had been badly wounded during the withdrawal and it was not anticipated that he would return), and had been given command as an acting Lieut. Colonel—an appointment that had been welcomed. It came, therefore, as a surprise when a message was received stating that Colonel Buxton would shortly be returning to re-assume command. Remembering the situation in the Saar, and during the weeks which followed, I wondered what the future might hold. At that time too, chaplain volunteers were required for several overseas theatres including the Middle East and North Africa. Three times this notice was published in Divisional orders, and on each occasion my name went in, but nothing happened. It later transpired that the Senior Chaplain had not forwarded my applications. In time, I realised that his decision had indeed been directed by the hand of God, and I never again volunteered.

To my intense relief, it soon became patent that the Colonel's attitude towards me had completely changed. The reason was never disclosed, but I was profoundly thankful!

Soon after Colonel Buxton's return, and three days before an important exercise, a message was received that H.R.H. the Duke of Gloucester would be paying the unit a visit. The date clashed with that of an important exercise. The Colonel heard the news from the Adjutant when he came into the mess after a long, wet day of reconnaissance on the moors, in preparation for that same exercise. All present watched, waiting for the inevitable explosion, but it never came. The C.O. read the message a second time, put his glass down, and there followed a silence both pregnant and purposeful. Then,

"This is damned inconvenient. The exercise must go on. Padré, you will have to be largely responsible for the Duke. I will talk to you tomorrow."

The following morning, Command were asked to find out and report the Duke's interests. These, to my relief, included farming and shooting. The Duke was natural, talked easily, and was obviously interested in all that was going on. Far from being the ordeal I had anticipated, the periods when I was alone on duty with the Duke were most enjoyable.

The return of Colonel Buxton early in December meant to my joy, the inclusion of shooting (chiefly snipe and duck) in 'organised recreation'. The Colonel is the only man I have ever seen to have, and take, the chance of a right-and-left at woodcock. The following account of one of our organised shoots was published in the *Shooting*

Times for 1st January 1954. It was by far the most amusing day we had while stationed in Bodmin.

It was 1940, and the 5th Battalion the Severn-siders were in the far west. Christmas Day had been celebrated in the traditional Army manner, with Company dinners served in gaily decorated requisitioned halls where the N.C.O.s had waited at table. The Commanding Officer, Adjutant and R.S.M. (and in our case, accompanied also by the Quartermaster and the Padré) had done the rounds and, mercifully, had stood up to the repeated toasts demanded on these festive occasions.

Snow was falling as Boxing Day, (the officers' day off) dawned, but stopped before 8 o'clock. After a good breakfast, eaten with relish despite the sumptuous fare of the previous day, four guns (all from the Battalion), with two wives as beaters, set out for the water-meadows along the northern bank of the Camel. Three impromptu drives put eleven snipe in the bag, and brought the party to the reed-bed which formed the boundary of our shoot.

Here, a mallard was disturbed and, in his bemused and sleepy condition, flew back over the guns to fall right into the river. Two guns raced down the bank to retrieve the prized bird. The first failed to reach the mallard; and in straining to grasp the floating body as it sped past him, the second slipped and plunged headlong into the water, but the drake was firmly held. Bathing in June or July may be enjoyable, but on a cold Boxing Day it cannot be termed pleasurable! I know, for I was that second gun! Boots were emptied and stockings wrung out before continuing the day's sport.

A small tributary of the Camel was followed up for half a mile, and the hedgerows beaten out on the return journey. A teal and a rabbit found their way into the bag, but a wily old woodcock lay low until we had passed.

Back at the cars, an early lunch was taken, and off we drove to the moor, where permission had been obtained to shoot over two adjoining farms. The farmer, in whose yard the cars were parked, was in fine form and had obviously tapped his Christmas present, attacking it in a hearty manner. He pointed out the boundaries and wished us luck.

Two hours later, when beating out a likely dingle, a stranger appeared and, after appropriate seasonal greetings, said:

"So his Lordship isn't going out with you gentlemen after all?" to which one of the party replied quite truthfully: "No."

The newcomer, on learning that the afternoon's bag did not include a woodcock, said:

"Come on over to this spinney; I'm sure his Lordship would want you to have a 'cock.'"

He then beat out the small cover, and a fine woodcock was flushed and gathered. After the exchange of a few pleasantries we parted, his Lordship's keeper to attend his lawful business, well pleased with the additional, if belated, 'Christmas Box', and ourselves relieved that our boundary mistake had been covered by a merciful error of identity!

Retracing our steps rapidly, we obtained from the farmer's wife a clearer picture of the farm's limits.

A further short wander round resulted in a teal, which brought the total bag to seventeen snipe, three teal, two rabbits, a mallard, a pigeon and, of course, the woodcock.

In 1949, when lunching in Exeter with the Commander of a T.A. Brigade, I narrated this story. He appeared inordinately amused; it was only when he stopped laughing that the light really dawned, for he said:

"I really must remember to tell my cousin when I dine with him next Tuesday; he will be amused that his keeper assisted you in poaching his woodcock!"

It truly is a small world!

(reproduced, in part, by kind permission of the *Shooting Times*)

The South West was a defence area, and wives were not allowed to take up residence near the unit. One Sunday, late in December, Colonel Buxton summoned all officers and senior N.C.O.s to meet him after Church Parade. Speculation was rife; was it another invasion scare, or were we suddenly moving? The C.O. began by saying:

"I suppose you have read with interest that a very senior officer has been living in this Command not with his own wife, but with another's. I prefer that my officers and men should live with their own wives. I have today found digs for my wife who will be travelling down tomorrow. You, gentlemen, may also bring your wives down if you wish, provided I have your word that there will be no let up in training and discipline. If there are repercussions—and I cannot see that happening—I will carry the can. Good morning, gentlemen."

It was a fantastic statement coming from a C.O., and the Battalion showed its appreciation by its enthusiasm in training and exercise. Within a couple of weeks, more than a hundred and fifty wives were billeted in or near Bodmin.

The regular contacts with the local Methodist Minister at the Town Hall canteen, both in the services and at social gatherings during the autumn and winter, were extremely friendly. We discussed many subjects connected with our ministry. Some of his statements created a suspicion that a greater emphasis was being placed upon the Sacramental aspect of holy Communion by some members of the Free Churches than had been apparent since the death of Wesley. In Holy Week, an opening came for a clarification probe on the subject.

"What are your plans for Easter Day?" the Minister asked. I replied that an attempt would be made to give every sub-unit the opportunity to make their Easter Communion, and that the parade or voluntary services would have to be staged in the nearest town or village church.

Out of politeness, I asked him what were his services on that Easter. His reply was staggering, at least to me. He said:

"Well, I have put on an 8.00 a.m. Holy Communion, 11.00 a.m. Morning Prayer, and Evening Prayer at 6.00 p.m., and I have told my people that if they can only attend one service, they should try and come to the 8.00 a.m. for the Sacrament. I have hinted that that is the most important manifestation of public worship."

When questioned further, he said:

"Well, yes; certain of the younger men in our ministry tend to pay more attention to the Sacramental aspect of the Communion than do many of the older generation."

The remembrance of pictures of the Stations of the Cross and ornaments generally in Handsworth Theological College appeared now as but another manifestation of the same movement. Yes, in retrospect, it would appear that those 'winds of change', of which one heard so much in relation to Africa after the war, were already at work, ecclesiastically, in the South West Circuits.

During the period of December '40 to April '41, with so many wives and families in the area, life took on an almost parochial atmosphere, and a most happy one too![1]

The number of welfare cases, even before the advent of domesticity, was small. One of these, involving a member of another unit, shook my high regard for the Roman Church. The C.O. of the young man's unit telephoned and I went to try and help. We visited the girl (aged about eighteen) and her mother. The girl was indifferent to the fact that she was breaking up a home. At last, having found out she was Roman Catholic, I said we would go and see her Father Confessor.

This we did. At first, he was most sympathetic and promised to stop the whole affair. Then suddenly he asked, referring to the young man:

"Was he married in a non-Roman Catholic Church?" To my affirmative reply, he responded:

"Then I am afraid I can do nothing; we do not recognise that marraige."

I was badly shaken; and so was the young man when he was posted away shortly afterwards!

During the heavy bombing of Plymouth in the early months of 1941, several wives from the Battalion, including Vivienne, volunteered to take mobile canteens into that town. They did very good work and were, at times, in very considerable danger. I, personally, was relieved (much though I dislike leaving Bodmin) when the unit moved into the Plymouth area in May, and wives had to return home. We missed our wives very much but, frankly, I had been frightened every time they did canteen duty in Plymouth.

Notes

1. This parochial atmosphere was reflected even in Battalion: Part 1 Orders, e.g.:

   Battalion Part 1 Orders S/No. 77 dated Monday, 7th April, 1941.
   573, DIVINE SERVICES—GOOD FRIDAY, 11th April 1941.
   This is a full working day but facilities will be afforded for the attendance at service on Good Friday and it is hoped that many will take advantage of this opportunity and attend either the Ante-Communion Service at 1100 hrs or some part of the 3-hour Service from 1200 to 1500 hrs.
   It has always been the custom for people to come into this service, and leave at any time except during one or other of the addresses so there should be no doubt about coming out at any time between the hours of 1200 and 1500 hrs (except during actual addresses).
   Services for Easter Sunday, 13th April 1941, will be issued separately.

CHAPTER EIGHT

Devon

The move from Bodmin to the Plymouth area was also a two-stage affair, with a short stay by some of the Battalion in Uffculme and Willand, before Battalion H.Q. and two companies went under canvas in Kitley Park, and the other two companies into huts at Wembury.

The tented camp was not popular. Firstly, it was discovered that a decoy fire (to be lit when air-raids developed on Plymouth, which happened frequently and was one of the reasons for our move to the area) was sited alongside the wood in which our tents were erected. Representations were made after the first raid and the use of that decoy was discontinued. Secondly, the torrential rain turned the camp into a quagmire and because of the shade, the ground under the trees never dried out, so of necessity one became adept at channel-digging and the construction of drainage systems generally.

An amusing incident took place soon after our arrival. The owner of Kitley Park, an unfortunately-named Colonel Bastard, invited the C.O. and some other officers for a glass of sherry. Colonel Buxton, wishing to be polite when presenting his officers, referred to his host as Colonel Bast*erd*. The latter spoke up at once and said:

"Don't be afraid of offending, Colonel. It's bastard by name, and bastard by nature!" The party then went with a swing.

The Battalion, between exercises, sent parties into Plymouth to help in the clearing of the rubble after air-raids, and generally to assist in work of this nature. News came through late in May that the 5th Glosters were to be converted into a Reconnaissance Regiment. This resulted, it was believed, from the Battalion's performance in that type of rôle during a long and unpleasant Divisional exercise. It was an exciting prospect, and pleased everyone.

The Distance between the two main groups of the Battalion, the unit's rôle, and the various exercises, rendered Battalion services an impossibility, and church work had mostly to be undertaken on a company basis.

The Naval Hospital and Dockyard had to be visited, and the Saltash ferry linked us with Brigade and Divisional units on the other side of the River Tamar. These trips were full of interest because of the coming and going of ships of the Royal and Free French navies. The cruiser *Nigeria* and the large French submarine *Surcouf* were based upon Plymouth as, indeed, were several vessels of shallower draft. These ships were often to be seen moored at their berths, moving out, or returning from forays in the Channel and the Western Approaches. In the dockyard was the cruiser *Kent*. She had been torpedoed in the Mediterranean; after the gaping hole in her bows had been plugged, she had been towed via the Cape to the United States, and thence to Plymouth for major repairs. Colonel Johnstone of the 8th Worcesters was related to one of the *Kent*'s senior officers (the Captain, I believe) and an invitation came via the Colonel to lunch on board. This was an interesting interlude, in spite of a certain slowness in 'honouring' the Quarter-deck!

Nobody was sorry when, in June, the unit moved to Newton Abbot. Our stay was short, and marred by a tragic accident when a young trooper loosed off his tommy-gun in the billet, killing one of his room-mates and wounding two others. Training in the new rôle began, but at first (and indeed for some time) it was of an experimental nature.

From Newton Abbot, we moved in July to North Devon settling, after a few days in transit, in a group of villages centred on Winkleigh. In this village, the lads (on the first night) ran into Devonshire cider with a local variant known as 'Tanglefoot'. This was a cider, matured in old wine or brandy casks. It was smooth, but heady, and the non-country lads on that first evening drank what they called "this mild stuff" rather too freely. The Gloucestershire and true West Country boys went carefully, but a very large number of the new June drafts went out for the count. On Monday morning, the C.O. held a parade and dealt with the situation admirably:

In effect, he said, "you new chaps have learned a lesson the hard way. Do not treat lightly that of which you have no experience. You have had your punishment, and I will say no more, except Heaven help anyone who in future comes up on a charge of drunkenness!''

There was no more trouble from cider!

The company with whom I lived was billeted in Hatherleigh. I contacted the local Vicar the afternoon we moved in (the Saturday), and asked, having seen his service sheet in the church, whether I might take a celebration of Holy Communion at 7.00 a.m. the next morning, and a short Matins-type service at 9.30. He refused, saying he did not know me, or how I would conduct the Holy Communion or whether, in the second service, I would 'preach the Gospel'. I pointed out that the alternative to his church was the bar-parlour of the hotel which was Company H.Q.. He did not relent, so we held our Services in the pub. Later on in our stay, we were allowed to use Hatherleigh Church.

My father-in-law had been born in Fishleigh Manor nearby, and a call on the owner produced an invitation to fish a stretch of the *Lew* and the *Torridge*.

The water was low, and the daylight hours too few because of exercises and recreation at normal times. I fished, however, on several nights during the full moon periods of August and September, with more success than I deserved thanks to advice given to me years before by old William Elias, one of the greatest fishermen (and poachers!) in North Wales, on one of my holidays near Llannor. Success, however, was as nothing to the enjoyment I had on two nights when I encountered Tarka, face to face.

The first occasion, in August, was beneath a full moon in a cloudless sky. The first two hours, from ten o'clock till midnight, had produced just one fish, and that, a minimum which I lost. I had placed it up on the bank while I flogged a pool some yards away, only to find, on picking up the bag a few minutes later, that a rat had had an easy supper leaving precious little for me to grill. Soon afterwards, I cut across a loop in the river and made for a shelving shingle beach where, when the shingle came into view, I saw movement. I halted, peered, and saw that it was Tarka, dragging a fish on to the shingle. He stopped and at once, with his back arched, began his midnight meal. Still smarting from the loss of mine, my evil mind conceived a plan. Why not frighten Tarka and take his fish, and so replace the one the rat gnawed? Rod and bag were placed gently on the ground and, with as blood-curdling a yell as I could utter, I charged down the bank, confident that the fish was mine. Alas, alas! They say, truly, that pride comes before a fall; half-way down the gentle slope of my toe hit a small root, and I rolled the rest of the way to the shingle's edge. I got up at once, still intent on my brigandage, only to see Tarka, with determination, and I felt sure disdain, dragging the fish into the water and away. I laughed and gave him best. Would the L.D.V. or police, hearing the yells, assume a madman was at large, and converge on the spot? I quickly seized my kit, and made for billets.

Another night, it was September then, I was fishing the same stretch of river. Success, and that comparative, had only come with William Elias' 'Special'. Midnight had passed and I was drifting a home-made light moth down a large pool into the run below, when an otter whistled. Thrice this happened, and the sound seemed to be nearer each time. Suddenly, after a silence of some minutes, a silver ream appeared at the exit of the pool and in the moonlight, I saw Tarka swimming upstream. I froze and watched as, silent as a ghost, the otter approached nearer and nearer. Mercifully, no fish paid any attention to the moth, and the rod and line remained motionless. Finally, when Tarka was almost alongside me (a bare three feet away, maybe), I spoke. A sudden swirl, and Tarka was gone. I have often wondered whether it was the same otter I had encountered a month before, or the mate perhaps? If this was so, what discussions they must have had about the strange, uncouth intruder who at times invaded their demesne, interrupting their midnight activities.

It was during this period that our organisation and designations were changed and we became, officially, the 48th Reconnaissance Regiment.

In October, we took part in the gigantic 'Exercise Bumper' in which the 48th Division finished up near Bedford. For this operation, because the Recce Regiment was working as independent squadrons, I was posted to the 8th Worcesters. I was told at the end of the exercise (it was then late afternoon) that I should make my own way back to North Devon. Enough petrol for the trip was given, and also some hard rations. All units were to harbour where they wished for the night. I disliked the prospect of travelling alone, and even more the thought of sleeping in the car for the night; I had no money to put up at a hotel.

As I drove along, I turned over the idea of diverting and spending the night at home. I stopped and ate some sandwiches while doing the mileage sums and calculating the petrol. The plan was impossible because I would have needed another two or three gallons. I drove on, even more disgruntled. Four or five miles further on, a miracle occurred, or so it seemed; there in the middle of the road, battered but still holding its contents, was a square Army 4-gallon tin petrol container, which had obviously fallen from some R.A.S.C. vehicle proceeding homewards—a convoy had passed while I had been making my calculations. It was manna (liquid variety) from Heaven! I spent the night at home, and reached Hatherleigh before my boys the next day.

In November, the 48th Division became a Home Defence Division and were ordered to move to the East Coast, and the three Regular Battalions and the Recce Regiment were drafted to combat formations. I, as a Divisional Troops Chaplain, was destined for Lincolnshire. I had been with the unit now, in peace and war, for three years, and with the C.O. friendly now, I hated the thought of leaving my 'family'. The C.O. approached Divisional H.Q., but without success, and so I packed to go. The morning I left, the C.O. gave me a letter to deliver personally at the War Office, on the way to Lincoln (I was still driving my own car, it must be remembered), again asking for my retention:

5th Bn. The Gloucestershire Regt.
Winkleigh
N. Devon

10.11.41

Sir,

I respectfully bring the following to your notice; although the procedure may be somewhat unusual, I consider the case merits it.

I am giving this letter to my padré, Revd. Gethyn-Jones, to use as he thinks fit, and in the hope that it may possibly help in his being allowed to remain with this Battalion.

Throughout my service, and especially as C.O., I have always realised the immense value a padré, who has gained the respect and confidence of all ranks, is to a unit.

Gethyn-Jones has achieved this in this Battalion and it has been a great help to me as regards the happiness and general spiritual welfare of the Battalion. I first met him in June 1938, when Canon Helm sent him to me to interview with the idea that he should be posted to this Battalion, which he eventually was, and has served with us ever since, including in France and Belgium. He will be a great loss to this Battalion if he has to leave us now we are being transferred to another Division.

> A Territorial Unit is somewhat different to a Regular Unit and there are still a large number of men in this Battalion who come from parishes in Gloucestershire whom he knows.
>
> It is because I attach so much importance to his retention in this Battalion that I am writing this, and can only hope it may be possible to arrange it.
>
> I have the honour to be, Sir,
> Your obedient Servant,
>
> G.A.H. Buxton

The chances, however, seemed remote. I called at Taunton on the way to say good-bye to the D.A.C.G. (The Reverend D.D. Lloyd-Evans) who said:

"You sound pretty miserable!"

The C.O.'s letter was produced and read, after which the D.A.C.G. questioned me on the whole background of peacetime and war service. On hearing the full details he said:

"We'll soon fix that!"—three telephone calls followed in quick succession. The first was to the War Office, when strange Welsh words were passed between the D.A.C.G. and the Deputy Chaplain General (the Reverend Gethin Hughes). During this quite long conversation, my spirits began to rise, but the occasional introduction of rapidly spoken Welsh which I could not follow created slight apprehension. Calls two and three were, I imagine, in the nature of D.O.s to Eastern and South-Eastern Commands, informing them that a padré named J.E. Gethyn-Jones would *not* now be going to Lincolnshire, but would instead be reporting to the 43rd Recce Regiment in a few days. Then the D.A.C.G. said:

"Let's go to lunch; I think we've earned it!"

He had! I returned via Winkleigh to Hatherleigh that evening, a happy man, and set out with the Regiment on the 17th November for Kent and the 43rd Division.

CHAPTER NINE

Knowlton Park, Kent

The Regiment, after a long and tiring convoy across country, arrived in eastern Kent on 19th November at the commencement of 'Great Binge', a five-day Divisional exercise. It was indeed an exhausting week.

The Divisional Senior Chaplain, the Revd. Victor Pike (the one-time Irish Rugby captain), was surprised and annoyed to find that a chaplain had arrived with the Recce Regiment. He pointed out that he had his full quota of Divisional Chaplains and that consequently, there was no room for me. He added that I had better report to him in Canterbury the next day, in preparation for a move back to the 48th Division, who were now in Lincolnshire. That meeting was most uncomfortable. The S.C.F. state that the War Office had instructed him to post one of his chaplains away to make way for me. This was upsetting for him and, naturally, he was furious. I, the wretched cause of the trouble, caught the full blast of his Irish wrath.

A few weeks later, a message came from the S.C.F. ordering me to report to him the next day with my kit, for transfer to another unit within the Division. It was clearly the preparation for an outside posting. I reported as ordered, and found the S.C.F. extremely angry. His words were few:

"I have had a rocket from the War Office for trying to move you from the Glosters. They say you want to stay with them. Well, go and rot with them!"

I fled. It was a shocking and worrying start to life in a new Division.

The S.C.F. left shortly afterwards to become D.A.C.G. 11th Corps. We next met years later at Bagshot soon after he had become Chaplain General. The 1941 incidents in Kent were brought up, and caused considerable merriment amongst the party. The C.G. could not have been nicer to me that day and, indeed, throughout his time 'in the chair'.

On 6th December (1941) came the official order (still in my file) posting R.A. Hood to Aldershot area, and myself to the 43rd Division. Thus began an association with the Wessex Division which lasted, with but one break, until 1956, and in a slightly less intimate way, until 1961.

The unit was billeted in Squadron locations eastward of Canterbury from Wickambreux to Ash and Knowlton. This made close contact with the more distant sub-units in the appalling snows and frost of the winter difficult. We were, however, never completely bogged down, and church services, for example, were nearly always on time. The local clergymen were very co-operative and, because Knowlton Park was R.H.Q., the private chapel there became, literally, *our* church.

A second intelligence test (Recce personnel were required by the War Office to attain in these tests a higher standard than the Infantry) in December, following the earlier one at Hatherleigh, further depleted our numbers. These tests were repeated for all new drafts. The C.O. was permitted, especially when the invasion became imminent, to retain a few of the key specialists who had failed. The M.O. (Doc. Ellis) and I, and many others too, were a little sceptical of the validity of the premises behind these tests, but a check on the retained personnel who had not reached the prescribed standard showed that, in the stress of operations in Normandy, they had been more liable to battle exhaustion. The tests were thereby fully vindicated.

On 7th January 1942, a draft of one hundred reinforcements arrived direct from civilian life, and although thirty failed their matrix test, the remainder were good material and produced many excellent N.C.O.s. Lieutenant Colonel Buxton was soon afterwards promoted to full Colonel, and left to command a District.

Leave came round in early January, and on returning to R.H.Q. on the 20th, I found dinner in progress and the new C.O., Lieut. Colonel A.D. Ward, presiding. There was a vacant place at table next to him, and to this seat I was motioned. For the rest of the meal, the Colonel talked on many subjects; leave, family, parish and games. Dinner ended, and the real Dudley Ward spoke:

"Waiter, the padré and I will take coffee in my room." There, from 8.30 until nearly midnight, I was treated to one of the brilliant expositions and outlining of plans with which we (and later 12 Corps, 4th British Division, and 5 Corps) became familiar. Firstly, there was a detailed account of his talk on the previous day to all officers and N.C.O.s. It contained an appreciation of the Recce rôle, and a clear outline of his policy for the training of the Regiment, which included a major re-organisation of the unit. He then explained how he proposed to help me, as Padré, and what he expected of me. He had pointed out to the officers and N.C.O.s that they were leaders of, and examples to, their men in every way, and that they would be expected to give a lead in matters both secular and spiritual. He further informed them that he would be present, duty permitting, at 8.00 a.m. Holy Communion every Sunday. He expressed the hope that his example would be followed by many. Few padrés can have had a more terrifying, yet heartening, introduction to a C.O..

I rapidly acquired a great regard for Colonel Ward, both as a man, and as a leader. I have always considered him and General Wavell the greatest of leaders whom I met during the War.

I admired Montgomery's psychological perception, and his ability to 'sell himself' for the cause. By so doing, he laid himself open to the charge of showmanship which many, especially amongst the officers, levelled against him. This, I felt, was a loathsome and carping criticism of a deliberate campaign which was eminently successful. I remember one particular incident in December 1944 when taking prayers with the troops on the banks of the *Meuse* during the early stages of Von Rundstedt's Ardennes offensive. Conditions were chaotic and the rumours, especially among the Americans, were depressing. I had my back to the ice-bound road and was facing the men. Suddenly, as a vehicle drove by, they stiffened to attention and saluted. When they came down from the salute the Sergeant spoke, almost in soliloquy: "Monty. Thank God! Now we shall be all right!" It was clear from the attitude of the men that he really spoke for all present; such was the confidence that Monty had inspired in the majority of the 'other ranks' by his 'preaching tour' in South East England during the spring of 1944. I admired, too, Monty's obvious ability as a strategist and tactician, but to me he had not the human touch of Ward and Wavell.

Early in February the Colonel obtained Broome Park, Lord Kitchener's one-time home, as a training centre for potential N.C.O.s. Major

Charles Kinnersley was placed in command of this centre and assisted the Colonel in drawing up the training manual which they termed the 'Recce Bible'. This long course was eminently successful. The chaplain, to the surprise of some, was allocated a place in the instructional programme.

The preparations for the furnishing of the messes and recreational rooms in Broome Park were the direct cause of an unpleasant programme.

On 12th February, the day the *Gneisenau*, the *Scharnhorst* and the *Prinz Eugen* sailed so successfully up the Channel, the Broome Park Q.M. (Lt. Parry), the S.Q.M.S. and I were detailed to drive to Dover to buy the needed furniture. It must be recorded that we were ignorant of the heroic drama taking place just a few miles out to sea. The considerable air activity was assumed to be nothing more than a tactical exercise. In Dover, the second-hand shops were disappointing, so we decided to try Folkstone. Half way down the final approach to that town, and at the steepest part of the hill, there is a hair-pin bend. Well before reaching that point, it seemed to me the car was travelling too fast. The driver, Trooper Bridges, advised to brake, replied:

"I am, Sir, but they have failed... and the gear lever's stuck!"

"There's an escape road ahead on the right, near the corner. Try for that." was the next instruction.

Horror of horrors! An ascending bus barred the way to safety: Trooper Bridges, with commendable coolness, clung grimly to the wheel and strove to negotiate the bend. But at the speed we were travelling, it was hopeless. Centrifugal force won, the car overturned, tobogganed on its steel roof down, across the road, up the pavement and glanced off a tree. Had this tree not deflected us in our headlong flight we would have shot into mid-air only to drop into a deep quarry bordering the footpath. Bridges damaged an elbow, and we were all cut, bruised and shaken. The jack shot out of the boot, hit my head and knocked me out. Even so, we were extremely fortunate. The next morning, I blacked out on P.T. Drill, and was temporarily exempted from those early morning frolics. That order was never rescinded! After a week or two, however, I again attended those exercises, but not in P.T. kit.

General Montgomery inspected the Regiment in March, when two incidents caused amusement. He did a normal inspection, then ordered all hats to be removed. He then repeated his inspection with the comment: "Now I can see the *real* man!" The second amusement concerned new battle dress, of which the Regiment was in short supply. R.S.M. Capener, relying on detailed briefing and split-second timing, arranged for the first six or eight of the front rank, after they had been inspected, to move back in different order to the second rank. This scheme was duplicated at the other end of the second line where, after inspection, they exchanged with the rear rank. Whether or not the beady eye of the general spotted the ruse, we never knew, but no comment was made.

Sport, both as a relaxation and as an aid to fitness, was encouraged by Colonel Ward, who was himself an Army runner and an able hockey player. Daily P.T., and a weekly cross-country run, also formed part of the fitness campaign. There were no hockey pitches available (in any case, the snow and frost would have prevented play) so I took my recreational exercise on the Worth marshes and the water-meadows of the River Stour. The enjoyment was great, but the rewards were few for without a dog it was useless and wrong to shoot a duck or snipe unless they were over land, where they could be retrieved. There remain several amusing memories of these outings.

On one occasion, I met a farmer on the marsh who said:

"Make sure you shoot a sheep with your snipe, padré!"

I laughed and said:

"Will the police believe it was an accident?"

"Oh yes!" he replied, "They did when Major X... shot one last week, and Lieut. Y... shot one the week before."

The farmer obviously liked his un-rationed mutton!

Another time, some geese landed six hundred yards away alongside a rine into which I had dived when I heard their call. The ice was solid, so to my simple mind a goose was as good as in the bag. I marked carefully the position of a bush near where the geese were feeding, and crawled on my belly along the ice (having difficulty passing beneath a bridge) to a point some fifty yards from the bush. I was exhausted and soaking with perspiration, so lay for a few minutes to recover my breath before the final advance. Suddenly, a Spitfire flew over almost at ground level. With a cackle and roar of wings, the geese lifted and headed away from me—I would cheerfully have shot at the Spitfire pilot had he returned!

Winter gave way to Spring, and on the 16th May the Regiment left the Squadron Locations and came together as one unit into Old Park Barracks, Dover.

CHAPTER TEN

Dover

The Dover period was by far the most interesting and, in a way, the most satisfying of our many home stations. I believe this feeling was shared by the majority of the Regiment. If we could not go overseas, we could at least, in Dover, see and experience some little of the meaning of war, and our mobilisation seemed necessary. In addition, leave came regularly and, although it was a closed area, wives and sweethearts could obtain permits to stay in the area for two or three days.

Here in Old Barracks, for the first time since Bodmin, the unit was in a single location. This coming together was essential if the ésprit de corps, so important to a Regiment shortly to become involved again in a major campaign and which had been abundantly evident in the dark days of 1940, was to be fully developed.

The Barracks contained accommodation for two full units. Our Regiment was fortunate in that it was allocated the higher one, built almost entirely on the flat top end of a valley leading up from the town, and having a lane forming its north-eastern perimeter giving easy access to Dover or to the Canterbury and Deal roads. The parade ground was centrally placed and here, during an incendiary raid on the town, a most amusing incident was witnessed.

It was latish, 10.00 p.m. maybe, when we in the Mess realised that fires had started in earnest in the town, and that the majority of the unit were viewing the sight from the parade ground. A few planes could be heard droning round, and the absence of anti-aircraft fire indicated that the night-fighters were up. A move was suggested, and to a man the mess went out to view the spectacle.

Approaching from the Deal direction, a German bomber could be seen caught in the beam of a search-light and within a minute, several more probing shafts were brought to bear on the single aircraft which, in consequence, was brilliantly illuminated. It appeared to be, and indeed was, directly overhead when the belly of the plane opened, and an object, bright and silvery in the pool of light, began to fall.

The plane must have been comparatively low, for this was seen clearly by the whole unit. The object emerged, the single word 'Bomb' was whispered accompanied by, it seemed, a rustling of leaves, and lo! the parade ground was empty—not one of the 800 men could be seen! Never, repeat never, have I witnessed so rapid a dispersal and so complete a 'fading away' of a complete Regiment.

I watched, from the safety of the sand-pit into which I had dived, and saw the fragmentation of the bomb while it was still high up in the beam. A few of these component parts (incendiary bombs) fell on the camp, but the majority landed in the fields behind the Officers' Mess. No damage was done.

The German cross-channel batteries regularly shelled Dover and the cliff batteries, while a few fell in the village of Whitfield where the Barracks were situated. One of these 'overs' made a huge crater in the Rectory garden. The incumbant, Revd. J. C. Fortescue-Thomas, was a god-son of my grandfather. On another occasion, when motoring along to take evening prayers for a group of Batteries on the cliffs east of the Castle, the *Bosch* dropped a shell a hundred and fifty yards ahead of the car. It was safe enough, but too close for comfort and was, all things considered, a most unfriendly act!

During these shellings of the town, life became quiet to some degree, all except at the Crypt. Here, in an underground restaurant kept by Mr and Mrs Evans, life went on. The proprietors' boast was 'We never close—meals at all times'; and what meals they were too! It was generally felt, and rightly so, that Mr and Mrs Evans did more to provide social amenity and maintain morale than any other agency or organisation in the town and evirons of Dover. If anyone ever deserved a decoration, those two did. Although they received nothing of this nature, they had at least the satisfaction of knowing that they had won the admiration and gratitude of thousands of service people.

(In April 1947, my wife and I were going over to photograph some of the graves of the 5th Glosters/43rd Recce Regiment in France, Belgium, Holland and (we hoped) Germany, and I called in and asked

Mr Evans to reserve us a table for three on May 8th, the day of our return, adding: "Please reserve, if possible, three large Dover Soles, really large, because it will be my wife's birthday." The boat was very late docking on the 8th, and we did not arrive at the Crypt until nearly 10.00 p.m.. The bar was crowded, but the tables were empty so I went to the kitchen at the back to apologise to Mrs Evans. There on a large blackboard, used to record order details, were chalked in big block letters 'PADRE—THE 3 LARGEST SOLES'—they were! They dwarfed the plates, overspilling on every side!)

Padré's Hours, Confirmation classes, discussion groups, and general pastoral work figured frequently in one's programme while services, both Sunday and weekday, could now be held centrally. On some Sundays, the services (following the practice established during the Knowlton Park period) were voluntary, while we experimented in the matter of Church Parades. When these took place the men, dressed to Parade standard, were not inspected, but reported to the N.C.O.s on duty at the door of the hall where the Services were held. Thus the irritation of Platoon, Company, and Regimental inspections where removed, and the men came (I fondly believe) in a much less hostile frame of mind.

General G.I. Thomas took over command of the 43rd Division in March 1942, and some time later called a conference of all his chaplains. This took place in Canterbury and the General, with very few preliminaries, stated that he wished his chaplains to preach a *Jihad* (a Mohammedan word for a war against unbelievers) crusade. Furthermore, he laid down during this 'pep' period that the addresses given throughout the Division on each Sunday should be identical; that every chaplain would receive a copy of an approved address and preach or read it verbatim.

The storm broke.

It was pointed out that chaplains were individuals who varied considerably in thought and outlook, and that such a method, imposed from above by a layman, was totally unacceptable. They said furthermore that they believed they were commissioned by Christ to preach the Gospel and not a *Jihad*. They conceived that it was their duty to inculcate into the personnel of their units the recognition and acceptance of Christian faith and practice, and also to prepare them to face the strain of battle and, if it should come, death itself. The General, understandably angered by this flat refusal to accept his policy, banged the table with his cane, saying that never before had he encountered such an unco-operative, indeed rebellious, body of chaplains, and stormed out.

The Senior Chaplain then took over the conference, and a short scheme of sermons, in keeping with the expressed feelings, was outlined and agreed. Every chaplain was to receive a brief subject sketch for each of the addresses. He would, however, work out his own approach and interpretation. It must, in fairness, be pointed out that the General did, in time, come to understand the chaplains' point of view, bearing them no malice and backing them strongly.

Although we were 43rd Divisional chaplains, we were also temporarily part of the Dover Garrison, and several Divisional padrés assisted with the static units such as anti-aircraft, shore and cliff Batteries. My occasional extra commitments included certain Cliff Batteries and a Battery set in one of the Harbour Moles. To the services of the latter came, now and again, some members of the A.S.R. service, and on more than one occasion, when the Service was over, an operational trip out to sea became one of the pleasant 'perks' of the padré!

The D.A.C.G. held a Staff meeting every Monday morning which the 43rd Division chaplains stationed in the Dover area were expected to attend. The D.A.C.G., a very good man, rattled me on one occasion. He had preached Harvest Festival at Whitfield Church the Sunday night before and in the congregation he had spotted my wife and myself. At the Monday meeting, thinking perhaps of security regulations, he said:

"Gethyn-Jones, what is your wife doing here?"

The reason was an operation which a Harley Street man (resident in or near Whitfield) suggested should be done in the local hospital so that I could see Vivienne almost every day during the early post-operative period. I disliked the D.A.C.G.'s public interrogation, and merely said it was a personal matter. He pressed for a more definite answer, and so one word led to another. Finally I told him that it was no business of his and that in future I would not be attending his Staff meetings, nor would I be taking any further orders from him. I then walked out.

My S.C.F. saw me the following day and I explained the situation, saying that I had no intention of having my private affairs discussed in public. In the end, after more than two months and an exchange of apologies, I once more attended the Monday meetings.

I fully realise that I must have been a difficult padré to handle at times, because I have always been quick-tempered and resentful of what I considered autocratic or dictatorial attitudes or unwarranted interference. I suppose I have always been a rebel at heart, and just wished to be left alone. It was during this same period that I had a flare-up with a new S.C.F. of the Division.

The new S.C.F. arrived at Divisional H.Q. in 1943 and within two days had broken his leg. There was a Staff Chaplain, but I was pulled in to act for the S.C.F. when it was realised that he would inevitably be 'Y' listed. Leave came round first for the Staff Chaplain, Rev. A.E. (Bertie) Edwards, and then for me. It was arranged that I would not leave until the evening of Edwards' return. At 5.00 p.m. that day, when I had written a brief report to Bertie, a message came through that a new S.C.F. (Rev. Raymond Clayton) had been appointed and would arrive in two days time. I stayed at the office until nearly 11.00 p.m. writing out all details relating to Division and Corps, and tried generally to put him in the picture about chaplains and the future, as far as was known. I then telephoned Edwards and went over to see him so that he could be fully briefed and able to amplify my report, if necessary, to the S.C.F.. Finally, I wrote a note of welcome to the new S.C.F..

During leave I heard nothing from the S.C.F., despite the full report and detailed position relating to chaplains I had left for him. On returning to Old Park, I was told by the Mess Corporal that the S.C.F. had telephoned several times asking me to report to him directly I returned, and to report to him in person at his office at 9.00 a.m. the next morning. I failed to get him, so I telephoned Edwards who painted a grim picture of an autocratic S.C.F. who was riding his position.

I arrived at Divisional H.Q. at ten-to-nine the next morning where the C.M.P. said the S.C.F. had been down twice to enquire about my arrival, and had left orders that I was to report immediately. I was well before time, so this cracking of the whip following on from the peremptory messages of the night before irritated me, and I decided upon a show-down. So I went to the lavatory and read the morning paper until 9.30 and then reported.

The balloon went up.

I said nothing until he had finished, when I merely said that we in the Division were fellow priests and that the accident of his new appointment was no justification for his autocratic and ungentlemanly behaviour, and that if he desired the loyalty and co-operation of his chaplains, he had better treat us as adults and not as irresponsible children. He took it well and we arrived at a fair *modus vivendi*. Unfortunately for him, he fell foul of the Divisional Commander, and soon afterwards a new and more acceptable S.C.F. arrived in the person of Revd. Ivan D. Neill. Some chaplains feared this latter, but as far as I was concerned, he was by far and away the best S.C.F. I ever served under. He was able and considerate of his chaplains, and never spared himself in battle.

Recreation in the form of dances was a major problem in Dover as it had been at Knowlton Park. The Navy at Dover, and the R.A.F. at Hawkinge, were the only real sources of supply for partners, and duties in both Services often made it difficult for their young ladies to come. It usually fell to the padré to contact the unit and obtain the consent of the senior officer (female), assuring them that their charges would be well watched and brought back (under my personal supervision) by the stipulated time.

The first contact with the Senior Service, Female Branch, was an occasion for an appalling 'clanger' on my part. I asked the C.O. and the Adjutant of whom I should seek permission for the girls to come. Neither knew, but suggested that I should ask for the 'Senior Wren'. The lady Flag Officer (I believe that was her rank), to whom I made the request, blew up and informed me that the Chief Wren was an N.C.O., or something equivalent, and not the Senior Officer! She calmed down, and the girls came, causing a terrific hit—the Wrens were always more popular than the girls of the other Services.

I will never forget the 'Passing Out' dance, at Broome Park, of the civilian intake course. On that occasion, I collected two bus-loads of W.A.A.F.s. The evening was fine and warm for May, and all went well until the time came for the girls to be shepherded home. I called the roll, and half the girls were missing. Half an hour later, having combed the Park and the Mansion, we had all but one. She turned up eventually, having been to a pub some miles away for a drink. I could have wrung her neck because it got the Regiment a bad name, and that particular source of dancing partners was cut off.

The Very Reverend Hewlett Johnstone, one of the most able, colourful, but controversial clerics, the 'Red Dean' of the day, was Dean of Canterbury. I invited him to talk to the Mess after dinner one evening, and he willingly accepted. He gave a brilliant exposition on the bible and its meaning but (out of politeness, I learned later) held back on politics, a subject which had been the *raison d'être* for the issued invitation. He came again, later, ranging over a variety of subjects. This was greatly appreciated, and it was with reluctance that the party was broken up after midnight.

The Dean also gave a talk at one of the Sunday evening services and sing-songs in the Town Hall at Dover. His impact there was not as great, chiefly no doubt, because there were not the searching questions and cut-and thrust of argument that there had been in the Mess at Old Park.

A story concerning the Dean, but which has no connection with the Regiment, is worth narrating. It was the night of one of the big raids on Canterbury and many houses, including the Deanery, had suffered hits. At the height of the attack, and while the fires were still blazing, the Dean, his pyjamas showing under his cassock, toured the bombed area and chatted with victims, wardens, and others on duty. An old lady, being dug out of the rubble that had been her home, spotted the tall, bushy-haired figure and asked him whether the Cathedral had been damaged, adding that he should go back to bed before he caught a cold! The Dean replied to the effect that the Cathedral still stood and pointed to Heaven, and that they would both be able to say their prayers there when daylight came; to which the old lady is reported to have said: "God is good!" This story may have been exaggerated but it was in circulation the following day.

Exercises from now until the actual landing in Normandy were frequent and, increasingly in their size and nature, indicated our rôle in the invasion and subsequent breakout from the bridgehead. On these exercises, and in the more basic training, we had some accidents, some of which were fatal. Two officers were wounded, Major Blood losing a finger and part of his hand, and Captain Day an eye. Both rejoined us later, the latter telling a good story of the acquisition of his glass eye:

Discharged from hospital, he was given a chit to obtain a replacement from an opthalmic shop. Here, the girl (none too clean, and with a frock that needed washing, said John Day) took the chit, looked at his remaining eye, presumably for colour and size, and murmered:

"Tray seven, I suppose."

She returned from the cabinet and held up the false eye alongside the good one. After careful scrutiny, her verdict was that it was a splendid match whereupon, said Day, she 'harred' upon the eye, polished it on her none-too-clean skirt, and popped it into the waiting socket. It was so unexpected, and so deftly performed, that poor John had no time to protest and demand prior decontamination for the eye! Anyway, he suffered no ill effects.

Colonel Ward, to give variety to our programme and add spice to our training, arranged with the Senior Naval Officer in Dover that the Regiment should send some Officers and Other Ranks on board the anti 'E' Boat patrol boats at regular intervals. Each party consisted of two Officers and about twenty O.R.s, who took ·50 'Boys' rifles and Bren guns with them. Ostensibly, they were to give additional fire power, but interest and battle experience for the men were the real reasons. These trips (on which I was allowed to take my turn) were greatly appreciated even though casualties, including fatal ones, were suffered at times. Other units followed suit, but the practice was eventually vetoed by the War Office because (so they said) the occasional heavy casualties could not be accepted as justifiable on what was, after all, not a really necessary operation.

Colonel Dudley Ward left the Regiment to become B.G.S. 12 Corps in July 1942. His 'reign' had been the making of the Regiment, while his 'Recce Bible' provided the text-book for all subsequent operations. In January 1948, while staying at Dymock for the Cathedral service when the 'Colours' were restored to the unit (once again the 5th Glosters), he took Colonel Charles Kinnersley (who, as 2 I.C. and from the middle of the Arnhem period as C.O. spanned the entire active service period of the 43rd Recce Regiment's life) for a five-mile walk round after church, and made him narrate in detail the events of June 1944 to May 1945. When the tale was fully told, General Ward spoke for the first time and said:

"Well, I'm glad that the (Recce) Bible teaching and theory worked in battle. Excellent!"

We all (or nearly all) held Colonel Ward in very high esteem; we also feared him in the sense that we did not wish to let him down. I remember one grim moment on the South Downs. An exercise without troops had been set for all officers and senior N.C.O.s. The C.O. had gone on ahead and we were scheduled to meet him at 9.30 a.m.. Vehicles had been detailed by the M.T.O., but these were late. As we drew near the rendezvous, we saw the C.O. pacing up an down, tapping his leg with his cane. The poor wretched M.T.O., Captain John Ellis (known as 'Mechanical John' to distinguish him from Captain John Ellis the M.O., who was known as 'Doc John'), said:

"Hold tight boys; here it comes!"

"Sit down, gentlemen." said the C.O. quietly, "What has happened this morning happens only once in the life of any good unit. It has happened in the 43rd Recce Regiment. Now let us get on with our exercise."

During our long stay in Dover, with so many sports fields available (the Duke of York School's among them), games on a wide scale were played. The Regimental record was good, and many of its members played in representative games; Lieuts. Taylor and Crawshay at cricket, Captain Scarr and two others in rugby, several at soccer, while Lieut. Faulkner and I played hockey for South-Eastern Command, and I went on to play in the 1942/3 and 1943/4 seasons for the Army against, among others, the R.A.F., the Hockey Association, and the South of England. In these games, I renewed many old friendships of my first-class playing days; Kirkpatricks (Scotland), Lewis (Wales), and Dodds and Slack (England).

Shooting, despite the fact that we had almost one-and-a-half wild-fowling seasons in Dover, figured only twice in my diary, but both outings were, in their own way memorable. These two occasions were in 1942. In 1943, during the summer, my gun was in for repair at a shop in Canterbury when the city was heavily blitzed. The shop was destroyed and my gun lost—perhaps that was why there were no shooting entries in my diary for the 1943/4 season.

The one day coincided with a Saturday afternoon light bomber raid on Canterbury. Vivienne, who was staying for the weekend at the local Rectory, was with me, and we were walking up some ditches looking for duck or snipe. We could see and hear the raid taking place, and had seen planes crossing and re-crossing the coast. Suddenly, two Messerschmidts tore directly at us (it seemed) at no more than fifty to sixty feet altitude. we dived into the ditch, out of the way of possible machine-gunning, and a few seconds later, the two aircraft passed almost directly over us. I put my gun up, as at a goose, but refrained from pulling the trigger (much though I wanted to) because of the Geneva Convention. Perhaps I was foolish?

The second occasion formed the latter half of the article published in the *Shooting Times*, which is here reproduced verbatim with permission:

> 'It was 1942, and the Dover air was warm with the bright September sunshine when Colonel Biscuit of the 99th Severnsiders returned to the Mess. A quick drink and lunch was served. Over coffee, the C.O. turned to the padré, whose parish was Leadonway in the West Country, and said:
>
> "You shoot, don't you? What about a walk round after tea?" He then spoke to the Adjutant, "Cole, we have lent farmer Brown twenty men for harvesting this week. Pop round and persuade him to allow us to walk his stubbles, will you?"
>
> After tea, in answer to the C.O.'s question, Captain Cole replied that that would be alright. "Good. Arthur and Padré be ready by 5.15." Major Arthur (whose prowess on the tin whistle was recognised by the entire Regiment; did he not regularly compete with the Band at Officers' Mess dances, and just as regularly drown the caterwauling of the Mess felines on Saturday nights, in a benevolent attempt to sooth his brother officers to sleep?) was a keen shot, and was ready in the hall before either of the others.
>
> The first stubble, next to the Mess, produced a large but very wild covey, and a single bird to the parson's gun was the only casualty. As it was being gathered, a figure was seen approaching over the rise in the next field, and recognised as that of the bluff farmer. In the cause of friendship and co-operation, it was decided to thank Farmer Brown and offer him the bird before following the covey across the road.
>
> The cheery greeting of the C.O. was stifled at birth when, at twenty yards range, the bucolic child of the soil shot out:
>
> "What the h... are you doing poaching on my land?"
>
> To say that this broadside was unexpected does not meet the case; it was devastating. Gone was the confidence with which the first approach had been made, and the Severnsiders were left in a completely untenable position. There was no defence; only abject capitulation loomed ahead. In vain did Colonel Biscuit repeat again and again that he had sent his Adjutant to ask for permission, and had been assured that all was well. And just as often, back came the explosive reply:
>
> "Lies! Lies! all a pack of b..... lies! I ain't given on-one no permission!"
>
> Out came a piece of paper and names were demanded that the Law may take its inexorable course. The announcement of the padrés calling produced yet another outburst:
>
> "A b..... poachin' parson! I hope the perishin' Bishop twists yer perishin' tail!"
>
> The nominal Non-Conformist agrarian had the representative of the Established Church where he wanted him. Apologies, explanations,

promises and threats were all useless. Farmer Brown had seen others shooting but failed to come up with the culprits who, using dead ground with the skill acquired on manoeuvres and at battle schools, had slipped away. He did admit he believed they were not Severnsiders but members of the other Battalion in the Barracks. He would, however, now make an example of those he had caught, and so ensure a peaceful future for his farm.

A deflated C.O., a crestfallen Squadron Commander, and a very worried padré, returned to the Mess. A summons in a civil court was not a pleasant prospect, and might have a damaging effect on their future.

The Colonel's face was thunderous when, an hour or two later, the unfortunate Adjutant was asked for an explanation. This was quite simple. Captain Cole had been to see Farmer Brown, but he had not been at home. However, in his previous dealings with Brown, the Adjutant had found him quite friendly, and had been certain in his own mind that, in return for help freely given for the harvesting, there would be no difficulty over an hour or two of shooting. At tea, faced with the fact that he had failed to see Brown, and feeling confident of the farmer's goodwill, he had said that it would be all right.

That evening, and twice on Sunday, Captain Cole pleaded with the stubborn farmer to refrain from pressing charges, but Brown was as stubborn as the proverbial mule. It was not until the fourth visit, early on the Monday morning, that the Adjutant's efforts were rewarded, the explanation accepted, and the charges dropped.

That night, a contented Colonel and a relieved Squadron Commander celebrated on the C.O.'s native beverage, and the officers living in Mess were once again lulled to sleep by the tuneful melodies of the tin-whistle and the plaintive, soulful wailings of the bagpipes.

Meanwhile, in his room, a very shaken padré returned thanks that history had not repeated itself, and that he would not follow in the footsteps of his predecessor Geraldus de Leadonway (who, in the 13th century, was involved in a case relating to the poaching of peafowl).'

Welfare cases occurred with some regularity, and occasionally presented considerable problems. One night over a cup of coffee, the local Rector said:

"Sergeant 'X's wife, or fiancée—I have forgotten which—is staying the weekend with one of our Mothers' Union members. She seems a very pleasant lady."

I had had considerable correspondence with Mrs 'X' and felt that a personal chat might do more good than many letters, so I decided to call and see her. The request to speak to Mrs 'X', Sergeant 'X's wife, was met with a blank look, and the statement:

"I haven't got a Mrs 'X' staying here."

Suddenly, a second voice from within said:

"Sergeant 'X' isn't married. I'm his intended, and we hope to marry shortly."

The next half-hour was one of the most difficult I have ever experienced. On returning to Barracks, Sergeant 'X's Squadron Commander was awakened, records were carefully checked, and at 1.00 a.m. a court of inquiry was held in the Squadron Office. Bigamy was, for the moment at least, nipped in the bud, and a week or so later, Sergeant 'X' joined a draft being sent to a Regiment overseas.

One day, a young trooper arrived in floods of tears. His story, when he was able to speak, was distressing. He was a Roman Catholic, somewhat lapsed, but had married a non-Roman in a Welsh chapel. A local O.C.F. (R.C.) chaplain had looked him up and had tried to persuade him to remarry in the Roman rite. What was actually said was uncertain, but our lad received the impression that his existing marriage was no marriage at all, that his two children were bastards, and that his 'wife' would receive no pension for herself or for the babes if he should unfortunately be killed. His AB64 (the O.R.s' record of status and service) was produced, and the entry 'Married' was pointed out. Even so, over half-an-hour was needed before he accepted the assurance that his family's status was legal, and that their pension rights were incontrovertible.

Yes, welfare cases were indeed very varied and in aggregate took up a lot of time.

Quite often in the Dover days, I would cycle down to Whitfield Rectory after Mess to have a chat with the incumbent and his wife. The road, after leaving the Barracks and the village, passed through a wood and then over very flat country. When crossing this open land, I always had at a particular gateway a strange feeling of unease, with my hair metaphorically standing on end. This happened in daylight too. Eventually I spoke to the Rector about it, enquiring if anything unpleasant had ever taken place there. He tried all his old people in the parish, but drew a blank. But then in May 1944, by which time we were in Eastbourne, he wrote saying that a very old ex-parishioner had returned to visit her daughter. The latter had asked her mother about the matter, and the old lady had replied:

"Oh yes, that was where old... committed suicide."

Could this have been the cause of the strange feeling?

In October 1943, we left Dover and moved to our final home station, Eastbourne.

CHAPTER 11

Training—the Final Phase

The Regiment left Dover for Eastbourne on the 4th October in 1943, beginning there the final phase of its training tour around the South West and South East coasts. It was billeted in groups of requisitioned houses, the majority of which were in or near Heathfield Square. The unit was thus considerably nearer the South Downs Battle Training Area, thus saving valuable training time and avoiding a great deal of wear and tear on both men and vehicles.

A Buckmanite family living within our billeting area at Eastbourne made a great impression on certain members of the Regiment. They, unlike so many of that persuasion, were not emotionally inclined and were indeed quiet and devout Christians. Their kindliness and hospitality was such that very soon their house became a popular meeting place for many of our men, and the influence of the family was entirely beneficial. They continued to correspond with several members of the Regiment for many months.

Late in November, my wife visited Eastbourne and we had a most pleasant forty-eight hours leave at Pevensey. The weather was kind, but our ability to travel and sight see was limited. We still have a Chinese wall plate which we bought as a souvenir of that enjoyable break.

The padrés of the 43rd Division also had their final battle preparations during this period, over and above the routine training which the unit's simulated battle exercises and procedure provided. We had attended, while in Kent, an 'acclimatisation to blood' course at Chartham Military Hospital. It was intended that the operations to be watched should include amputations, abdominal surgery, and other messy 'repairs'. There had been no exceptions; even those who had had previous battle experience were required to attend. This Divisional policy of specific courses of personal preparation culminated in a Chaplains' Study Week, held near Tenterden between 17th and 21st January. The subjects included:

a) Vehicle maintenance, fault detection, and general repairs.
b) Cooking under battle conditions.
c) Voice production.
d) Mines, booby-traps and gas.
e) Camouflage.
f) Security.
g) Soldiers' welfare.
h) Hygiene and First aid.
i) Map reading, including a night compass march exercise.

All these were of great value. Finally, there came the full 2nd Army Battle Training School course for chaplains, at Church Stowe.

To this course were sent many of the chaplains who were scheduled to land with their units within a set period after 'D' Day. All were grateful for this opportunity of professional tuition and guidance. Each chaplain, before he was accepted for the course, had to undergo a thorough medical and fitness test, after which a certificate was issued stating that he was 'fit for strenuous training'. Those who had served under Montgomery in South Eastern Command had probably grumbled at his physical fitness campaign for all arms of service, but most of those selected for the Church Stowe course were thankful for that preparation.

The battle school training not only acclimatised us to the noise and conditions of warfare, but served even more to instruct one in the methods of self-preparation, personal protection, and the evacuation of wounded under fire. A cartoon in the Mess ante-room at Church Stowe warned chaplains that in battle 'there is no Divine Right of padrés'. The basic principles of use of cover, camouflage and movement were taught. Its inestimable value was fully recognised and, short though the period was, it must have saved many lives. Furthermore, it gave confidence and prepared the chaplain, mentally as well as physically, for the ordeal by fire. Six chaplains of the 43rd Division were detailed to attend the course, which began on

28th February, and ended with an exercise named 'Flat Out'; it did not belie its title.

The exercise course was of some length, and included a river crossing by two ropes (one for the hands and the other for feet), scaling a ten-foot wall, crawling under barbed wire while under fire (Brens firing on fixed lines) and many other such pleasantries. All this, as with most modern equestrian competitions with which television has made us familiar, was against the clock, but in addition we were harried by vigorous and vocal instructors.

Our course was enlivened by the fact that the chief instructor broke his leg while scaling a wall; the only major accident of the four days.

An Eastbourne vicar, Prebendary S.M. Warner of Holy Trinity Church, was most kind and made his church available for the Regiment every Sunday and, of course, welcomed us to normal parochial services. Occasionally other units shared the church with us. We were fortunate during that period in that we had two excellent organists, Doc Ellis and Trooper Goldthorpe, and another who was with us for a short time. The congregation of Holy Trinity Church, too, were friendly and many of our men speedily got their feet under local tables.

One of the highlights of this period, and to my mind one of the finest boosts to invasion morale, was a talk given by General Montgomery. General Essame, in his history of the 43rd Division, gave an admirable description of the scene that morning:

> He (Montgomery) appeared in person to inspect the greater part of the Division, drawn up in a hollow square at Rye on 4th February in the early winter dawn. All had risen long before daylight. As he walked along the ranks, snow began to fall. Finally, he mounted a jeep and, calling on the men to break their ranks and gather round, addressed the troops all around him hanging on his every word, he resembled one of the great missionary Bishops of the Middle Ages, calling upon the soldiers to embark on a Crusade. His bearing with the troops at this time always contained a hint of the ecclesiastic. If he had been born in another age, he would probably have been a towering figure of the Church. As a great political Cardinal of the later mediaeval period, he would have been thoroughly at home.
>
> H. Essame, *The 43rd Wessex Division at War 1944–45*, London 1952, p.12.

Monty also said, but Essame unfortunately omits mentioning it, that he had never yet lost a battle, and nor did he intend to.

He then promised that he would not commit the 2nd Army to the campaign until he had, at least, parity in men and weapons. It would then be up to the men and their fighting spirit to ensure that victory was theirs.

The effect of this speech, especially on the O.R.s, was very considerable. Some Officers felt it was a gross example of showmanship; I have already indicated my feelings on the subject. In conclusion, let me say that the speech and Monty's whole attitude did an incalculable amount of good that day.

Leave was discontinued towards the end of February, and preparation became more definite. Lectures were given on various aspects of the invasion, including relations with the people of the countries to be liberated or invaded, hygiene and many kindred topics. Films were also shown on such subjects as First Aid and security. In this programme the padré had his place. I talked on, among other things, God and Man, death and its meaning to the Christian, the physical temptations which might be faced, and the foolishness of superstition. This latter talk was given because of the reluctance of some to wear their identity discs.

I also asked permission to speak to all Squadrons on burial procedure. In the 1940 withdrawal, many of our men had been compelled to bury their friends because no chaplain had been in that particular area, and time had been short. Naturally they hated this, but they disliked even more (as they said to me later) not being able to say the right thing and give them a 'proper' burial. The men were aware at Eastbourne that, in action, Squadrons might have to operate many miles apart, and that they might again have to perform the last rites for their comrades. It was in consequence of this apprehension that I asked for a lecture on burial procedure to be allowed. At the same time, I prepared a brief form of burial service which was submitted to my Bishop. After the episcopal approval had been given, the form was printed on a small postcard with, on the reverse side, instructions on the choice and marking of sites, and the disposal of discs and effects. These cards were distributed to the men after the talk to the Squadrons. As far as I can recollect, I do not believe they ever had to use them until I left the unit at the end of March 1945; this fortunate situation was the result of the ease of wireless communication, and the speed with which I was able to move from Squadron to Squadron.

I also drew up a folded card of simple prayers for daily use. On these, too, I talked. Within a week, there were hundreds of requests for a second card, the first having been sent to wife or sweetheart, and plans having been made to say the same prayers every night at, if possible, the same time. The card was reprinted and this daily link worked in many instances and was, I believe, helpful. I explained my plan to move from Squadron to Squadron as frequently as possible, but pointed out that operational exigencies might make this difficult at times.

I asked, in consequence, for volunteers (below S.S.M. rank) who would act as 'Padré's Helpers'. They were to be of two grades. The first would gather the men together for prayers and Communion when I wirelessed ahead that I would be with their Squadron at a particular time. The second were to be prepared, in addition, to take prayers once a day in my absence for any who wished and were off duty. These volunteers were given a booklet entitled '*A Pocket Padré*'. It required courage to come forward and have one's name published in Orders as a Padré's Helper, yet over fifty did so, and more than half were prepared to read the daily prayers. These 'Helpers' did splendid work, especially in the early days before our ranks were reduced to a single figure—twenty-six were killed, drowned or wounded in the landing.

All this was possible, I believe, because I had been with the unit for six years and had known many of all ranks in parish life.

The final Confirmation course began at this time, and the candidates were confirmed in Canterbury Cathedral in May. One of this course was 'Hal' Bagwell, the West of England lightweight boxing champion.

One of the men developed warts, large warts, on his hands. After local treatment had failed, he was sent to the Field Ambulance and thence to General Hospital. He was returned before the expiration of the twenty-one days which would have 'Y' listed him, but it was clear that he could not go overseas in his condition. The lad was worried at the prospect of leaving his friends and pleaded with the M.O. to cure him. A further week of ineffective treatment followed, after which the M.I. Orderly (Corporal Smith) suggested psychological treatment. Doc Ellis agreed to try the plan. The 'build-up' consisted of the eulogisation of a 'rare drug' (in pill form), then being produced in America in very small quantities, for just such warts (there was, of course, no such thing!). It was emphasised to the patient that these pills were extremely difficult to obtain in the U.K., but that the M.O., through certain influential channels, would try and obtain some. This mental preparation went on for some weeks until the poor lad, with the certainty of the Second Front being really imminent, was in a very dithery state. Finally, Smith said to Doc Ellis:

"Let's try it today, Sir."

"Well," replied the M.O., "What do you propose we do?"

"Oh," said Smith, "I suggest we dip six aspirins in Flavine, and spin a good story!"

Later that morning, long after sick parade had ended, the wart-infested patient was sent for. He came at the gallop. He was informed that as a concession, a very *special* concession, six of these rare tablets had been sent over from the States. He was given two, to be taken at twelve-hourly intervals, and told to report back at 10 p.m. the following evening for two more. The last pair would be administered twenty-four hours later.

Within three days, the warts had gone. Psychology? Black magic? Witchcraft? Well, whatever it was; it worked!

Early in the Spring, Doc Ellis received a new, white, half-track medical truck, and was anxious to test its climbing abilities which were claimed to be considerable. After a few trial trips to familiarise himself with the gears and general handling, he invited me to be a passenger in the climbing trial. I readily agreed, but a little later began to doubt the wisdom of my decision. The chosen site was on the cliff approaches near Beachy Head. We drove down a gentle slope to the bottom of the valley and then, to my amazement, turned right-handed and drove straight at the steep valley side. The grass was short and the surface reasonably even, and for the first twenty or thirty yards the tough caterpillar tracks at the back made light of the task, but the increasing steepness of the ascent caused John to run rapidly through his changes until bottom gear was engaged. By that time, the angle of ascent was acute, and the top was still some forty or fifty yards away. The point of no return had been reached, and we had to go on; it was as simple as that.

The only problems were; a) was the engine powerful enough to drag the half-track to the top, and b) would the vehicle, with its heavy rear half, do a backwards somersault?

Slowly, the half-track crept forward and then, quite suddenly, the slope became easier. At the top, we stopped and Doc climbed out, lit a cigarette, and said:

"I'll not attempt that again!"

The real driver, who had been sitting in the passenger seat and sweating from every pore, and I, fully agreed!

One afternoon, while returning from a Divisional exercise on the South Downs, I called in at Berwick Church to see the recently finished modern murals painted by Duncan Grant, Vanessa Bell, and Quentin Bell on the orders of Bishop Bell of Chichester. I was amazed at the colours and at the Flemish appearance of some of the characters. In spite of a predisposition towards the mediaeval, I was impressed by these examples of 20th century ecclesiastical art (a reaction not experienced when, long after the war, I saw the Epstein 'Christ' at Llandaff Cathedral and the Sutherland 'Majesty' at Coventry).

The facade of normality was advocated, indeed insisted upon, well into May and farewell parties and like festivities were strictly forbidden. These did take place, however, in a modified form. The Regimental tailor, Trooper Greenberg, an all-in wrestler in civilian life and a quiet, friendly man by nature, was returning from one such conviviality when he ran into trouble. He was nearly home, thanks to the support and assistance of the tall railings around Heathfield Square's park-like gardens, when two C.M.P.s patrolling the area, pounced. Greenberg assured them that he was all right and that he knew where he was going, but the C.M.P.s were persistent. They were warned repeatedly by Greenberg to keep their hands off him, but did not, and in consequence, they suddenly found themselves on the inside of the Park fence, the gates of which were firmly locked.

The C.O., the Adjutant, and I were in the Orderly Room the following morning when the C.M.P.s arrived and reported the incident. With one voice we said,

"If it was a Recce man, it could only have been Greenberg!"

The thought of two burly C.M.P.s being tossed lightly over the high fencing was almost too much for our composure, and that of the Regimental Orderly Room staff. The offender was summoned, and gave his account clearly and honestly, much to the amusement of the Recce members present. The C.O. thanked the C.M.P.s for their diligence and report, and said he would deal severely with the case. This he did, after the departure of the C.M.P.s, by telling Greenberg to return to duty and not to be such a b..... fool again, adding,

"You might get hurt yourself next time."

"Thank you, Sir," replied Greenberg and then, as he turned to go, the 'professional' spoke with utter contempt for his assailants, "but they could *never* hurt me, Sir!"

The Regiment had been commanded since August 1943 by Lieutenant-Colonel J. Lane-Fox of the 'Blues', a man of great charm who later showed the bravery and resolution associated with members of the Sovereign's Body Guard. The C.O. was naturally an able horseman, and had hunted for several seasons with the Taunton Vale pack. In May, an uncle (George) by marriage, who was commanding a balloon regiment which was to sail with the 'D' Day forces from New Haven, and who years before had hunted with the Taunton, moved into the area, and I invited him to dine in the Mess.

It was for me an evening never to be forgotten, during which the uncle and I dropped three very large 'clangers' (the worst of which I dare not mention!). George arrived as the C.O. came into Mess, and I began the introductions.

"Colonel, let me present Squadron Leader or whatever rank he was Angel. George, this is Colonel..." and my mind went completely blank! The C.O. stepped in and said,

"Lane-Fox, padré, and you should know it by this time!"

Worse was to follow.

The C.O. and George discovered that their times at Taunton had overlapped a little and when reminiscing, George said:

"Do you remember a funny little Subaltern who rode so well and played polo?"

"No," replied the Colonel.

"You must," George went on, "because he was such a superb horseman, but a funny little man all the same. Ah, I remember his name; it was Ward-Jackson."

"Well," said the C.O., "*I was* that 'funny little man'."

The C.O. had had to change his name to Lane-Fox when he married a niece of Lord Halifax! The third brick was a veritable mountain, and I was pleased when George announced that he had to return to his unit.

Aerial activity from both sides of the channel increased significantly as 'D' Day approached. During one of these 'hit and run' German light bomber raids, a bomb fell near the billet shared by Doc Ellis and myself. We were awakened either by the explosion itself, or by the ceiling falling in on top of us. The amazing thing was that, although the entire roof was blown off, and the ceiling collapsed, the windows in our room remained intact except for a few cracks.

I was returning from a chaplain's assignment at Dover one evening early in June and by chance, stopped to have a look at the church and Martello Tower in Dymchurch where Dr. Sin, the 17th century pirate turned parson, had been vicar. Again by chance, I climbed the high sea wall, and saw out to sea a strange contraption. It looked like a gigantic box being towed along. Noah's Ark came to mind, but it had no obvious prow or stern, nor was there a steeply pitched roof. Later, in Normandy, I learned that what I had seen at Dymchurch was a section of Mulberry (code-name for an artificial harbour) being taken down the Channel to join the invasion fleet.

Rumours were rife on the morning of 6th June when members of the Regiment went down to a 9 a.m. lecture in the town. I fear that the talk received scant attention, for the thoughts of most people present were far away on a foreign beach where Allied troops were said to have landed. When we came out from the lecture, the wirelesses were blaring out in shops and through open windows, and our progress back to billets took the form of a series of quick moves from one loudspeaker to the next.

The official news of 'D' Day came as a great relief. All the uncertainty was over and our programme was now clear. The Regiment knew (at least the C.O., Adjutant and a few senior officers did) that provided things in Normandy went according to plan, we were now in the 'pipeline', and would land as a follow-up Division on 'D' Day plus twelve, or thereabouts.

There was suppressed excitement tinged, naturally, with some apprehension as, during the next seven days, the final preparations were carried out, the water-proofing of vehicles checked, and all the last minute details carefully studied.

The wheeled vehicles left Eastbourne late on June 13th and the carriers by rail the following morning.

The night convoy was a rehearsal for things to come much later in the year—a slow-moving column, stopping for ten minutes every hour, and occasionally unintentionally due to mechanical breakdown or traffic congestion. I travelled in the M.O.'s 'white' half-track because my thin-skinned P.U. had been left behind and was scheduled to come over with the Divisional residue in a few weeks time. One hold-up occurred when Trooper Wayman, a Don R., had an accident and broke his leg. The Doc splintered him up and wirelessed for a vehicle to take him to the nearest hospital. Wayman pleaded pitifully to be allowed to go with his pals, saying that the Doc could plaster his leg and that he (Wayman) could do many useful odd jobs until he was once more fit to act as a Don R.. John was (rightly) adamant and, weeping like a child, Wayman was put into the waiting ambulance and so left the unit. After the war, I unveiled a memorial tablet at Blakeney in the Forest of Dean. In the congregation was Wayman. Had he had his wish on the night of 13th/14th June 1944, his name would undoubtedly have been inscribed upon that tablet, because *all* his companions were to die in the landing a few days later. Incidentally, on that Blakeney memorial was the name of the plane-spotting officer attached to our ship. This amazed me, because on his death I had written to his mother who had lived in Yorkshire.

The convoy arrived at West Ham, the marshalling area, on the 14th, having enjoyed a foretaste of the welcome of tea, refreshments, and general bonhomie which was such a feature of events during the liberation of certain parts of France, Belgium and Holland.

The tented transit camp, near the greyhound stadium, was sited on an old rubbish dump and, with complete absence of amenity, was dirty and depressing. Here we had our first experience of V-1s (the flying bombs nick-named 'Doodlebugs') which we endured again in the Liège area during Von Rundstedt's Ardennes offensive in December. Services were held in camp each day. These were days of boredom and discomfort and we were delighted when, on the 17th, activity recommenced.

The vehicles left for the docks that day, and on the following morning, equipped with lifebelts, French francs, and brown bags listed as 'Bags, vomit', the unit too moved in. The Sunday services were held on the quay, when most of those not actively involved in loading of vehicles and kit, attended. Later that afternoon we went aboard, and at dusk the *Derry Cunihy* cast off, and we knew that the next land under our feet would be the sands of Normandy.

CHAPTER TWELVE

The Return to France

What were our thoughts as we slipped away from the quay and steamed slowly down the Thames estuary? In January 1940 when we crossed to France many of us had felt that we could not hope to survive the war, basing our estimate on the casualties in the earlier German conflict. Added to those facts was the awareness that more sophisticated weaponry had been developed, technological advances in aircraft and armour were taking place, and finally there was a strong suspicion (rarely referred to) that chemical warfare of unbelievable horror could break out. This last spectre had been engendered no doubt by the knowledge that Major Over's (our 2.I.C.) previous employment had been in that field. Yes, the future prospects had not been very attractive.

This time, however, having had a little experience of the new type of 'war of movement', and with some knowledge of the losses sustained even during the less fortunate campaigns such as Dunkirk, the Far East, and certain of those in North Africa, we thought that if victory were not too long delayed, then there was a more than fifty-fifty chance of survival.

That night, we anchored off Southend pier, and remained there until the following evening when, with the large convoy that had assembled by that time, we began the purposeful voyage to Normandy.

One of the ships in the convoy was hit by shell-fire from the German cross-Channel batteries at Cap Gris Nez as we passed through the straits of Dover, and was beached near Deal.

Off Eastbourne, which we had left almost exactly a week earlier, the convoy turned out to sea and made for the French coast. The approach, in spite of deteriorating weather, was interesting, and the scene as we sailed almost the whole length of the British bridge-head to the Easternmost extremity was fascinating but awe-inspiring. Ships were there in their thousands, or so it seemed: warships such as the massive *Rodney* and *Warspite*, smaller cruisers and destroyers, strange vessels firing banks of rockets from what looked like large steel window-frames, landing-craft for tanks and personnel, and merchant ships by the score, carrying men, equipment and stores to the great adventure. My letter written the following day to my wife contains the passage:

> ... we are anchored off the coast but, as the wireless told you, we have not unloaded. Last evening, there was a wonderful sight, in fact one of the greatest sights in the world. There suddenly, in the grey of the evening, was the biggest gathering of ships of all kinds... literally hundreds of them, ranging from big battleships down to tiny craft the size of M.T.Bs.. The run across has been rough but uneventful.

At moments of great emotion, if opportunity allowed, I not infrequently recorded impressions, occasionally even in doggerel verse. The following was written on the back of the above letter to my wife:

Our Convoy

We crept through the grey of gathering night
We tramps and ships of the line.
When through the pale of the fading light
Unfolded a sight sublime;
East and West, and North and South,
As far as the eye could see,
Line upon line of transport and tramp
And the might of the King's Navy.

The Cardiff, the Ajax, the dark Dido,
The Rodney, that giant of steel,
And many another one did not know
Was anchored on even keel.
We passed through the first and outer ring
Of escorts and watchdogs grey,
Swinging to rest with the turn of the tide
To await the dawn of day.

The *Derry Cunihy* dropped anchor off the village of Ouistreham, where the Caen canal and the river Orne came to the sea. By morning, the weather had worsened, and for several days we sat there riding out the storm which so upset the schedule of the whole enterprise. We saw in the distance the beaches, strewn with wrecked landing-craft and other debris. Away at the East, on a cliff top a mile or two beyond the river, a German coastal battery continued to fire on the invasion fleet throughout our time aboard. The *Derry Cunihy* was not hit, but a small landing-craft was sunk by shell-fire near the ship on the 24th.

The men spent much of their time reading, writing letters or playing cards, with a number of thriving poker and pontoon schools almost perpetually in session. The result was, of course, that a few men were virtually 'skint', having lost every franc they were issued with before they had had a chance to spend them. 'Char' too was constantly on the boil both on deck and in the holds.

From the padré's angle, this was a period of rare opportunity, for the 'parish' was the ship, and then parishioners had few duties and much spare time. The normal early morning Communion and also the evening prayers in groups, to which the unit had become accustomed on schemes and exercises, were maintained. Even more important, perhaps, was the constant contact with individuals and small groups, when discussions often developed, problems were talked over, and fears faced.

The long wait, riding out the storm, was a time of relaxation and considerable interest. We were sufficiently far from land not to be a primary target of enemy gunners (except in the case of the battery to the East), and yet near enough to see a great deal. It was like being in the wings of a vast theatre where one was witnessing a drama and standing by for one's own entry, for we realised, of course, that when calmer conditions allowed the unloading of our armoured vehicles, then we too would be on the stage, but for the moment, we took our ease.

Thousands of dead fish floated by, freshly killed by exploding bombs, mines and shells. Many of the men threw down buckets and baskets on the end of ropes to catch them as they drifted past, and the more venturesome climbed down the scrambling or landing nets, or down ropes hanging over the ship's side, and scooped up the silvery booty in buckets, wash-bowls, mess-tins and even steel helmets. The vehicles' tommy cookers then came into their own, and the aroma of fried fish became commonplace and at times pretty powerful, and many were the references to the 'fish and chip shop round the corner'. All this added greatly to the general amusement, and gave variety to the menu.

On the 23rd, the weather changed rapidly for the better, and the prospects for landing on the next day appeared brighter. There was an incident that afternoon which, trivial though it seemed at the time, had a marked effect the following morning. When storing kit under the bunk, a strange contraption fell out. It was made of cane and webbing, and looked for all the world like a part of the old-fashioned stays of a gigantic woman! The Doctor was present, and said it was a Neil Robertson stretcher, explaining further that it was a recognised medical 'prop' used to hoist badly injured persons up or down cliffs or from high buildings, especially when rigidity or immobilisation of limbs or the spine was desirable. He then demonstrated, with me as the 'victim', the method of wrapping it round the patient, strapping him in and then fixing a rope to the head end, by which he could be hauled up or lowered.

That night, a heavier than usual air-raid on the anchorage developed. One heard the roar of the engines, the noise of anti-aircraft guns of various calibre, and occasionally the explosion of a bomb. Because of the danger from falling anti-aircraft shell fragments, and the possibility of a direct hit on the ship, only the Duty Watch were supposed to be on deck.

At around 3 a.m., I heard a plane diving. Suddenly there was the noise of metal against metal on the ship itself, accompanied by an awareness of an impact, slight maybe, but positive, as the plane pulled out of its dive and sped away. I waited for the splash, convinced that the plane had hit our mast or some part of the superstructure and might plunge into the sea. Nothing happened, so I got out of my bunk and went on deck. Nothing appeared wrong with the mast, or any other part of the vessel, so I sought out the Watch and asked the cause of the noise and the slight feel of vibration in the ship. He replied that there had been no metallic sound, and that I must have dreamt it. Vehement protests that I had been wide awake met only with the firm declaration that one often imagined a bang when one suddenly woke up. There was no point in arguing, so I went back to my cabin and dropped off to sleep.

Several hours later, and after the usual service, I took a brief walk round the decks before returning at about 7.00 a.m. to the cabin where, contrary to standing orders, I took off my boots before lying down on my bunk.

An hour before Reveille (put back to 8.30 a.m. to conform with ship's routine) a landing-craft came alongside and orders were given to steam to Gold beach and unload in greater safety. A few moments later, with the first throbs of the donkey engine, there was a violent explosion and the whole ship heaved and shook.

Scrambling back onto the bunk from which I had fallen, I thrust my head through the porthole. The mental impact was strange, producing an almost dreamlike reaction, when I saw the aft rail disappearing in a swirling foamy turmoil reminiscent, on a large scale, of a pot of boiling water. To verify the facts, I opened the cabin door leading to the aft deck. Confirmation came as the door flew open.

The shock was bewildering because of the suddenness of the unexpected and catastrophic turn of events. An hour before, I had walked out of that door, across the deck, and climbed down the ladder into No. 4 hold to return my communion set to the Doctor's 'White' half-track. Now there was no deck; only a foaming and turbulent patch of water in which objects, some human, were bobbing about.

The top of the mast stuck out of the water at a jaunty angle, and I saw the jagged sides of the ship which had, clearly, split in two. The stern rails, visible when I had looked out of the porthole moments before, had now disappeared. The stark reality produced a peculiar feeling, for suddenly everything seemed to be going in slow motion as the realisation came that No. 5 hold was under several feet of water, and that No. 4 hold was represented by a gaping hole into which, from the doorway, one could not see.

What were my reactions and thoughts?

I remember, first, saying to Doc Ellis "The ship has split in half!" to which he replied "Come out quickly, padré" and second, being terribly frightened and wanting to panic. I was, I suppose, as near to cracking point as one can be without crossing the fateful line.

I picked up my boots, put them on and laced them up. This foolish action (I ought instead to have followed Doc Ellis out of the cabin at once, in case the forward section keeled over and sank) gave me time, like Nehemiah of old, to pray 'to the God of Heaven' and to steady my nerves, and enabled me to act rationally when I came out on deck.

There was bustle, but no noise or panic, while in the sea I saw masses of floating debris, some bobbing heads, and patches of oil spreading rapidly. The Doc and I ran aft and discovered that part of No. 4 hold was still above water and that inside there were three figures floating. A small raft was thrown down and a rope fixed to the rail of the superstructure on which we stood. Then a R.E.M.E.

Staff Sergeant and I went down. At the same time, a large M.G.B. drew alongside the wreck.

In the hold, the three wounded men were collected on to the raft. Two had broken arms, while the third man was much more seriously injured. We called up to the M.G.B. for a rope. This was tied around one of the men, under his arms, and we shouted, "Pull!"

Rough on the poor chap?

Well, yes; but it would have been rougher still had the fuel-oil, which now covered the water in the hold, been ignited by the ammunition lorry blazing on deck a few yards above our heads, or if the final plunge had taken place. The second arm-patient received the same crude treatment.

The last case was indeed a problem; he was unconscious and in a bad state (I suspected a broken back). The heavy-handed method used for numbers one and two would, most likely, have killed number three. Suddenly, 'a still small voice' seemed to whisper 'Robertson stretcher'. At the same time, the cabin scene of the previous afternoon flashed through my mind. I shouted: "Robertson stretcher, quickly!"

A few moments of silence followed, then suddenly came a shout, presumably from the M.G.B. overhead:

"Depth-charge overboard!"

I thought, "Well that's settled it; we've had it!" I suppose that, in scrambling for the Robertson stretcher (which, providentially, they had with them) they must had dislodged a depth-charge which had toppled overboard. Naturally it was not primed, or triggered (or whatever they do to these things before using them in anger), but *I* did not know that!

The stretcher descended, and a few minutes later, trussed up like a fruit tree in transit, the injured man was pulled up gently and taken aboard. The Staff Sergeant followed and then, from the still floating half of the ship, they lowered a rope ladder down to me. Less than a minute later the fuel oil in the hold was alight, ignited, no doubt, by a tracer-round from the ammunition truck, or a burning fragment.

To me, the sequence of events (the accidental instruction in the use of the Robertson stretcher, and the presence of one on the M.G.B.) constituted a modern miracle which certainly saved the lives of three men; the badly injured trooper,[1] the Staff Sergeant and myself.

It was clear now that the water-tight doors between the engine-room and holds 1 to 3 were intact, and that that part of the ship was in no immediate danger of sinking. All non-essential personnel had been ordered down the ropes into the waiting boats. Only the C.O., the Quartermaster, and one or two others remained, busy removing important papers. I ran back to my cabin to collect some kit; the bulk of it had been in the M.O.'s half-track in No. 4 hold, and was now on the seabed. The cabin was ablaze and all I could rescue was my mackintosh. I then slid down the rope, followed by the Quartermaster and the C.O.

A few survivors were taken direct to the beaches that day, but the majority were transferred from the rescue boats to the *Cap Tourain*, a large depot ship that had been a French luxury liner in the days of peace.

The wounded, numbering some 150, were placed in lounges, dining rooms and cabins; anywhere, in fact, where a stretcher could be rested. All through that day, and the following night, surgeons, doctors, and orderlies from the depot ship and from many Royal Navy ships, along with the R.M.O., did all that they could to save lives and relieve pain. It is a tribute to their skill and hard work that only three died of wounds while on board.

The unwounded were soon given dry garments (sailor's suits from the ship's Quartermasters' Stores and Survivors' Outfits supplied by many a town and village at home) to replace the oil-blackened vest and pants which was the only covering of the majority. Cigarettes, hot tea, and stacks of food awaited the first boatload, and were at hand the whole time.

The dead and wounded had been identified and, when it appeared that no more survivors could be expected, the roll was called. Just under two hundred were accounted for. Later it was learned that some twenty had been landed on the beaches, and one or two bodies had been brought ashore and buried.

The situation facing the Colonel following the roll-call was grim. He had less than three hundred survivors of our 500-strong light scales party, of whom about 150 were wounded, the majority of them being non-operational. Should he ask to return to the U.K. to reform, or should he build up the unit in Normandy?

Colonel Fox-Lane rightly decided upon the latter course of action, and requested that our rear party, 'B' Squadron, and the remainder of the H.Q. Squadron, should be brought over as soon as possible and that he might have direct access to R.H.U. (the Regimental Holding Unit; a pool of reserves ready to replace casualties in the various Regiments).

What of the 180 missing? Piecing together the stories of others, and remembering what I saw for myself, one can arrive at a fairly definite conclusion. Most, if not all, of those who went down with the ship, were either killed outright or so stunned by the explosion that they could not have known that this was the moment of their passing.

During the day, a number of bodies were brought aboard, but because there were no facilities on the *Cap Tourain* for burials at sea, I took our dead over to a nearby cruiser *H.M.S. Sirius*, and asked to see the padré. On being ushered into his cabin, I found to my amazement that he was an old Oxford friend, the Revd. M. Martin Harvey, with whom I had often played hockey in the past. He said that *Sirius* was returning to England the next day, and that he would conduct a burial service for our men who had died of wounds, and those whose bodies had been recovered from the sea.

That evening, a small party headed by the C.O. set out in a landing-craft, and a burial service was held over the wreck by myself and an R.C. padré from the depot ship. Much of the rest of the time was spent with the wounded and those who had swallowed fuel oil before being rescued from the sea; some of these latter were suffering badly, and a few were critically ill.

We were not the only ship casualty during that period (though our losses were probably by far the greatest), for Admiral Vian's flagship, the cruiser *Scylla*, had been badly damaged by a mine on the previous day, while we saw a destroyer (said to have been the *Swift*) break in two and sink, yet another mine victim.

On the 25th, the majority of the Regimental survivors were detailed for disembarkation, but even this operation was not without incident, for the German battery on the headland to the East found the range of the *Cap Tourain* and two of our officers, Lieuts. Cammell and Charlton, were wounded when the ship suffered a direct hit.

We landed on the beach at Ouistreham, quite near the entrance to the Caen canal, and were welcomed by the occasional salvo of mortar bombs. Thus our return to France was finally accomplished.

That same afternoon, a hospital ship took the majority of the wounded back to England, and our dead were buried at sea by Padré Martin Harvey. The padré wrote:

> At 4.30 p.m. on Sunday 25th June, we had the burial at sea, with full military honours, at a point 15 miles north of the coast of Normandy. The Ship's Company was present, as were a number of soldiers and Royal Marines who were taking passage with us.

On looking back at those grim hours from Saturday morning until Sunday, what memories stand out?

The first thing that impressed me was the calmness and discipline. There was no vestige of panic, and very little noise. It was as though all realised that every breath was needed for the hard and demanding task of getting everyone to safety. 'Self' was forgotten; and one saw badly wounded men rising above the pain of their own wounds and struggling to help their less fortunate comrades. For that time, they became super-men, not bound by the normal limitations of the body; I saw so much bravery and forgetfulness of self in those few minutes that I was amazed that human nature could rise to such heights. One example is enough:

A little man, clad only in vest and pants, and with one arm useless, his head bleeding, and he himself nearly unconscious, was seen struggling to support a badly wounded comrade. He was gripping him by the hair, and holding the lad's head above water until they were both handed to safety.

The second impression was of the promptness and whole-heartedness of the Royal Navy's aid. Without their quick action and skilful handling of the situation, many more lives would have been lost, and much added suffering would have resulted. All that could be done *was* done, speedily and well. No praise can be too high for those men of the Senior Service.

The third point was the weather. Had the accident taken place in the hours of darkness, or had the weather not changed in the preceding 24 hours, many of the survivors would never have lived to see the depot ship.

In retrospect, one realises that three factors (the magnificent discipline of the men and their efforts to help each other, the promptness and skill of the Navy, and the favourable weather) prevented a major disaster from becoming the extinction of a Regiment.

Notes

1. In July 1982, this same trooper called to thank me for helping to save his life. I was greatly touched; up to that moment, I had not known whether or not he had survived. Because of the crude oil in which we were all plastered, I did not even know his name.

CHAPTER THIRTEEN

Normandy—The Early Days

The journey by truck from Ouistreham to our assembly area was full of interest. The route at first lay largely along tracks through cornfields where the evidence of war lay strewn about. The stench of dead and decaying animals, with which we became sickeningly familiar in July and August, was something new and very unpleasant. Finally, the convoy stopped in an improvised camp near the village of Pouligny two miles North East of Bayeux, where it was said tents would be soon available, and where it was forecast the Regiment would reform. The site was a sparsely treed orchard which became the unit's home base for several weeks, indeed until it had been re-equipped and brought up to operational strength.

Soon after the landing, I went to a nearby convent, and asked the nuns of their Christian charity to give me a cup, plate, and some purificators to enable Holy Communion to be celebrated in camp for the unit; we literally had nothing except what we stood up in.

The Community were friendly and generous, producing what was required, and suggesting a call on the morrow when further supplies would be available. They were as good as their word, for a neatly labelled parcel contained more purificators and also a small green burse and veil. (That burse and veil, together with a red and gold pair made a week or two later by my wife Vivienne, survived the war and were used at all T.A. camps which I attended from 1947 to 1961, and are still in my sick communion case for use in hospitals and at sick communions.)

There in that makeshift camp at Pouligny, the remnants of the Regiment began to take stock of itself while the C.O., Squadron

Commanders, and the Quartermaster mapped out the camp. The survey completed, the digging of slit trenches and deep latrines followed. This physical exercise helped considerably. It not only gave some measure of protection but, momentarily, it took the men's minds off the events of the landing. The repercussions of the tragic events on the 24th (over and above the mental and physical sufferings of individuals and families) were in certain cases sudden and totally unexpected, as Major Tom Carter, O.C. rear party, soon discovered.

The unit had been compelled, by reason of the light scales landing table, to leave behind in Eastbourne one fighting Squadron and certain other H.Q. Squadron troops. These, numbering nearly three hundred men, were scheduled to follow within three or four weeks when the bridgehead had been sufficiently enlarged, and the supply situation assured. Major Carter had, within ten days of the departure of the Regiment, completed the water-proofing of vehicles and the general preparation for eventual embarkation. This effectively brought tactical training to a standstill. Major Carter, realising the possibility of boredom arising, assembled his party on Friday 23rd June and explained that, although he could not grant official leave, if any wished to go home or visit friends and could be back by Sunday night or early on Monday morning, they might go, provided they left their addresses and (where possible) telephone numbers at the Squadron office.

A number went. Late on Saturday night and totally unaware of the fate of the advance party in Normandy, Major Carter was horrified to receive orders instructing him to be at Gosport marshalling area on Monday the 26th. He went at once to the Police, with the names, addresses and where possible, the telephone numbers of those on leave. They were instructed to report back to Eastbourne forthwith. They were told, however, that if they could not be there by midday on Sunday (and some had no hope of being so) they were to report direct to the Gosport marshalling area, and not later than early on Monday morning.

The result was remarkable, for they came by train, bus, taxi and one even on a bicycle, with not one missing or even late. It was a magnificent effort and reflected great credit on Major Carter and the Police, and demonstrated the remarkable loyalty and morale of the men.

On Monday 26th, over in Normandy, tents began to arrive for the unit, and within two days, all were under canvas. This was a great relief for, sparsely clad as many still were, sleeping on the ground or in slit trenches without covering was none too pleasant. Because of the nightly air activity, and the possible hazards of anti-aircraft shell fragments, orders were issued to dig out the tent floors to 'a reasonable depth'; four feet was suggested, but not always achieved.

On the same day, the C.O. and I discussed the question of letters to next of kin and decided, in view of the number of dead and missing presumed dead (nearly two hundred in all), the time factor, and because the details were identical in nearly every case, that each of us should write a general letter which would be duplicated. This was done, and the letters were sent off within a few days. Unfortunately, these, and all the other Regimental out-going mail, were held up back at base, to prevent the fact of our heavy losses becoming generally known. This action, of which we were not aware until some time later, caused fearful distress to the next of kin of almost the entire Regiment, and great bewilderment to us within the unit when, by mid-July, hundreds of letters began to arrive asking anxiously for information about Tom, Dick and Harry in view of the non-arrival of any letters from them, and the fact that, through the 150 wounded now back in England, news of the disastrous landing had now spread far and wide. In view of the fact that, since leaving, no word had arrived from any member of the unit in Normandy, and no official announcement had been made, the picture in general to those at home appeared very ominous.

On Tuesday 27th June, a memorial service was held in the quiet of a Normandy orchard. The Assistant Chaplain-General of the Second Army, Reverend J.W.J. Steele, took prayers, and the Deputy Chaplain-General of the Allied Army in the field, Revd. Canon F.Ll. Hughes, preached. It was a most impressive service. Afterwards the D.C.G. asked me to make a list of the things I needed most, which my wife could send. He explained that he would be flying back to the U.K. the next day, and would be returning probably on Friday. His Staff Chaplain sent the following telegram to my wife on the Thursday morning:

> Send immediately to DCG Rear HQ 21 Army Group No.1 APDC London W1, old cassock and surplice clerical scarf sleeveless sweater shoes thin.

The Staff Chaplain telephoned later that morning and said that the D.C.G. had seen me and that I was fit and well but added, euphemistically, that I had 'become separated from my kit'! My wife replied,

"Just like my husband! He's always careless with his things!"

This conversation saved Vivienne a great deal of worry a week or so later. Joan, a maid in my father's vicarage (my wife was then staying with him), went to Hereford Hospital to visit a boyfriend. In a nearby bed was a wounded member of our Regiment. In conversation, the sinking of the *Derry Cunihy* was mentioned, and Joan was told that I had gone down with the ship. When she broke the news to my wife, Vivienne, remembering the Staff Chaplain's remarks, guessed the truth, and was spared much anxiety.

On Wednesday 28th June, the Doc and I, still garbed partly in survivors' outfits, and partly in our own oil-soaked battle-dress and boots, reported as ordered to 2nd Army H.Q.. The poor Doctor received a rocket for presenting himself to the D.M.S. in such a condition. He and I, and indeed the whole Regiment, were livid at the refusal of medical officialdom to face the realities of the situation. The chaplains' H.Q., in contrast, were sympathetic and helpful. John Steele, for example, dug out some spare kit and a Communion set. In view of this last item, I broke and buried the cup and plate which I had used temporarily for the celebrations since our arrival at Pouligny.

Those early days at Pouligny were a time of emotional tension. Maybe many were not fully aware of their condition, while others recognised the symptoms and strove nobly to control their feelings and appear completely normal. This condition was mainly evident at night, when the subconscious took over.

The Doctor's large M.I. tent accommodated the medical staff, a few patients, and the padré. It was not unusual to be awakened by the sound of someone sobbing or crying in his sleep. The victim, when roused (as he usually was), said that he had been reliving those fateful events of the 24th. Both the M.O. and I experienced these uncontrollable reactions during our sleep. When walking through the camp late at night, as I frequently did, those cries of anguish were often heard, and I felt deeply for the sufferers. These nightmares continued in some cases until operations recommenced, which understandably had the effect of dulling earlier memories. I believe those involuntary nocturnal outbursts were nature's way of releasing the emotional tension; in line with the sentiments behind those well-known lines of Arthurian romance:

Home they brought her warrior dead
She na swooned nor uttered cry
All her maidens watching said
She must weep or she will die.

Though it may sound contradictory, the morale of the men was excellent, although there was at times a feeling of apprehension. This was understandable for, without having fired a single shot or seeing even a solitary German soldier at close quarters, the unit had suffered staggering losses. The inference was clear, but rarely expressed: 'What will happen when the Regiment becomes operational?'.

I fear I stuck my neck out and said that I felt and believed (and indeed I did feel and believe it) that we had had our big trial by fire, and that for some time at least, our losses would be slight. Mercifully this was to be the case, for the first twenty-two vehicles (armoured cars, bren-gun carriers and so on) destroyed resulted in only two fatal casualties. Our foot casualties, too, (until after the Arnhem episode in September) were remarkably few, and four of these resulted from failure to take adequate and available precautions.

During this period, as during the phoney war days of early 1940, the Germans dropped propaganda leaflets in night air-raids. The design of the leaflets was varied, but the intention was clearly to induce anxiety for the safety of loved ones at home, and so lower morale and the determination to fight. While in the transit camp in London, the unit had experienced the V-1 'Doodlebug' flying bombs, and so they understood the colourful leaflet on which was an artist's impression of a giant, bearing a flaming torch, striding over a devastated and burning London with, underneath, the message *Berlin—now London*. All this propaganda was a psychological blunder, because it angered our men and made their resolution to fight all the stronger.

On the 10th July, 'Jupiter' was mounted; an attempt by the British forces to clear the high ground between the rivers *Odon* and *Orne* and capture pt. (hill) 112, of which the Germans said, 'He who holds 112, holds Normandy'. The 43rd Division, in addition to its own three Infantry Brigades, had under command the 46th Infantry Brigade, the 4th and 31st Armoured Brigades, the guns of the 11th Armoured Division, the 15th Scottish Division, and two Agras. To help cope with the heavy casualties anticipated, a large composite surgical unit was established in Château Mouen, just behind the forming-up line. During the forty-eight hours of July 10th and 11th, about eighteen hundred casualties passed through this unit. At the height of one of the several counter-attacks, we were warned that we might be over-run in the next hour. All ambulances still operational were loaded up and evacuated. Mercifully, the counter-attack was finally held, but the casualties amongst patients and unit (including cooks, orderlies and drivers) were heavy. Eighteen of the unit were killed by shell or mortar fire, mainly during the closing stages of that counter-attack, many of whom were among the forty-nine I buried on that second morning.

While with the surgical unit, and later with the Somersets, it was pleasing to realise that respect for the Geneva Convention in respect of ambulances was being observed by the Germans. There was one stretch of the road alongside Hill 112 (which often had to be used by ambulances) that was overlooked by the enemy. If the ambulance was on its own, no attention was paid to it, but if it was in convoy with other vehicles, it had to take its chances. This seemed to be fair enough.

My most vivid memory of that Normandy baptism by fire was of an incident during the first night. I was assisting a doctor in a cowshed when three new wounded were brought in. Two had abdominal wounds, while the third had multiple wounds in the arms and chest. The doc took a quick look at the three and, pointing at the third, said:

"Padré, put a torniquet high up on that left arm, and take it off. The elbow joint is completely shattered, and nothing can save it. Then dress it and dress the other wounds. And hurry, or he'll bleed to death!" I was thankful for the pre-war simple St. John's training and for the Chartham Hospital experience, slight though it had been.

Later, when the party was over, I went to Divisional H.Q., and thence back to my unit.

A few days later came a posting to the 4th Somerset Light Infantry to replace their padré, who had become a casualty. Here I was amongst old friends, although many of my closest associates of Dover days (when I had taken many services for them and played hockey with them) I had seen passing, wounded, through the surgical unit at Mouen during July 10th and 11th.

I joined them at Eterville during the preparations for yet another attack upon Maltôt on Hill 112. The unit was deployed on two sides of the Château, in a series of section posts which were rather wide apart—the result, perhaps, of the casualties already sustained. It was possible to visit the most forward posts by using cover, so prayers were taken daily with each group. Three incidents are imprinted vivdly upon my memory.

The first occurred at a forward position alongside a road. It was 11.00 a.m. and all was quiet. We talked together in the ditch (all, that is, except the look-out), and then began our prayers and reading. Suddenly there came the moaning wail of the *nebelwerfer*, a five-barrelled mortar which, because of the wierd whistle of its bombs, became known as 'Moaning Minnie'. Depending on the range, there was a time lag of perhaps several seconds from the first sound of the whine to the explosion of the bomb. We scattered and flattened in the ditch and slit trenches. The bombs fell unpleasantly close on the road and bank, but mercifully none landed in the ditch. A second discharge was also close, but equally ineffective. After a couple of minutes of silence, I said: "Well, boys, what about it? Shall we continue now, or would you prefer postponing the prayers until tomorrow?"

"Cor, sir! We're not going to let the Bosch stop our prayers!" said one of them, and so we continued.

On one occasion, from some operational necessity, no movement at all was allowed in the forward area until after dark. Thanks to the Tannoy system, we had our prayers by remote control!

The third event took place in the night of 22nd and 23rd of July. The 4th S.L.I., still in the woods and fields near Château Eterville, were in reserve, while the 4th and 5th Wilts. made the final assault on Maltôt. That evening, orders were laid down that there was to be no movement at all within the Battalion areas unless a stand-to was ordered. All, including M.O., orderlies and padré, were to remain in their slit trenches or dug-outs, even if casualties occurred. I hated every minute of that night of inactivity and, lying there in the solitude of the slit trench during the anticipated 'strafing', I was scared stiff. I put my greatcoat doubled over my chest, and my tin hat over my stomach, and hoped for the best!

During my stay with the Somersets, my driver who had recently come over to Normandy with the remainder of the Divisional troops, joined me at Eterville during a lull in the battle. The sun was shining, and behind the wood in the centre of our Defence Area, most of the unit were brewing tea. Poor Owens drew up, and as he got out of his P.U. a shell dropped twenty-five yards away, killing one and wounding several. Two minutes later, a second shell landed even nearer. It was a very bad baptism for the lad, and one from which he never fully recovered.

Familiarity, they say, breeds contempt. Often, it also engenders a feeling of security, while a lack of full comprehension can produce the opposite effect. This was well illustrated as a result of the temporary posting to the Somersets. On arriving with that Battalion, several asked, "What unit have you been with, padré? On being told "The Recce Regiment", the response, in almost every case, was: "Cor! I wouldn't want to be with that suicide mob for all the tea in China!"

On returning to the Recce, our men said almost the same thing of the Somersets. It was an interesting, but understandable, attitude.

On the 25th July, the 43rd Division was withdrawn from the line, and the chaplains were called to a conference at Corps H.Q. by the D.A.C.G. (Revd. G. Druitt), and after spending a pleasant and relaxing day, during which three replacement chaplains joined the Division, we all returned to our units in preparation for the anticipated breakout from the bridgehead.

CHAPTER FOURTEEN

Normandy—The Break-out

As a reminder that prayers and services (short though these often had to be) formed an integral part of the daily round of the chaplain's life, even during 'active' conditions, a few entries from my small pocket diary covering such periods as the break-out, the *Seine* crossing, Nijmegen and Arnhem, will precede certain chapters. These brief memoranda are recorded exactly as written in pencil on most days. All services were, of course, voluntary. Squadrons are often indicated here merely by their letters; H.Q., A, B, or C.

July 30:	H.Q., 30+2 H.C. (remained for Holy Communion). C, 100+8. B, 150. E.P. (Evening Prayers) H.Q. and Mortars. 11.30 (p.m.) (new) A arrived (Graham).
31:	Dig in new area. Visited A and B. Saw Bevan—Dennis has D.S.O.
Aug. 1:	Buried Germans (Smudge) A. Midgley and Macalister (?) wounded. E.P. H.Q. & A.
2:	A. H.Q. 4. buried 3 Germans in C's area E.P.C., Tac H.Q. and A Ech.
8:	3 Tp. A Sqn 15. Buried Sgt. McCoy. Services. Harvey died.
9:	asked by Vinnicombe (R.A.S.C. Officer) of Jeffreys.
10:	12 Admin H.Q. R.A.S.C. 40 2.504 Coy R.A.S.C. 50. E.P. B.Sqn. then with Ivan (SCF) to see Jeffrey's grave. Then on to D (anvu) found 7 dead (in dark).
11:	C.O. refused to allow digging party—Frank and I went & found large number—buried them. Returned found 3 Staffs (South Staffordshire Regiment) buried (the 3). 505 R.A.S.C. 40+7 H.C.

12:	H.Q. 9 H.C. C.Sqn 3. 10B (Sung Eucharist really) 10. 11A 4 H.C. Shells & mortars on farm.
13:	7.2nd army H.Q., Recce H.C.10. V.S. 350? H.C.12. B.ech 506.30+9. Lunch with Ben (Q.M.)
14:	515 out with B (Sqn) in orchard all day. Buried 2 Germans. 730 called to A.Ech.
15:	Frank told me of booby-trapped bodies. saw D.A.C.G. on road. Div.—Ivan. heard of Tal's death (chaplain who had replaced me at Somersets) 5 Service 504 R.A.S.C. E.P. B. and C.

It was heartening finally to be back with my own unit, not that the temporary attachments were unhappy periods, indeed quite the reverse. The Somersets were old friends and gave me a warm welcome. Their morale was excellent and everyone seemed cheery even when the pressure was really on. A chaplain was fortunate to have such a posting and such support from all ranks.

The scratch surgical unit had integrated quickly, but because we had come together for a specific operation which turned out to be far busier than even the most pessimistic had forecast, the settling down was purely a rapid 'teaming', with constant changes of personnel due to casualties and emergencies. There was neither the time nor the opportunity to forge any real personal relationships during those forty-eight hours and, understandably, one experienced a feeling of aloneness. There had been many moments of comparable danger and discomfort in the past, but then I had been amongst the tested friends of my own unit, which somehow made a world of difference.

The Recce Regiment was now approaching full strength. 'B' Squadron and the residue of H.Q. Squadron were delighted to be back in training with the rest of the regiment. The whole unit was in fine spirits and eager to go into action.

On July 28th, 'B' and 'C' Squadrons moved to the Divisional concentration area ready for the hoped 'break-out' from the Normandy bridge-head. The following evening, R.H.Q. and H.Q. Squadrons joined them at Conde sûr Seulles. The next day, Sunday 30th, was quiet—the lull before battle—and voluntary services were held in all Squadron areas. The turn out was remarkable, with 'B' Squadron 150 strong (see diary). One of the new men in that Squadron, seeing the number present, suspected a 'Parade', which of course it was not, and said: "Is this a compulsory service? If so, I'm not coming!" At 11.30 p.m., a complete replacement Squadron, fully officered, arrived and became our new 'A' Squadron. One felt extremely sorry for Major Graham M.C., who had trained them in England and brought them over believing that he would remain in command. Major Scott-Plummer, who had commanded the 'lost' Squadron, had agreed to step down. The General and the C.O., however, insisted that to ensure continuity of regimental operational tactics formulated and long-rehearsed, Major Scott-Plummer must take over command, so Major Graham returned at once to England.

The Regiment moved at 4.30 a.m., and at Jerusalem crossroad we met the 2nd Battalion and saw, amongst other old friends, Colonel Dennis Biddle (a Company Commander with the 5th Battalion in the Saar days) and Sergeant Bevan, who asked me whether we still sang *Cwm Rhondda*. We dug in at 7.30 a.m. and 'B' and 'C' were soon operational.

The battle moved rapidly for the first few days. At Briquessard we suffered our first casualties, amongst whom was Sergeant Stan Midgeley, one of the Padré's helpers. The Midgeley family had been most unlucky; Clarence, serving with the Durham Light Infantry, was killed near Dunkirk, another brother was taken prisoner in Crete, and Percy (Stanley's twin brother) was killed with us on 24th June. The final blow came when Stanley stepped on an anti-personnel mine and lost his leg. He now lives in Cam in Gloucestershire, and regularly attends Berkeley Church, where he is a sidesman.

An even more tragic case had links with the 5th Glosters in May 1940. A gunner Observation Officer was killed while seconded to the Battalion during the withdrawal. Later, his mother wrote to me and said that her husband and all three of her sons had been killed in Belgium or France during those three weeks in May.

Booby traps, including one attached to a body, were encountered on August 3rd, but fortunately warning of this latest macabre device of the S.S. had already filtered through to all ranks, so we suffered no casualties. When a body was found in suspicious circumstances, the routine suggested was to avoid it if at all possible and later, when time allowed, to fasten a cord or chain to the belt or some other part of the equipment on the body, then to attach the other end to a carrier or armoured car, and move the body a yard or two. Captain Moreland was one of the few who encountered and successfully dealt with these rare but grisly, ghoulish and lethal snares for the unwary.

At La Lande, German flares turned the night sky into daylight, and on the 5th, 7 Troop lost both officers (Lieutenants Monty Banks and Frank Vascha). Monty and I had eaten our hard 'tack' the previous evening, leaning against his vehicle near Ondefontaine, and discussed 'home' and what we would do when this was all over. I was badly shaken by Monty's death. The personnel of 7 Troop reacted well under their new officers, and maintained their spirit and drive.

Even in battle humourous incidents occur, as when Captain John Ellis ('Mechanical' John) woke the M.O., Captain John Ellis ('Doc' John), in the middle of the night when the latter was trying to snatch some sleep, and announced that a fly, nicely nestling in his ear, was buzzing so loudly that he could not hear clearly the chitter-chatter and messages over the regimental intercom. The M.O. syringed and syringed with water, oil, and goodness knows what, but still the fly (which was later found to be a gnat) sat snugly, but continued to be very vocal. It was not until a third visit the next morning that the insect, now dead, was washed out.

August 6th found the Regiment on the stubbornly defended line of Duval Crossroads—Danvou, Horondel, and St. Jean le Blanc, while slightly to the north-east lay Mont Pinçon, the last of the major bastions of the German defence system in Normandy. The assault of this commanding position was a grim and costly period. Considerable though the contributions of the armoured and artillery elements were, it was upon the infantry (the 'P.B.I.' in common parlance) that fell the major burden of this bloody business. Their determination and courage beggars description but, I suppose, can be exemplified by the story of the remnant of the 5th Wiltshires who, led and inspired by their Colonel, walking stick in hand and red rose in his lapel, took and held the vital crossroads and village of La Verinière at the foot of Mont Pinçon[1]; but at what a price!

Our own men, fulfilling their normal rôle and occasionally doubling on foot for the heavily depleted infantry, were magnificent and took everything in their stride. This final phase of the battle for Normandy revealed the sterling character of all ranks helped, no doubt, by the quality and leadership of the officers and N.C.O.s Observers in all other units will, I am sure, subscribe to these feelings. The chaplains, too, had their casualties. During those few days, three out of thirteen unit chaplains of the 43rd Division were killed. These were the Reverend Jamie Douglas, one of the best of our original team, and two recent replacements for earlier casualties, Reverend Tal Davies (who had taken over from me with the 4th Somerset Light Infantry when I returned to the Recce Regiment) and the Reverend F.W. Musgrave. One of the last two unfortunately lost his life through inadequate training. He did not recognise the moan of a mortar bomb, and so failed to take cover in time. Was it coincidence that the 43rd Division chaplains who had attended the 2nd Army battle school had a much lower casualty pecentage than those who had not had that advantage? Even in the fighting arms, this lack of training, this insufficiency of knowledge or appreciation, maybe, of when and when not to take cover, from time to time had tragic results.

Those early days of the breakout have left many memories. The dust of Normandy during that hot summer had to be seen to be believed, while the drive through the thick cinnamon dust of the narrow wooded valley leading up from Le Mesnil Auzouf to Duval was a wierd experience. For me, however, the most eerie sensation occurred in the empty village of Danvou. The previous day, a certain battalion had suffered heavily and I had gone over to lend a hand by searching for casualties and burying the dead. Walking up a lane to an orchard where many bodies were lying, I passed an isolated detached house. This building oozed evil, and it took considerable resolution to approach, enter, and finally search it for possible wounded or dead. Even when it was known to be empty, it retained that same creepy, almost sadistic atmosphere, similar in some respects to the feeling of revulsion experienced near the Old Park Barracks outside Dover. I have often regretted the inability to investigate the previous history of that house.

On another occasion, an urgent wireless message came through, asking the padré to go at once to a certain troop area. The situation upon arrival was quiet and the men appeared their normal selves. The Squadron Commander was in the forward edge of a wood overlooking a steep valley. The German positions were across the brook on the lower slopes of Mont Pinçon. An infantry attack had failed in this area a day or two earlier and there were apparently still two British dead lying in an orchard three or four hundred yards down the road. This, so said the Major, was upsetting the morale of his men; a statement I did not, and never have, accepted. He then asked me to go down and bury the dead. On the assurance that it was necessary, I agreed.

Two volunteers were called for. The response was interesting (particularly in view of the previous suggestions of affected morale) for almost everyone was prepared to come and soon, with clerical collar fully exposed and white handkerchief held high on a spade, the column of three set off.

The Germans 'played ball' (as they usually did under such circumstances) and let the party get on with their task. A few minutes later, the Major also came down the lane, but instead of coming into the orchard to us, he surprisingly made for the farmhouse. By this time, the necessary documentation had been completed and all that remained was the grave-digging and the actual burial. Suddenly the Germans, no doubt made suspicious by the disappearance of the officer into the house, began mortaring the orchard and house. The bodies were quickly placed in a nearby slit-trench (which possibly they themselves had dug), the brief burial service was said, the grave partly filled in, perhaps to a depth of a foot, and a rapid return was made to the troop positions, followed by the Major who, it appeared, had made a recce for wine! I am still convinced that the wine, rather than the morale of his men, was the reason for that request for burial in broad daylight and in full view of the enemy. I was furious, and went straight to the C.O. and told him that I did not mind, as he well knew, sticking my neck out when necessary, but that I strongly objected to being used as a stalking horse in a wine-foraging lark.

The next day, the grave was fully filled in, and the usual wooden crosses placed in position.

Late on the 12th, with Mont Pinçon in the hands of the 43rd Division, the Regiment withdrew into harbour. There, a huge pile of letters from next of kin awaited the C.O. and padré, asking almost frantically why there had been no reply to repeated requests about sons, husbands and brothers serving with the Regiment; rumours in the U.K. had by this time reached damaging proportions.

It was 5.30 a.m. when the Regiment pulled in and within 15 minutes I had seen the C.O. and received permission to drive back at once to 21 Army Group H.Q. and seek an interview with Montgomery himself. I arrived at his H.Q. at 7.00 a.m., unwashed, unshaven, and very angry, and went at once to see the D.C.G. (Reverend Canon F. Ll. Hughes) and demanded that I should see Monty right away. The D.C.G. replied that no-one could see him before 9.00 a.m.. I exploded, but was finally calmed down by the D.C.G. who promised that *he* would see the great man at 9.00, and gave his assurance that the matter would be settled with all speed, and a ruffled and only partly-pacified padré returned to his unit and the pre-arranged Sunday services. Later that morning Monty himself ordered the immediate release of all letters of the 43rd Recce Regiment. This was a great relief to all concerned.

There was for me, when I heard of it, an amusing sequel to that release of the Recce mail. Weeks earlier, when visiting some of our men at the 75th or 76th General Hospital in Bayeux, I bought and posted home a Camembert cheese. Storage in the held-up mail for weeks in that summer heat had had its effect, and when the package arrived, it more or less swam through the letter-box, and its effluvium haunted the house for days!

With the capture of Mont Pinçon, German resistance in Normandy began to crumble. The Regiment, after thirty-six hours to rest and refit (during which time there was a full Regimental Service), moved to a new harbour on the Conde road. On the 15th, 'B' Sqadron recced forward but were held up by mines near Clécy. Two of their armoured cars were knocked out, and a supporting tank also lost a track. Luckily, among the three crews there were no serious casualties. While the road was being cleared of mines for the main advance (the leading cars and tanks, having gone through the mined area, pushed on quickly towards the river *Noireau*), the remainder of the Regiment relaxed, and some of our men 'inspected' the knocked-out tank. Just before the Regiment moved off, the tank recovery vehicle arrived. Five minutes later, the R.E.M.E. sergeant in charge, after he had been into the tank, shouted to his mates:

"My God! If we'd been another ten minutes, there'd have been no b..... tank left to recover; they'd 've nicked the b..... lot!"

It was interesting, later in the day, to see a strange and more powerful machine-gun mounted on one of our light armoured cars in place of the normal Bren, and a tank periscope adorned another car. Perhaps the R.E.M.E. sergeant had been right in his assessment. Our men learned quickly to remove, if possible, anything that was not a permanent fixture when they had a car knocked out, knowing that an abandoned car was always fair game for replacements. The tank crew had apparently not learned that basic lesson!

The crossing of the *Noireau* marked the end of the German resistance in Normandy west of the *Seine*. Caught between the twin thrusts of the 21st Army Group, and shattered by the news that the American and French Divisions were in Paris, the retreat of the German Army began in earnest, and ended with its disintegration in the shambles of the Falaise Gap. At that moment, we were not fully aware of the effectiveness of the hammering of the British and Canadian Forces in the previous eight weeks, nor of the extent to which the strength and morale of the German Army had been sapped. The truth began to dawn a few days later from the interrogation of prisoners.

At Conde, we were halted, and the 11th Armoured and 49th Infantry Divisions passed through to continue the chase. Two incidents come to mind.

The first was told by Trooper Youell, who had retired to attend to nature's call and, at the same time, to read newly arrived mail. Suddenly, when he was at his most vulnerable, a party of Germans intruded upon his privacy and, to his surprise, insisted upon surrendering. Probably few soldiers, so indelicately situated, can boast of having 'captured' so many prisoners!

The second event took place on August 20th. The whole Regiment had assembled in a field for a service of thanksgiving. The men were seated in a semi-circle when, during the reading of the lesson, a dear old Norman farmer or farm-hand came up and sat down with them and later, upon his knees, prayed shoulder to shoulder with them. At the end, he came up and, with tears in his eyes, shook several of us by the hand and walked off.

On the 22nd, the unit was ordered forward and told to get to the *Seine* at Vernon with all speed—a distance of 120 miles.

The advance, via Bréteuil and Paçy-sûr-Eure, occupying approximately twenty hours running time, was militarily comparatively uneventful, with few delays apart from a major bridging operation at Paçy. A few hours after the completion of that task by the Royal Engineers, from the heights above Vernon, the first elements of the 43rd Recce Regiment saw the waters of the *Seine* and another phase in the armed struggle for Europe's freedom was about to begin.

The rapid movement of the 43rd Division in the final stages of the battle for Normandy had meant that the villages tended to be fully inhabited and little damaged. This had a marked effect on the men, and the spontaneity of the applause and fêting given by those suddenly liberated country folk lent a fantastic carnival air to the triumphal progress. At the same time, though the physical pressure was still great (we continued to operate from dawn to dusk of the long summer days), the mental tension was, for the moment, eased and a sort of sensory recharging took place.

Two other vivid memories, both very trivial, also remain from that period of the dash from the *Noireau* to the *Seine*. Both occurred on the same evening.

We had travelled far and fast through Athis, smoking Argentan, and ended that day at Bréteuil. Here, the Assault troops took over for the night, and the armoured cars withdrew to a laager outside the village. The welcome for our troops was magnificent, with the poor Colonel embarrassed by the attention of the ladies and little children. Within minutes, however, female shrieks were heard above the cheers of the crowd, and a party of several girls appeared with their heads completely devoid of hair. These, it turned out, had been collaborating with the Germans, living in the lap of luxury while the normal villagers were not so lucky. These Norman equivalents of the American Gun-Man's 'Moll' (film version!) were not physically harmed, but the indignity of their shorn heads and complete ostracism was punishment enough.

I went round all squadrons in harbour, taking prayers and talking, and I returned to R.H.Q. at about 10.30 p.m.. It had been a long and tiring day which had begun before 5 a.m.. The Adjutant, Captain 'Cole' Packer, saw me and said:

"You need a drink, Padré!"

I replied that I could do with a good glass of water, and I meant it. He handed me a tumbler which, in the light of the Tilley lamp appeared to be water. In my parched state, I put the lot down in one gulp—or attempted to. For the next few minutes I coughed and spluttered, eyes streaming and stomach and gullet burning. 'Cole' had given me a tumbler of neat Calvados. It was not a joke; he genuinely thought that I realised that it was spirits, and not water!

Those hectic four weeks of operations had proved several things:

a) That the morale and efficiency of the unit had not been affected by the tragic landing and by the introduction of nearly three hundred strangers. This may be attributed in part at least to the wise handling by the officers and senior N.C.O.s of a very delicate situation, but I believe too that the sound country character (and we were mostly West of England and Welsh lads), and the 'family feeling', regimental spirit, or ésprit-de-corps, call it what you wish, which had developed over the years, were important factors.

b) That the Recce 'Bible' drawn up by Colonel Dudley Ward (later General Sir Dudley Ward) in 1942, and ably interpreted by Colonel Lane Fox and Major Charles Kinnersley (2.I.C.)—the latter undoubtedly the finest military brain (with the exception of Colonel Dudley Ward) in the Regiment during the six years of war—was eminently workable.

c) That the policy (as far as possible) of daily prayers in some section of most Squadrons was both feasible and welcomed, and that the Padre's helpers were a very great help, and it is true to say that even after most of the helpers had become casualties, their spirit and the influence of their example lived on.

Notes

1. See: "The 43rd Wessex Division at War, 1944–45", pp. 67–9

CHAPTER FIFTEEN

Vernon to Nijmegen

Diary Notes:

Aug 27:	Rev(eille) 5 am (crossed) bridge V(ernon) Service 50+ H.C.12. Mortars Booth killed. Edge killed by sniper, dig in on railway. Saw Kinns (chaplain)
28:	Moved to forest of Vernon. It is thought (flying (V1)) bomb site. Massey killed, Shutler & Jones wounded
29:	RAIN! & puncture! maternity case! Buried Sgt. Davies (R.C.) Broken neck case at Gasnay Back 430
Sept 3:	(Sunday) Recce H.C.—8 (3) 930 HQ 200—H.C.17 1045 C 45 (H.C.5) 1215 A 70 (H.C.9) RASC 3 HQ = ? 30 H.C.4 415 506 70 H.C.10
4:	Talk by Div Com(mander) & P(resentation) of medals. Took rest of day off except for letters to N.o.K. (next of kin) etc. E.P. at R.H.Q. at 840
11:	0545 left forest. Beauvais, Amiens, Arras, Lens, Thuméries, T.L. H & Brussels. (saw) 2 man sub(marine) outside Albert – R.A.F. kill? Night with 504 coy. Story of jeep in hall.
12:	F.D.S. of 15 Div. Saw Tony. Called on Mère st. Aldegonde posted 3 letters for her. News of move E.P. 9 & 11 Tps.
13:	Mike & stores 12 C 90 -H.C.6 Brussels saw (?) & grave of Martin (killed in May 1940) Saw Hughes re (?) no go. E.P. HQ & 10 Tp

The Vernon period provided amusing as well as grim moments. The bizarre conditions under which the final reconnaissance for the bridging and assault were made should be read in *The 43rd Wessex Division at war*. The strictest secrecy was enjoined, because of the German forces at Vernonnet on the other bank of the *Seine* (less than

300 yards away) and on the steep escarpment behind, a feature which dominated the area selected for the crossing. Heavy bridging equipment for Class 9 and Class 40 bridges had to come from far in the rear, while the Dukws and stormboats, in which the actual crossing were to be made, had to be brought from Arromanches. American Recce troops, members of the Maquis, civilians armed to the teeth, masses of spectators as well as a squadron of the 43rd Recce and large bodies of Divisional, Corps, and Army R.E.s milled around; the French Police even ran up the Tricolore, the Union Jack, and the Stars and Stripes on one of our observation towers! Now that no element of surprise remained, the prospects for the assault crossing and the bridge-building operations appeared more than usually hazardous, and the boat crews, their 'passengers' and the engineers, faced an unenviable task. Progress was, however, better than expected (or feared!) and by dark on August 26th, the Class 9 bridge had been completed.

Soon after dawn, 'B', 'A', and 'H.Q.' Squadrons crossed the bridge. 'B' moved left-handed through Vernonnet but, because of heavy congestion in the lodgement area, the others were ordered to turn right and harbour temporarily; 'A' in the local sports field, and 'H.Q.' under cover of the hedges in an adjoining field, and await orders.

Almost at once the 'moaning minnies' were heard. At that time, most of the unit were talking in groups around their armoured cars, and brewing tea—it was ever thus during moments of inactivity! They say great minds think alike; certainly there was unanimity at that moment, and with one accord each dived under the nearest vehicle—in my case the medical 'White' half-track in which I had crossed the bridge. I thought I was not slow in reaction, but a kick from a boot still attached to the M.O. showed me that he too knew the form!

R.H.Q. had several wounded while the C.O. and the Divisional Commander had narrow escapes. One of our front wheels was hit by a fragment, but we underneath were unhurt. After we bandaged up the wounded, I ran over to 'A' Squadron and found that Trooper Booth, with whom I had talked only a short while before, had been killed by an almost direct hit. Several others had been wounded. I started the preparation for the burial and then, telling the Sergeant I would be back in a moment, I went round a nearby building and, for the only time in the whole war, I was violently sick.

Before I returned to R.H.Q., engines had started up in the next field and H.Q. Squadron began moving out. The orders, naturally, were to disperse and dig-in. The medical vehicle pulled out, turned away from the bridge, and drew into an orchard some distance along the road. Here we dug our trenches between the road and a railway cutting which bordered the orchard, after which the Doc and I set out to locate the others. Seeing movement along the railway bank, we strolled over and ran head-on into a fighting patrol of 4th Wiltshires led by their C.O., Colonel Ted Luce, looking for the enemy. Apparently, because we had been the last vehicle out of harbour as a result of the damaged wheel, we had not heard the full briefing, and had driven too far. We learned that the bridge over the *Seine* had been hit and that the R.E.s were experiencing difficulty in linking up again. Later that morning, the Sappers ferried four tanks over, and everyone felt a little happier.

Slowly the bridgehead was broadened. The infantry who had made the assault crossing, and the follow-up Brigades, were attempting to push northward and up into Vernon Forest, supported by 'B' Squadron of the 43rd Recce and some tanks of the $^{4}/_{7}$ D.G.s. 'A' Squadron with the 4th Wiltshires moved southwards along the river towards Giverny, where amongst our casualties was Lieutenant Peter Edge, a one-time N.C.O. in the unit, who had served with distinction, and who had been commissioned a short while before rejoining the unit in Normandy. By nightfall, the German counter-attack under General Macholtz, slow in developing, had spent itself, and the lodgement area was secure. The 40 Class bridge too had been completed, and the remaining tanks of the $^{4}/_{7}$ D.G.s and $^{15}/_{19}$ Hussars began rumbling over.

The next morning, the 28th, R.H.Q. and H.Q. Sqaudron moved into a small hutted camp in Vernon Forest, midway between the operational squadrons. It was soon obvious that the area had been one of the V-1 launching sites. So well was it positioned that the ramp was hidden from the air for almost its entire length. It is little wonder that the R.A.F. often experienced difficulty in locating those magnificently camouflaged, and occasionally half sunken, hornets nests. On the following morning, there came a sudden call from 'A' Squadron for the M.O., saying that they had moved into the next village and were meeting stiff opposition. The thing that worried them, however, was that they had on their hands a maternity case which needed urgent attention.

Ellis shouted across to me, adding:

"Padré, for goodness sake come along! I haven't done a midwifery for years, so you may have to bury mum or child!"

Luckily for us, as we drove up we saw a company of the Wiltshires and their M.O., moving in to take over from 'A' Squadron. Ellis, again quick in reaction, went over to the Wiltshires' M.O. and said:

"There is an urgent maternity case in the second house on the left. As my boys are being withdrawn, I'd better hand the case over to you. Good luck!"

Later that morning, resistance broke completely, and the enemy faded away. Speculation was rife as to whether the end of the war was almost at hand; some even talked of possible German capitulation within days. Monty, seeing the situation right along the *Seine* from Paris to the sea, advocated (as we now know) an all-out thrust into Germany, which might well have ended hostilities before winter. This plan, however, was not accepted, and the scale of his thrust in the 21st Army Group area was reduced.

To increase the speed of the breakout from the Vernon bridgehead, the fighting units of the 43rd Divison were rested in Vernon Forest and all our divisional R.A.S.C. companies and our own 3-ton lorries were taken to ferry petrol and rations for the armoured divisions now pouring over the bridge and sweeping forward towards north-east France, Belgium and Holland. We were peeved, tired though the whole Division was, that we could not be (as we fancifully imagined) in at the death. This feeling soon died, however, when Welfare took over. E.N.S.A. parties arrived which included such stars as Flanaghan & Allen, Florence Desmond, and Kaye Cavendish, who played to Brigade audiences. Fishing in the *Seine* had its patrons, while the Doc and I, picking up discarded German rifles, set out one afternoon to try and shoot a boar—many had been seen. Our success after four hours was limited to the sight of an old sow and a small litter crossing a glade! Naturally, we did not shoot. Such a foray was, perhaps, a little foolish, for at times the bracken and undergrowth was chest high, and a chance encounter with an old 'tusker' under those circumstances could have been most unpleasant. The Divisional Staff obtained permission for a small party of leave personnel from every unit to visit Paris each day. Any spare time I had, I preferred to spend in and around the forest, and so I never applied for a Paris trip.

The church life continued, if numbers are any criterion, to flourish. On Sunday the 3rd of September, forty-eight made their communion

Cover (greatly reduced in size) of the revived 5th Glosters' Gazette which appeared November 1939. The original 5th Glosters' Gazette appeared for a time in the 1914–18 war.

The sketch specially drawn by H.M. Bateman for the 5th Glosters' Gazette, December 1939.

Soldats français!

Pour qui vous battez-vous?

L'effort des Anglais ne correspond pas à l'effort et au sacrifice demandé au peuple et surtout aux soldats français. Votre gouvernement a suivi aveuglement les conseils de Londres en proclamant la mobilisation générale pendant que personne — les faits l'ont prouvé — ne menaçait vos frontières. Contents de vous avoir engagé dans la guerre totale, les Anglais se sont bien gardés de vous envoyer de véritables combattants

Beaucoup mieux payés, mieux nourris que le pollu, les Anglais, qui veulent rester des milords, se sont bornés a se cantonner quelque part en France, pas trop près des premières lignes.

Le poid de la guerre pèse donc beaucoup plus lourd sur vous que sur les Anglais. Cependant ce sont eux, qui vous ont poussé à la guerre.

Vous rappelez-vous comment cela fut fait?

Ils ont fait signer par la France des accords et confirmer des garanties. Vos politiciens déclarèrent après, que les textes, rien que les textes commandaient la déclaration de guerre. Mais en fin de compte les Anglais se trompent.

La raison qui n'a jamais manquée aux soldats français sera plus forte que les textes. Nous ne sommes plus au temps, où un gouvernement pouvait engager à fond les forces de son pays pour la politique d'un gouvernement voisin, si l'opinion publique, si l'armée le déprouvait.

Il n'y a pas de raison de guerre entre Français et Allemands!

An example of the propaganda leaflets dropped by the Germans in the Lille area, 1940.

Below The 5th Glosters in the Maginot Line under French Command. Front row l to r: Col. G.A.H. Buxton (CO), French Commander, Major F.W. Priestley (2 I/C), Padre. The large figure to left (behind) was C.S.M. George Hill.

16th April 1940. The first three Glosters' fatal battle casualties: Cpl. F. Cleverley, Pte. A. Gardner, Pte. J. Young.

Visit by a senior French padre, Rev. Jean Dautheville Guibal, 7th April, 1940.

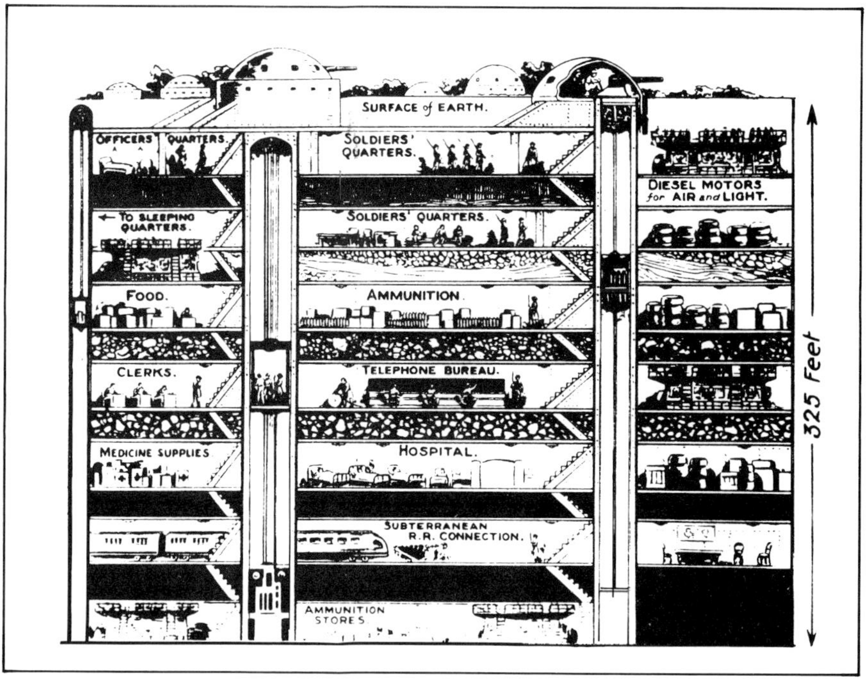

The architecture of the Maginot Line below the earth's surface. *Picture Post*, April 1940, N.22893.C.3 (1940) 24, Bodleian Library.

Returned from France May/June 1940. Padre Gethyn-Jones, Majors Mason, Priestley, Captain Hauting, Lieuts. Jenkins, Carter, Henn, Lymath, and Liversidge.

Army v. RAF, Uxbridge 11 Dec. 1943. Goal: I.M. McEwan HLI. Backs: G. Slack RASC, A.D. Lewis RAC. Halves: J. Balmer War Office, C. Woodford RMC, F.G. Self 421 Heavy A/A. Forwards: J.E. Gethyn-Jones RAChD, J.C. Dodds Army Dental, P.C. Webb Army Dental, P.C. Gray RE, C.G. Sandys RA.

St Come de Fresné Church near Arromanches, where the bells rang out on June 6th 1944 (D-Day) claiming to be the first thus to greet Allied Forces.

RETURN TO FRANCE

Ships in convoy. Note the barrage balloon being raised.

Sgt. Jones, (?), Lt. W. Moreland on the *Derry Cunihy*. It was sunk (acoustic mine) coming in to land.

A typical German propaganda leaflet designed to lower our morale. It had the reverse effect.

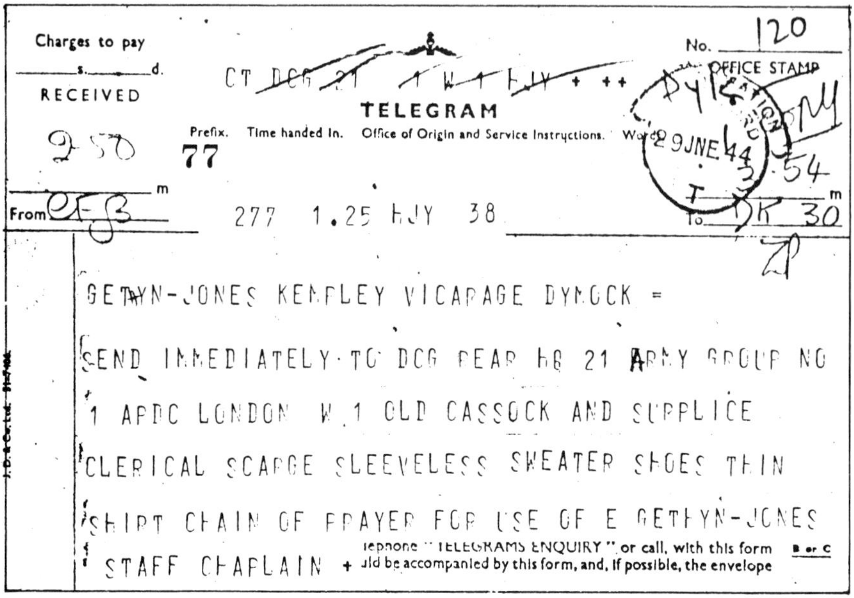

Charges to pay

s. d.

RECEIVED

9 50

Prefix. 77

Time handed In. Office of Origin and Service Instructions. Words

TELEGRAM

CT DCG 21 A W A F JY + + +

No. 120

OFFICE STAMP

DYMOCK 29 JNE 44

From CFB

277 1.25 HJY 38

To DK 30

GETHYN-JONES KEMPLEY VICARAGE DYMOCK =

SEND IMMEDIATELY TO DCG REAR HQ 21 ARMY GROUP NO 1 APDC LONDON W.1 OLD CASSOCK AND SURPLICE CLERICAL SCARGE SLEEVELESS SWEATER SHOES THIN SHIRT CHAIN OF PRAYER FOR USE OF E GETHYN-JONES STAFF CHAPLAIN +

...lephone "TELEGRAMS ENQUIRY" or call, with this form ...uld be accompanied by this form, and, if possible, the envelope

Telegram which saved Vivienne much worry a few weeks later. It tied up with a phone call from the DCG later that evening.

St George's House Chaplains' retreat (July 1944) after final capture of Hill 112. Front Row l to r: J.H.F. Wilson; I.D. Neill, SCF 43rd Div.; F.L. Hughes, DCG 21 Army Gp; G. Drewett, DACG; J.E. Gethyn-Jones, 43rd Recce Rgt., H.V. Prytherch; C.V.B. Haddelsey. Back Row l to r: I.J. Richards, D.W. Spiers, T.A.L. Davies*+, E.B. Gibbins, A.R.C. Leaney, J. Douglas+, K.H.F. Kinns, F.W. Musgrave*+, E.H. Etherington.
*—Replacement for casualties during Hill 112.
+—Killed in action between July 30 and August 5.

Vernon – crossing point, R. Seine, in August 1944. New bridge

Nijmegen Bridge drawn by D.J. Gethyn-Jones from an old print, with armoured cars added.

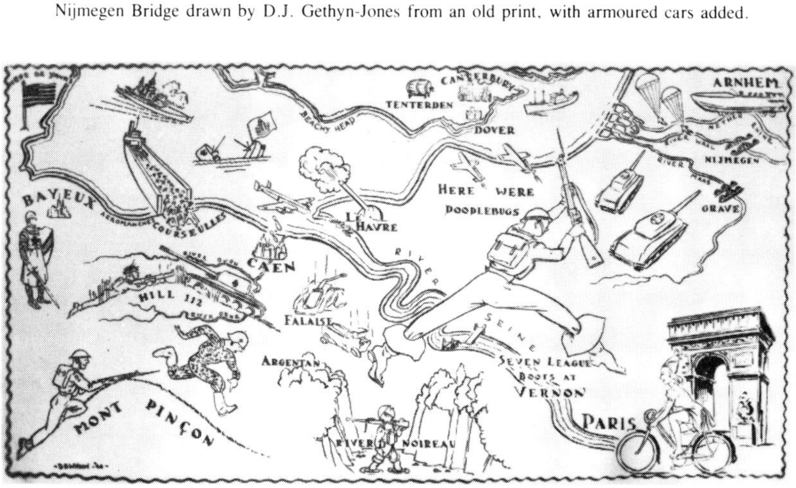

The 1944 Christmas card for the 43rd (Wessex) Division, drawn by Major Donald Wilson (Div. HQ), who added the sinking of the *Derry Cunihy* on my personal copy.

THE LAST GREAT BATTLE WEST OF THE RHINE: A "COMBINED OPERATION" TO SMASH A POWERFUL GERMAN FORT.

Kleve Schloss 11th C., associated with the legend of Lohengrin (Knight of the Swan) immortalised by Richard Wagner, also the home of Anne of Cleves 4th wife to Henry VIII.

Sgt. Darvel's original roadside grave with the wooden cross bearing his helmet.

The Battle between the Reichswald and the Rhine was the last set battle of the war in Europe, and centred on Kleve and Goch. The losses on both sides were very heavy. After the war most bodies were reburied in the vast Reichswald Military Cemetery.

The grave of Sgt. J.F. Darvel in the Reichswald Cemetery.

Reichswald Cemetery.

HISTORICAL TOURS FOR TROOPS of 21 A.G. Troop 1945

The Extern Rocks (near Horn).

The famous 11th C. descent from the Cross.

Arminius or Herman Monument in the Teuteburge Wald. He was the German leader who, in AD 9 combined the tribes and annihilated three Roman legions. Hence Caesar's cry 'Varus, Varus [Roman C. in C. in Germany], give me back my legions.'

An early party.

Bielefold Viaduct wrecked by the RAF.

(*Left*) The Mohne Dam Breached by Guy Gibson VC, but soon repaired.
The rubble below the dam is the remains of the villages and buildings swept away by the dam waters.
(*Right*) The top of the dam after repairs. Note the anti-bomb net.

BERLIN (*Russian Zone*)
September 1945

Russian Grand Stand bearing portraits of Truman, Stalin and Churchill erected in July 1945, located on Unter den Linden.

The national monument, Freiheit (the Liberty Memorial), facing the west front of the schloss.

Looks like A/A Zoo Flak Tower (88s were atop).

Ruins of the Reichstag (statue of Bismarck originally stood at the centre of the view in front of the building).

The Dom, Berlin's cathedral, seen between the statues outside Kaiser Wilhelm Schloss. Really three separate churches under one roof. In its crypt are entombed nearly a hundred members of the Hollenzollern family.

Tiergarten.

(*Above*) Technische Hochschule, ruined school of engineering on Charlottenberg Strasse.

(*Left*) Strasse des 17 Juni (formerly Charlottenburger Chaussee) with the Victory Column am Grossen Stern. The figure atop is 30 ft high, was unveiled in 1873 and originally stood in the Konigsplatz.

THE OLYMPIA STADIUM

The stadium was given festive outer facing of Franconian shell-limestone. Built by Werner March in 1934 – 36 for the XIth Olympic Games to a design which allowed a stadium to be filled and emptied amazingly quickly even with an enormous crowd. The chief means to this end was the sinking of half the stadium below ground level. Thus the people can move in from above to below and vice versa.

IN MEMORIAM

The monument at Bayeux to the British and Commonwealth forces who died in the liberation of Normandy (6 June – 26 August), but have no known graves. Of the approximately 1850 names on the panels, 168 were our men – 43 Recce/5th Bn The Gloucestershire Regt.

(*Right*) A section of one of the panels of the Bayeux monument. Midgley and Barge were brothers of two Berkeley Church sidesmen.

Memorial to 43rd (Wessex) Inf. Div. sited at summit of Hill 112, south of Caen. The battle began 10 July and ended on the 25th, and resulted in the most ghastly carnage of the Normandy campaign.

Grave of Lt. J.R. Banks.

5th Glosters receiving back their Colours (18.1.48). C.O. of party, Major H.G. Mason; King's Colour, Captain S. Wilcox; Regtl. Colour, Captain J. Collet; Colour Guard, R.Q.M.S. G. Hill; Sgt. Brown and Sgt. Hodges.

5th Glosters TA Camp — Post-War
Major Mason, Col. Waller, Col. Chalmers, Captain Wilcox.

Unveiling of the first memorial in England of the 43rd (Wessex) Division at Mere, 21st May, 1949, by General Sir Ivor Thomas.

Post war TA Southern Command Chaplains' Conference at Bagshot. Front row, l to r: E. Eynon (SCF), A. Bradley (Warden), D.D. Lloyd Evans (DCG), C. Williams (ACG), J.E. Gethyn-Jones (DACG), J. Goode (DACG), S. Shaw (SCF), P. Malins (Staff Chaplain).

Pembroke Castle 8 June 1958. Consecration of Guidon which H.M. the Queen was presenting to the Warwickshire and Worcestershire Yeomanry.

The medallion struck for the 'Normandy '84' commemoration, the 40th anniversary of the June 1944 landing (British, Commonwealth and Allied) to begin the freeing of France and Europe. Note (1) the broken chain symbolizing the release from four years of enemy occupation, (2) the cross of Lorraine, (3) the cathedral and above it a scene from the Bayeux Tapestry.

43rd Division War Memorial at Wynyards Gap, Dorset. A service for the Dorset Regt. in September 1987: *Left to right*: Padre Gethyn-Jones, Brig. A.E.C. Bredin, Major T.H. Wyllie, Mr. H.T. Bragg.

while three hundred and ninety-five attended voluntary services. The daily prayers, too, were welcomed.

On the 6th of September 'C' Squadron were called forward to provide protection for the Tactical H.Q. of the 2nd Army, under General Dempsey.

On Monday the 11th, I left Vernon Forest at 5.45 a.m. to act as 'floating' chaplain between 'C' Squadron of the Recce, and the forward R.A.S.C. Companies. The route through Beauvais, Amiens, Albert (where I saw a two-man submarine on its trailer, ditched—no doubt shot up by the R.A.F.) and Arras, was most interesting. Passing Lens, I stopped and consulted the map. Thuméries, where we had been billeted in early 1940, was only four or five miles off the main road. Despite the warning about pockets of enemy by-passed by the main axis advance, I turned off and drove to Thuméries. Madame 'Beurre et Oeufs', where I had been billeted, rushed into the street and kissed me, much to the amusement of my driver. An exchange of cigarettes for wine and we were on our way, and before 5 p.m. we were in Brussels. The city, which was *en fête*, presented no problems. Six of the seven people from who I asked directions replied in English while, slap in the middle of the Avénue Max, I spotted a vehicle of 504 Company R.A.S.C.. I followed him to his Company H.Q. and there spent the night.

The following day, September 12th, was indeed a lucky day. I was talking to some of the men of a Field Dressing Station of the 15th Scottish Division, at the roadside on the Louvain side of Brussels. There was a rattle of tracked vehicles and into view came a column of bren-gun carriers, and in the first of these was their Platoon Commander, a cousin of my wife Vivienne! A wave, and he was gone. Ten minutes later I set out along the same road to try and locate my 'C' Squadron.

A few miles further on, I noticed a strange name on a sign-post: Saventhem 1½ km. It seemed to ring a bell. I stopped, took out my diary, and there was the same word and, in brackets, 'Mère St. Aldegonde'. Vivienne had been a pupil at this Ursuline Convent and Mère St. Aldegonde had been her School House-Mistress. Impetuously (and foolishly) I left the main road and drove along the track to the Convent. In response to a knock on the central door, a grille opened and a wimpled face peeped out and my business was demanded. I asked whether Mère St. Aldegonde was still alive and if so, whether I might speak with her. The grille closed, and after some minutes the door opened and a stately old lady with a kindly face said in English:

"I am Mère St. Aldegonde. You wish to speak to me?"

I explained that I was the husband of Vivienne Angel and that she had asked me, should I ever be near Saventham, to call in and give her love and best wishes. The old lady's reserve dropped and, grasping my two hands she said:

"And how is my lovely Vivienne?"

And before I knew what was happening, I was seated in their reception hall surrounded by a noddering of nuns (or whatever the collective term may be), all speaking at once, all asking for news of the battle or of people of whom I really had no knowledge; school companions of Vivienne. I quickly said I must go and find my unit, but was firmly thrust back on my chair by Mère St. Aldegonde who turned to two nuns and rattled off something which sent them bounding away—if nuns bound!

They returned after a few minutes bearing a wine bottle and a square cake tin, both coated in earth. These were solemnly presented to me. Inside was a splendid fruit cake which looked as if it had come straight out of the oven. I protested that I could not possibly accept these gifts, for we had plenty of rations, and that they were in far greater need. To this Mère St. Aldegonde replied:

"But Father, you *must* accept, for this is the fulfilment of a covenant, a vow made to God. In May 1940, when we were overrun, we buried these and swore that they would be given to the one who should liberate us. You are the first Allied soldier we have seen, so they are yours with all our real thanks and Blessings." I gave them, in return, a 14-man ration pack.

Later that night, I shared the gifts with the officers of 'C' Squadron and we drank a toast:

"To that charming Irish nun, Mère St. Aldegonde!"

The next day I wrote home, and from that time forward, Vivienne and her school 'mother' corresponded regularly, and they met again in 1947.

On the 15th, 'C' Squadron's rôle with Tactical H.Q. 2nd Army ended, and that evening we rejoined the Regiment who, with the rest of the Division, had moved up on the 13th/15th from Vernon. Here, near Dièst, the sudden appearance of Browning machine-guns on some of 'A' Squadron's half-tracks may have had a connection with a wrecked 'Flying Fortress' (U.S.A.F. B-17 Bomber) alongside their harbour area.

The stiff opposition encountered by the 2nd Army along the waterways of eastern Belgium made it clear that the Germans' rapid withdrawal from the *Seine* had been to new logical defence lines based on the rivers and canals which intersected eastern Belgium and southern Holland.

That evening my batman, Trooper Peter Owens, a Herefordshire lad, showed me the grave of one whom I had known in Herefordshire before the war. A Belgian woman, who was putting flowers on the grave as I approached, said that Captain John Thorneycroft had been killed by an S.S. prisoner who had flung a bomb which he had concealed in his hand until he was only a matter of yards away from his captor. I wrote to the family a few days later.

The following day we set out early and by 10 a.m., we had crossed the Albert Canal at Berengen, where the 53rd (Welsh) Division had forced that great waterway. The 43rd (Wessex) and Guards Armoured Divisions were waiting for some major move that we knew was imminent. Rumours suggested that soon, very soon, the Allied forces were going to embark upon an expedition unparalleled in its imaginative perception. The facts, when they were revealed at the various 'O' groups, substantiated, indeed surpassed, the wildest rumours. The stakes of this proposed military gamble were high but, if fully successful, it might well have put British, Canadians, American and Allied forces into Germany along a wide front before the winter set in, and might even have broken German resistance and forced complete capitulation. As far as 30 Corps (of whom we were part) were concerned, it would be an extremely hazardous exercise.

American Airborne troops were to be dropped behind enemy lines to seize Eindhoven and the important bridges at Uden, Grave and Nijmegen, while the British 1st Airborne Division would land at Arnhem and secure that vital bridge over the lower *Rhein*. Along this line of Allied-held river crossings, 30 Corps, consisting of the Guards Armoured and 43rd Divisions, were to drive northwards to Arnhem and then fan eastwards with Deventer, Zutphen, and Doesburg as the first objectives of 'A', 'B', and 'C' Squadrons of the 43rd Recce Regiment.

The air armadas passing over on the 17th were a sight never to be forgotten, and with that gigantic 'drop' came the order to blast our way through, aided by air strikes by Typhoons and other pleasantries of the R.A.F.. To my mind, the Typhoons were the most demoralising of air attacks. The scream as they dived, followed by the whoosh of their rockets, culminating in the deafening impact explosions, was a nerve-racking sequence that I felt had no equal, at that time, in warfare. I saw a Tiger tank, of the type that had been holding us up in Normandy, lifted clean over and its gun and turret, weighing several tons, hurled twenty or thirty yards into a field.

At Eindhoven, the Regiment formed a screen on the east side of our corridor, from which direction a counter-attack was expected. On the night of September 21st/22nd, we continued northward over the bridges of Uden and Grave. Around midnight, we were hindered by a minor battle in a small village, and a short distance beyond, by small-arms fired from both sides of the road which represented, for most of our drive, the entire width of the British 'corridor'. Despite these irritations, the column pressed on and soon after dawn, when five kilometres south-west of Nijmegen, we harboured to await further orders.

The spirit of the men of the Division was terrific. They felt that they had proved themselves in the protracted fighting around Caen, Mouen, Hill 112 and down to Mont Pinçon. They had blasted their way across the *Seine* at Vernon, and now they knew for a fact that they were the equal, and possibly a great deal better than the members of the much vaunted German war machine. The fact that 30 Corps was right out on a limb with the certainty of violent armoured counter-attacks which might cut off our narrow corridor (which of course happened) was accepted calmly, indeed nonchalently. Set-backs there might be, but the end was certain. And these boys, at least most of them in the 43rd Recce Regiment, were not professional soldiers according to the accepted definition. They had, however, become highly 'professional' in the real sense.

We were visited while in harbour by a former member of the Regiment, Lieutenant Jeremy Taylor, who was now on the editorial and administration staff of the Recce Corps. Here, too, we learned that although the Nijmegen road bridge had been taken by a massive attack of American Airborne troops and the Guards' tanks, the road some distance beyond was blocked and, worse still, that the 1st Airborne at Arnhem had run into serious trouble in the form of counter attacks by tanks, and that the vital bridge was still in

German hands. Finally we learned that because of the weather, the scheduled 'drop' of a Brigade of the 52nd Lowland Scottish Division with their anti-tank guns could not take place, and that much of the badly-needed supplies of food and ammunition had landed in the German-controlled area. The 1st British Airborne troops were indeed up against it.

CHAPTER SIXTEEN

The 'Island'

That morning it was realised that Stage One of the grandiose scheme of the thrust through Holland to the Zuyder Zee had been completed successfully, with American airborne troops valiantly holding the vital centres and river crossings of Veghal, Uden and Grave, and awaiting the certainty of German counter-attacks on our essential but single road corridor. At Nijmegen, the American Airborne and the Guards Armoured Division had captured intact both the rail and road bridges over the wide *Waal* and had established a bridgehead on the 'Island'.

For us, ahead lay the prospect of great potential and excitement, for the Regiment had been ordered, directly the crossing at Arnhem had been secured, to lead the 43rd Division through that bridge-head, then swinging north-east to capture the *Jessel* river crossings at Doesburg, Zutphen, and Deventer; and possibly to organise the local resistance groups in each town to assist in their defence. In retrospect, that next fortnight proved to have been perhaps the strangest, most varied, frustrating and, overall, the most bizarre operational period of the whole war—at least that was what I felt.

Soon after harbouring, and while awaiting operational orders, the Regiment was detailed to collect the intact parachutes which were scattered everywhere and dump them centrally. The damaged ones were to be destroyed. Large segments of two of the latter, one a green comouflage mixture and the other a palish blue, found their way into my vehicle for future use. I still have a wildfowling scarf made of the former, and a pair of pyjamas from the latter, of which more anon!

For 30 Corps, frustration had already begun, and in consequence the 43rd Division were called forward to assist the Guards in the battle at Elst to clear the route to Arnhem. 'A' Squadron crossed the Nijmegen bridge at about 5 p.m., and around midnight the main body of the Regiment began to move, and by dawn, we had crossed the Nijmegen railway bridge and harboured in the fields near the *Waal*. My first task was to bury the enemy dead. At 11.30 a.m. part of the Regiment moved forward to Oosterhout House. This was a fine building but, surrounded as it was by woods containing snipers and booby-traps, the area was unpleasant, and before long we rejoined the squadrons already in the dyke-side fields, awaiting the next move.

The thrust along the main road to Arnhem, where it was known that the Airborne were closely beseiged, was checked at Elst. The task now given to the Regiment was that of clearing the narrow area to the west between the *Waal* and the *Neder Rijn* (Lower *Rhein*) and, if possible, to secure that flank from attack. Some miles to the east, the *Rhein* divides into two channels: the *Waal*, running through Nijmegen, and the *Neder Rijn*, flowing past Arnhem. It then re-unites in the delta country miles to the west. The only routes over these two branches of the Rhein at the eastern end of this large 'Island' were at Nijmegen and Arnhem. To the west, in German-held territory, there were many bridges. At Arnhem, the road bridge was intact and in German hands, but the railway bridge had been destroyed. We in 30 Corps were conscious of the vital nature of the Nijmegen bridges, which represented our only effective lines of communication, and realised that their destruction could spell disaster.

During the following day (Sunday 24th), although the Regiment was fully operational, short services or prayers were possible with some Troops of all Squadrons; and with the permission of a Dutch clergyman, the Reverend K.O. Finkenseiper, held the Holy Communion and shortened Matins for 'B' Squadron in Andelst Church. My diary records that this was an 11th Century building, but I fear I cannot picture it today although I remember the incumbent. In the afternoon, Mr Finkenseiper and I went over to another of his churches at Dodewaard, where there was a delightful old sexton. I enjoyed their 5.30 service and took them back afterwards, promising to collect on the morrow the kit of some R.A.F. personnel killed during the previous few days, and whom they had buried. 'A' Squadron had by this time established O.P.s overlooking (in the distance) the *Lower Rhein*.

The 25th, beginning at 4.30 a.m., was a day of mixed fortunes. Three of 'B' Squadron's armoured cars were knocked out, and Trooper Hawes was killed. I asked permission to bury him in the local churchyard at Opheusden, a tiny rural community at the edge of which Hawes had been shot. The Burgermeister, however, insisted instead that the burial should take place in a flower-bed at the town centre, and that he would attend. The reason he gave was that 'the people of Opheusen would wish to honour our liberator', and well they did.

On the way to Nijmegen to collect cigarettes and chocolate for the Regiment, I spotted a Messerschmidt 109 coming (as it appeared) straight for me on the bund road. I dislike being machine-gunned, so I stopped and dived for the ditch. The ME 109 had in fact sighted a low-flying British spotter plane cruising along close to the road. I watched, expecting the worst. Suddenly, the Auster banked sharply, and dodged round a tree. The ME returned to the attack, and again the spotter plane performed its aerobatics. These evasive tactics were repeated several times before the end came in an unexpected manner. During the fourth or fifth attack, the ME passed directly over a slit trench some five hundred yards away. To my amazement, a khaki-clad figure bobbed up, bren-gun in hand, and opened fire on the German fighter only thirty or forty feet above his head and, *mirabile dictu*, the ME crashed half a mile away. A few minutes later, I saw a Mitchell bomber brought down over Nijmegen by enemy fighters, two of which were themselves shot down. It was a grim sight as the game but crippled plane suddenly stalled, lost a wing, and spiralled into the houses.

During the day, several members of the Dutch Resistance swam over from the Arnhem side of the *Lower Rhein*, bringing news of the desperate plight of the Airborne. Amongst those who came through 'A' Squadron lines was a young Dutchman and his girl-friend Kitty. Both were given battle-dress and stayed with us for several days. Finally the lad became one of the four attached Resistance guides.

A contrast to all this is contained in a letter to Vivienne that morning, when I commented on the wild life to be seen of that Island: "*The number of partridges we have around us is terrific, and...duck flying about...couple of heron floating overhead, and in addition, I nearly ran over a weasel...*"

At that moment, I was thinking of a poem by Wilfred Gibson, one of the Dymock poets:

"And such a morning for cubbing—
The dew so thick on the grass!
Two hares are lolloping just out of range
Scattering the dew as they pass.

A covey of partridge whirrs overhead,
Scatheless; and gets clean away!
For it's other and crueller, craftier game
We're out for and after today!"

The following day was grim and gloomy. The beleaguered British and Polish airborne (to be exact, two thousand of them) had been ferried over the Lower Rhein during the night, but the losses had been heavy; of the relieving force, the 4th Dorsets alone lost thirteen officers and two hundred men. We helped lift some of the walking wounded, and the fit who had lost their bearings in the dark, back to Nijmegen. Following this evacuation, Lieutenant-General Browning, Commander of the British Airborne Forces, sent a letter to Major General Thomas, Commander of the 43rd Division, in which he wrote:

> Thank you and the Division for the most skilful and gallant action in effecting junction with, and subsequently withdrawal of, 1st Airborne Division. I do not hesitate to say that no Commander or Division in the Army could have done more than you did, and I am intensely grateful on behalf of the British Airborne Forces for all that you have done.

Rumours began to circulate that our narrow corridor from Eindhoven, cut for more than twenty-four hours on the 22nd/23rd, had again been severed for two days, and that heavy concentrations of the enemy were moving up. Basically this was true; the corridor had been cut north of St Oedenrode on the 24th, and five German Divisions had been identified to the east and west of the break, but the rumours became wilder and wilder. The news however that a combined operation by the 7th Armoured Division and the American Paratroopers had re-opened the lifeline effectively muted those lurid tales.

During those somewhat difficult days, our dwindling food supplies were supplemented by captured German rations. These, however, were far from appetizing, consisting largely of tea (made of chopped, dried beech or laurel leaves), very hard dog-biscuits stuffed with carraways, and tinned black puddings. Variety to the menu of my 'parent' squadron was achieved by taking twelve 'Mills' grenades and one '75' grenade to a backwater of the Rhein. By means of three 'boxes' (four Mills grenades thrown in quick succession to the four corners of a large imaginary square) and the single '75', and with the use of a borrowed (in the loosest sense of the word) punt, more than 50 lbs of fish were collected and very much appreciated! It was good fun, too, but an infantry patrol (of whom I had no knowledge), thinking that a battle was in progress, dashed up and reprimanded me for taking unnecessary risks. The actual nature of those risks was not specified and rather puzzling for it was certain that there were no Germans nearer than across the river, and grenades were familiar pieces of 'ironmongery'.

"Thank you very much; I must be more careful in future!" was the hopeful diplomatic reply. The report later received by R.H.Q. caused considerable mirth.

Amongst other German military stores captured on the 'Island' by the Regiment were several thousand sheepskin jackets, and others without sleeves. Such news travels fast, and orders were quickly received to send the entire stock to Divisional H.Q. for distribution. The Regiment interpreted the instructions sensibly, with the needs of the unit receiving priority. All members of the Regiment were most grateful for those garments during the bitter weather from November to February, and applauded the Colonel's ruling.

On the night of 26th/27th, 'A' Squadron were faced by a massive enemy assault force, seeking to establish a bridgehead on the 'Island'. Following a bitter containing battle, the remnants of the five hundred enemy were driven back across the river by a mobile column of the 8th Armoured Brigade and a reserve Infantry Battalion.

At about this time, the Colonel, a very gallant gentleman, had a serious disagreement with the Divisional Commander and, on the 28th, resigned. That evening, the C.O. talked to me of this sudden crisis. Later, Major C.H. Kinnersley came and joined in the discussion, and finally took over command. The news that Colonel Lane-Fox, on the recommendation of the Corps Commander, had been given command of another Recce Regiment was received with great pleasure. On the 29th September, German Naval frogmen who had been trained in Venice, swam with explosives down the *Waal* from the east, to destroy the road and rail bridges over the river at Nijmegen. Our Recce patrols saved the more important road bridge. Several frogmen were killed, others captured, while some escaped down-river to German territory. The fine watches worn by the frogmen were highly prized souvenirs.

One of the most vivid memories was of a stormy night spent sharing a cowshed (my slit-trench was flooded) with five of the guards, two cows, a goat, eight pigs, and some cats. These last were apparently flung in each night to keep down the rats. When the doors were closed, the atmosphere was somewhat malodorous, but one was dry, and the straw was warm. At 3.30 a.m., there came a kick in the ribs and a heavy whisper:

"Get up; you're b..... well on guard!"

I did so, but after half an hour visiting the posts, and wet through to the skin, I retired to the straw.

Both Vivienne and I were magpie-like over letters during the overseas periods of the war, i.e. *January* to June 1940, and June 1944 to the end of hostilities. Even so there were occasional breaks in my correspondence when, for operational reasons, field postcards were all that could be managed. In my case also, the problem of storage meant that letters from next of kin of casualties had to have priority, and were filed to enable me to recall at later dates details which would otherwise have been forgotten. Many of those letters have been deposited in the archives of the Gloucestershire Regiment.

Late in September, no doubt because of the Germans' earlier cutting of our lines of communication, an accumulation of letters arrived. They even include one from my old senior tutor, H.L. Drake; I had not seen nor heard from him since, when on exercise late in 1940, I had nipped in to Pembroke College, Oxford, late one evening and enjoyed a glass of port with him. It appeared from several of the newly arrived letters that the Press and wireless reports of the early 'Island' operations had been over-colourful, for in that batch came the one and only letter from Vivienne expressing extreme anxiety over my safety, and asking me not to take foolish risks. There was also one from Major George Mason, which concluded thus:

> I have a great affection for Vivienne, and I don't want to see her in widow's weeds, so don't go and do anything bloody silly!"

I do not know what I said to George, but the reply to Vivienne is extant:

> You say you are worrying—of course you are—you must however school yourself and try not to worry unduly. When my life's work is over, whether I'm in Kempley, Holland or Timbuktoo, I will Pass On. Until that time, however tight a corner I may happen to get into, I will

> be safe—1940, the boat, Caen area, Vernon etc. have not been strokes of luck, but the hand of God.
> You know perfectly well that I will not take a single unnecessary risk—I hate war, and love life too much for that, and I have had all the excitement that I desire long, long ago.
> With God's help, and with the knowledge that you all are praying hard for me, I will try and do my duty, and take any risk that that entails, but anything unnecessary or foolish—definitely no! So, Sweetheart, please try not to worry too much; we are all in God's hands and will be safe.

This feeling of the umbrella of Prayer was further strengthened a few days later when a letter came from Mère St Aldegonde in which she wrote:

> From all accounts you are not having an easy time. My prayers are following you; every morning at Mass, I name you and ask Almighty God to bring you safely home. I know that the other Mères are praying for you also; we all seem to have taken you to our hearts...

Vivienne mentioned in the above letter that Uncle George (contrary to orders) had gone over to Normandy on D+4 with the Americans and had been (a) reprimanded, and (b) sent to command a Pioneer Battalion 'picking up potatoes near Birmingham'. As an aged veteran of the 1914–18 conflict, he had at once demanded, and obtained, an immediate discharge to grow food on his estate in Ireland. Commanding an operational Battalion had been interesting and worthwhile, but a Battalion of potato-picking pioneers had no attraction for that hard-riding, mad-cap of an old war-horse!

One afternoon, when returning from visiting our wounded in Nijmegen Hospital, the car was hit by shell splinters on the approach to the bridge. Fortunately the driver was unhurt, and I only suffered a scratch on the cheek and knee. The engine still worked, and so the bridge was crossed before inspecting the damage. This luckily was comparatively light; 'Bostik' sealed the small hole in the petrol tank (thank Goodness the petrol had not ignited!), a punctured tyre was changed, and we were soon 'home'.

A chaplains' conference (with a three-line whip) was held on the 2nd October at an hotel in Nijmegen. It soon became apparent, however, that the D.A.C.G. of 30 Corps had summoned this meeting to give the chaplains a short break. The morning session was minimal, and the lunch was excellent. The meal ended, the Commander addressed the party for a few minutes, after which a film ('*Fanny by Gaslight*') was shown. Later, tea was served, and at five, 'carriages' arrived to return the chaplains to their units. It was a kindly thought, for some of the chaplains had had a really rough time.

On the 3rd, the Regiment handed over the defence of the left flank to the 101st American Airborne Troops, and the move south began in the early minutes of the 4th. My diary adds that I hoped the Americans 'are awake and do not let the locals down'. Our Allies believed we were too thick on the ground and decided that only one or two Companies were needed where we had deployed our whole Regiment, a Company of K.R.R.s, and some tanks under command. Later we learned that the expected German attack had developed and achieved considerable success, and that the 5th D.C.L.I., who were still on the 'Island', were thrown in to assist in the counter-attack to regain the lost village.

Nijmegen Bridge was being shelled when the Regiment crossed it for the last time, and we gratefully crept into our blankets between 3 and 4 a.m. in some large houses in the western suburbs of the town, to begin a short period of rest and re-fitting. At 7.15 a.m., bombs fell; the beginning of a short period of considerable activity by the Luftwaffe.

Soon after 8.30 a.m. a fracas blew up which involved a Roman Catholic priest and the local Protestant vicar, and related to certain of the bodies of the crew of the *Mitchell* bomber I had seen shot down over Nijmegen on the 25th. This dragged on for several days.

The final diary entry (on October 6th) reads:

> Request from C Squadron to go down and bury R.A.F. body. Whole affair not satisfactory, so spent morning sorting it out and making full report.

To return to the 4th:

After dark, a battery of American 'super heavies' (155mm guns) moved in near our billets. Around midnight, an ear-splitting explosion accompanied (now that we were awake to see it) by a vivid flash, told us that the 'heavies' on the front lawn were in action. A few more salvoes were fired before the crews packed up and sleep was once more possible. Altogether it was felt that the term 'rest' was slightly euphemistic!

During the next three days, shower-baths and E.N.S.A. shows were a pleasant change from the normal routine, while services were worked in with the now static R.A.S.C. Companies.

Reflections on the 'Island' Period

During the Regiment's defence of the western flank, and its watch on the two rivers lest fighting patrols should cross, it was possible to move freely around each Squadron each day carrying cigarettes and chocolate, taking prayers with small groups, and occasionally services of Holy Communion. The diary records that one morning at 7.30, eighty attended a brief service. Despite sometimes the grimness of the whole operation, and the reported presence of the *Panzer Lehr* Division lurking about on the western flank, the morale of the men was magnificent. There was a spirit of complete self-confidence; they knew that they were, at least, the equal of the enemy, and that the failure to complete the original hazardous scheme to drive north through Arnhem was due to two factors beyond their control: i.e., the weather (which prevented the Airborne being reinforced), and the unexpectedly high concentration of German troops in the Arnhem area before the operation began.

At the same time there was an eerie, uneasy feeling. There was nothing tangible; just an atmosphere that was weird and unpleasant. This indefinable extra-sensory perception was well expressed by a tough and battle-proved Troop Sergeant when he said that he was 'glad to get off that damned Island'—most people understood and shared his sentiments.''

South of the Waal

Operations began again in earnest on the 7th, when the Regiment, now under the temporary command of the 8th Armoured Brigade, gradually took over a largely defensive rôle on the southern bank of the Waal from Leeuwen to Dreumel, and from there across a narrow neck of land to the river *Maas* at Alfen. Here life was quieter than on the 'Island' and despite the regular patrol work and a 24-hour observation vigil, the static conditions enabled the Regiment to catch up on maintenance and also to rest by rota. From my point of view, it was a splendid time, for I could be certain of seeing most of the Squadrons in their respective areas most days.

The Regiment had under command a battery of S.P. guns of the Essex Yeomanry and, in a loose way, some two hundred men of the Dutch Resistance, a brave and enthusiastic band of men, but amongst whom there was at least one 'wrong un' who, undoubtedly, betrayed our positions and assisted enemy patrols which frequently crossed the *Waal* to our side. An example of this occurred on the 26th October.

A civilian reported that a 'fort' at St Andries, on the narrow neck of land south-west of Dreumel, had been evacuated by the Germans. Sergeant Oddy led a patrol of nineteen, which included Tommy Zwallo and a local Resistance man who offered to act as guide, to investigate. In open order they reached a point a hundred yards from the 'fort', when *Spandaus* opened fire on them from both front and rear.

Eight months later, Tommy described these events when I visited him in a Brussels hospital. He said that when the firing began, the second Dutchman (who had obviously led the patrol into the ambush) was standing up, laughing at the plight of our men. Tommy, lying on the ground with a badly smashed knee, promptly shot him. The battle was soon over; the wounded who could be moved were taken with the four unwounded prisoners over the river for interrogation. Luckily, Tommy was wearing British battle-dress with the insignia of a Lieutenant. This, and his excellent command of English, enabled him to pass himself off as a British officer; had his true identity as a member of the Dutch resistance been discovered, he would undoubtedly have been shot. He was still in hospital in Apeldoorn when that town was captured by the Canadians in April, 1945. Four of the wounded, lying in ditches and long grass, were missed by the Germans. Sergeant Oddy was able to get back to his own lines, while friendly Dutch civilians brought the others in. Later that morning I accompanied the C.O. and the Squadron Commander with three heavy armoured cars, seven carriers and one-and-a-half troops of the Assault Troops to within fifty yards of the 'fort'. There was no reaction; the Germans had obviously left, and the diary records that 'there was no sign of the missing'. Later the Germans announced that one of the patrol had been killed and that eight wounded were prisoners of war. They made no mention of Tommy nor of the other members of the patrol. This was the only major clash during our time in that area.

One of our officers, Captain Pat Badham, a keen wildfowler, bought an old 12-bore shotgun while on the *Waal* (for 20 Guilden, I think) and managed some duck flighting during his free periods. On one occasion, he lent it to me and, as it came up well, he said one day:

"Padré, I have had enough of this sleeping in ditches and generally living rough. I have applied for a job as Liaison Officer with the R.A.F.

where I can live in a civilized manner. If I get it, I will give you the gun as a thank offering, so pray for me!''

Not very long afterwards, Pat's wish was granted; he went off to his comfortable quarters, and the old bundook found a new home in the back of my vehicle.

One of the E.N.S.A. parties included Alice Delysia, the well-known French actress. For some reason she had to get back to Eindhoven after the show. Padré, the muggins, was detailed to act as chauffeur. Mlle Delysia was most amusing and interesting but even so, tired as I was, the long drive there and back with negligible lights was an assignment which I could well have done without—I hope I shall not be judged ungallant for having said so!

My turn on the two-day leave roster came on the 22nd of October. I chose Brussels in preference to Paris and left at 5.30 a.m., arriving at the Chaplains' H.Q. in time for lunch. A number of old friends were there, including A.L. Morrison, with whom I had been at Oxford, 'Bish' Snell of Hereford, and Geoffrey Lampe, who later became Professor of Divinity at Cambridge. I wandered around the shops and bought silks and lace for Vivienne, and some stamps for myself. Most of us attended the Opera on both evenings. It was a glorious time, and on the return journey, I called in to see Mère St Aldegonde.

The Doctor at Maasbommel was a cheery person, and an excellent pianist. Just before our departure, he invited four members of the Mess, including Doc Ellis, to dinner; the Duty Officer, poor chap, naturally could not come. Our spirit ration had arrived a day or two earlier and was almost untouched. Consequently, we contributed four or five bottles to the party. It was an excellent meal and a most pleasant evening, with the two doctors sharing the grand piano. The programme was varied, and greatly enjoyed. The final item was *Auld Lang Syne*, played as a duet by the Dutch doctor and our M.O., and sung by all of us—including the doctor's wife. By this time it was 3.30 a.m. and raining heavily. The half-mile walk to the vehicles was taken nonchalently; a feeling encouraged no doubt by our spirit ration and two bottles of Dutch gin. It is pleasing to be able to report that all four were present at their respective stations when stand-to came at 5.30 a.m..

Shortly after the party, we left the *Waal* and moved with the whole of 30 Corps down to the Geilenkirchen area. This, it was said, was for the purposes of political propaganda, so that it could be announced that British troops were fighting on German soil.

CHAPTER SEVENTEEN

Geilenkirchen and Von Rundstedt's Ardennes Offensive

On November 10th I went by ambulance to Dreumel (my own car was out of action) and saw the hand-over to the Canadian Unit. The place was stiff with gaping civilians, and many of us wondered how many German agents were amongst them. One of the Canadian officers obviously had the same idea, for he said:

"Say, civilians are expendable. It would be safer to shoot the lot."

The M.O. and I said goodbye to the local doctor late on November 11th, and by 11.30 p.m. that evening, the squadron convoy had left Maasbommel. These night moves, for security reasons no doubt, were unpleasant, especially so now that winter had really begun. The unlucky drivers, with lorries and vehicles nose-to-tail, strained to see the tiny light fixed under the rear floorboard and, supposedly, sited on a white circle painted on the casing of the crown wheel. It was a credit to their skill that so few collisions occurred. The drivers needed ten minutes' break every hour to rest their eyes and uncoil their nerves. The passengers, too, hated these night frolics. One loaded in the dark (and often in the rain), had little sleep on the drive, and at journey's end came the task of unloading and camouflaging the vehicle.

The column arrived at Schimmert near Sittard soon after 2 a.m., and by 3 a.m. most of the Regiment not on guard duty had dossed down in empty houses, barns, or their vehicles—sleep came easily in those days. I had a nasty dose of lumbago at that time, which lasted for several days, and was not improved by the move on the 11th, and the second one on the 13th to Puth.

We were now coming into the sector and, in a way I suppose, under the command of the American 9th Army, taking over American billets and positions. The move up was a slow and gradual process mainly because the early Corps attack (in which we had a minor rôle) became bogged down by the appalling weather, which greatly restricted the use of armour. As a result, 30 Corps was committed to a period of static warfare with patrol work on foot, and desultory shell-fire was almost the only overt enemy hostile action. In consequence of these conditions, the 43rd Recce Regiment was given a single Squadron holding rôle along the Geilenkirchen to Randerath road.

We managed, as a result of these changes in the operational programme, to work in some extra confirmation classes (they had been running for two months) in final preparation for the visit to Beek of the Bishop of Dover on Sunday the 19th. This was quite a social occasion when one met fellow divisional chaplains and friends in other units whom otherwise one rarely saw. There were some forty candidates, and the whole service, on the eve of another possible battle, was impressive. After the service, I was offered a short leave in Antwerp; I refused it in view of the fact that the Squadron was already operational, and the future was generally very uncertain. I said I would like the short leave (i.e. 48 hours in the leave centre) when the present tour was over.

One amusing incident occurred on the night the Regiment took over its first reserve positions in this American sector. All had gone well in the move up and everything was quiet until dawn. Then, suddenly, bedlam broke loose. A fusillade of small-arms fire, shouting, and the clatter of heavy boots on the metalled road, made one think that a running battle with a deeply penetrating German fighting patrol was in progress. The explanation was far simpler. The American unit, in its hurried handover, had left behind some chickens and pigs, which no doubt represented their private supplementary meat ration. At first light they returned for them to find that some had got out of their pens and were wandering around on the road and in the gardens. Time was obviously short, and the Americans probably also felt that the Recce

Regiment might soon commandeer the livestock as the spoils of war! The result was that they chased the escaped pigs and fowls in the gardens, through the empty houses, and up and down the village street, determined to capture them, dead or alive. The captives and corpses were then loaded into trucks and driven off. Our men, seeing that it was not an attack, wisely took cover until the 'party' was over.

On November 20th, because of the static nature of the operations, the whole Regiment, less one Squadron, moved back into Heerleheide, a small mining town on the Dutch side of the border. The operational Squadron (Squadrons changed over every three days) held defensive positions along the road leading north-eastwards from Geilenkirchen towards Randerath. These outposts represented the extreme right of the 30 Corps sector, and on our right, across the river *Wurm*, was the American left flank. Deprived of their armoured cars and carriers, our men were unhappy in the unaccustomed rôle of infanteers. The one good thing that can be said of that period was that when in reserve at Heerleheide, we enjoyed excellent billets in furnished houses.

There remain several vivid memories of that extraordinary month of a type of warfare for which we were not really trained and with which we had not been much acquainted.

The road up from Geilenkirchen to the forward positions was constantly being shelled, so armoured cars were usually employed for transport to the farmhouse in which the forward H.Q. had been established. One went on foot from that point on. The M.T.O., after I had nearly caught a packet in my P.U., and remembering my luck on Nijmegen bridge, kindly produced a light armoured car for my daily trips. Shelling of the forward positions took place on most days, and German patrol activity occurred frequently at night; yet despite this, casualties were light. The worst period was on the 27th and 28th of November. I arrived at 1.30 p.m. on the 27th, and found an unpleasant party in progress. I went round all the posts and was glad to find the men generally in good heart, despite being pinned down by heavy shellfire. The German '88's were the best guns of the war, and were used for anti-aircraft, anti-tank, and general anti-social work! Three members of the Regiment were killed and a number wounded that afternoon, and for the first time (except for a single instance in Normandy, when domestic anxiety was, I believe, the root cause) we had cases of exhaustion. In this war, thank goodness, this type of casualty was recognised by both medical and lay authorities, and it was accepted that, for some people, there comes a point when the nerves can stand the strain no longer, and that the man must be pulled out for a period of rest. Usually, he would come back to normal duty after a few days.

Later that evening, I called into Divisional H.Q. to make the funeral arrangements for next morning at the newly established Divisional cemetary at Brunnsum. I went up the following morning straight from the funeral to 'A' Squadron and found an even worse party in progress, with heavy mortar fire added to the '88's of the previous day. The C.O., the Squadron Commander, and I did the rounds, and were grounded for a period in the fort on the right flank near the river. There, and in some positions at the forward edge of the wood, one was shot at every time one stood up or moved. It was obvious that something had happened and that we were now under direct observation. I left at 3.30 to arrange a burial, and on my return at 4.30, it was clear that the position had worsened. The Corps Commander, General Horrocks, then arrived, and ordered our forward positions to be withdrawn after dark. The Americans had, apparently, fallen back on our right and neglected to notify the Regiment. Thus our right flank was for some distance fully exposed and at close range. It was no wonder movement had had such unfortunate repercussions.

That evening, when at Divisional H.Q. reporting to the S.C.F. and collecting crosses, I fell foul of the A.Q., Colonel Jo Macance. He asked what the latest situation was, and I told him, adding that it was hoped the position should improve on the morrow. In his talk to senior officers, the C.O. had outlined the operations which General Horrocks hoped would take place on the following morning. Colonel Kinnersley concluded by saying:

"This information is top secret, and must not, repeat not, be discussed or divulged until the operation is under way."

He then reported that the Americans would counter-attack in the morning and, it was hoped, retake the lost ground. The A.Q. asked me what this 'Improvement' meant. I repeated that it was hoped that things would get better in the morning. At this point he became angry and ordered me to tell him what was behind the remark. I replied that if he did not know it was unfortunate, but I had no authority to tell him. I then said that it was an order which I could not accept, and walked away. All this occupied several minutes and was extremely uncomfortable and acrimonious. The Colonel never forgave me.

Difficulty arose when two of our seriously wounded died in the American C.C.S. on the outskirts of Geilenkirchen. The first occasion was on the black 27th November, when Trooper Badman died of wounds; I called at the C.C.S. after dark and, hearing of his death, said that I would arrange for the burial in the Divisional cemetery the following morning, and would call for his body soon after 8.30 a.m.. The next morning, Trooper Badman's body was not there, and nobody knew where it had gone. Their office promised to check up. The same thing happened when Lance-Corporal Taylor died of wounds on 1st December; repeated inquiries produced nothing. Weeks later, after the Ardennes episode, we returned to the sector and, after a patient search in the large American cemetery at Margeretan, I found both Trooper Badman's grave and that of Lance-Corporal Taylor. It was a great relief to locate them.

One appreciated, when back in billets at Heerleheide, a proper bed and pyjamas. I had lost my only invasion-kit pair of the latter when the boat sank. Later, I bought a pair in the Officers' Shop in Brussels. Now, with semi-static conditions, a second pair was needed. A sewing-machine in use in the billet suggested a plan. I offered the lady of the house a few panels of blue silk parachute if she, or one of her daughters, would make me a pair of pyjamas out of another few panels. They jumped at the offer, and work began that same day. But tragedy (for me, at any rate!) followed, when one evening, a shriek came from the kitchen. The M.O. and I ran in, to find one of the daughters slumped in a faint over the sewing-machine, the needle of which had gone through her thumb, pinning it to the base. The rest of the family were howling their heads off but, perhaps wisely, doing nothing. We turned the wheel and withdrew the thumb, which the Doc then began to dress, and I fetched a bottle of Cognac which I had bought to replace the ration issue of whisky drunk some weeks previously at the medical party in Maasbommel. The M.O. gave the patient a drop of this, then placed the bottle on the table behind him. A few minutes later, when the thumb had been bandaged and the girl had more or less recovered, we noticed that the bottle was 'doing the rounds' from mouth to mouth, and that by that time, precious little remained. I reckon I paid dearly for my pyjamas!

30 Corps was due to be relieved on December 18th/19th and move to the Tilburg area for a short rest and the final preparations for an operation which, it was hoped, would clear the western bank of the

Rhein down from Nijmegen. It was to be a combined attack by the American Armies in the south, and the British and Canadians in the north. I arranged to take my deferred leave in Brussels from the 18th to 20th. Before I left, I made another exhaustive inquiry at American Divisional and Army H.Q. into the disappearance of the bodies of Lance-Corporal Taylor and Trooper Badman, again without success.

The weather was cold and foggy with snow almost everywhere when I set out for Brussels late on the night of 17th, and it was nearly midday on the 18th when I pulled in at the Chaplains' Centre in that city.

News was trickling in that the Germans had mounted an offensive in the Ardennes, but nothing was clear, and the weather prevented the air reconnaissance which would have established its strength and real direction. The rest of the day passed quietly shopping or gossipping at the rest centre, and in the evening several of us went and saw *Faust* at the Opera House.

The next morning, the news, while still confused, was disquieting. It seemed clear that Von Rundstedt had committed much of his hitherto held back Panzer striking force, and had achieved considerable penetration. The Americans, though fighting hard, were falling back along a wide front. Again, a quiet day was spent resting and doing little or nothing. When in La Grande Place the following morning (20th) I was told by Colonel Gadsden that plans had been changed and that the whole Corps was moving south-east. He was leaving almost at once so that he might find his Gunner Regiment before darkness and fog made things too difficult. I decided to do the same. Minutes later, when emerging from a shop where I had seen some silk stockings to send home to Vivienne, a C.M.P., seeing the Divisional flash, came up and said:

"Sir, all 43rd personnel are to report back at once."

When asked what the Divisional location was, he just said:

"I have no idea. Make for Hasselt, and the C.M.P.s there may know."

On returning to the Centre, I collected my kit and some sandwiches, and set out. I called in for a few minutes to see Mère St Aldegonde at Saventhem. The nuns were not a little worried at the news in the Belgian press and over the wireless, and felt that there was a very real possibility that they would be overrun yet again. I hoped that my assurances that this could not happen sounded convincing! I then made for Diest and Hasselt, in which area Gadsden and the C.M.P. had said they thought we should find some part of the Division. At 4 p.m., so records my diary, I located Divisional H.Q., and at 5.30, found R.H.Q. near Beverst. The sight of the familiar white 41 on a green background was indeed a relief—I was 'home' with my family. An hour later I set out for H.Q. Squadron and, despite the darkness, snow, and only having a 1/4 inch map to hand, arrived at their supposed location before they had all pulled in.

The next morning we moved to the the tiny village of Bérlo near Waremme, a few miles north-west of Liège. The Château there became Squadron H.Q. for the duration of our stay in the area. The Regiment's task was an impossible one; in theory, we covered the *Meuse* from Vise, through Lièe, down to Huy (inclusive) by a series of outposts, and were supposed to deny a crossing to enemy patrols and task forces. The Regiment had under command three companies of infantry and 112 Field Regiment; hardly an adequate force for a front of some 25 miles!

These outposts along the banks of the *Meuse* were bleak in the intense cold and recent falls of snow. The lack of both movement and of certain information (American rumours were rife and lurid), and having to wait and imagine what might happen, was unpleasant. The uncertainty was perhaps what most affected the men. But the unexpected appearance of Field Marshal Montgomery one morning changed everyone's whole outlook; the confidence which he had inspired in the men at Hastings in his pre-invasion talks was paralleled by his mere presence in the forward areas.

For example, one morning I was with an outpost on the *Meuse* bank, when a car passed on the ice-packed road to the rear of us. The sergeant shouted: "SHUN!"

When we stood down the sergeant was asked:

"Who was that?"

"Monty;" he replied, "Thank God!! Now we shall be all right!"

The 22nd was spent largely in locating the many sub-units of the Regiment, strung out along our very wide front. I went also to Divisional H.Q. to see the S.C.F. and to try and get something done about my car, which understandably, I suppose, after the appalling weather conditions of the past few months was giving great trouble. I went rapidly round the posts on the following day, taking prayers with a few groups, and making such arrangements as were possible for Sunday (the 24th) and Christmas Day. These services were, in most instances, a shortened form of Holy Communion and a few prayers and a hymn, taken with small parties in posts along the river bank. In the areas of the main bridges (Vise and Liège, for example) where there were larger concentrations of troops such as companies of Infantry and Anti-Tank Gunners in addition to our own men (and consequently more people not on immediate call), the attendances were far greater. These services were of course voluntary. The approximate numbers at the three services were 70, 100, and 70 with 10, 19 and 6 making their Communion. At Liège we were joined by a dozen or more Americans, both coloured and white. I had trouble with my water cruet, which froze more-or-less solid between services.

On the Sunday evening, Madame La Comtesse Elisabeth de Rénesse-Westerhalt invited the five officers billeted in the Château to dinner. We greatly enjoyed ourselves. Madame was a lady of dignified charm, possessing at the same time an iron nerve and a determination which swept aside all opposition. During the days of the occupation, she and her three nieces had played the dangerous game of helping escaped prisoners and airmen who had bailed out in the area. A number passed through her hands and returned safely home. The Comtesse was later decorated for her bravery. On one occasion, when her nieces had brought in three airmen whose plane had been shot down (one was wounded) and the Gestapo had arrived to search the house, Madame calmly did the rounds with the Germans (the Chateau was built in a square) while the nieces brought in their trail the three airmen two rooms behind. In the early days, so I was told by the locals, a German Major walked in and said he was billeting himself and his men in the Château. Poor man; little did he realize how wrong was his approach! Madame, pointing to the door, rapped out in polished German (she had lived for some years in Germany):

"Get out of my house! I have not invited you in. You and your men may find billets in the stables, but I will have not one of you in my house!"

The staff were terrified that their mistress would be summarily thrown into prison, or even shot, but such was her presence that the invaders treated Madame with considerable respect and some awe.

A friend of the Comtesse, Madame Simone van der Gracht, a perfect foil, was vivacious at the dinner and had endeared herself to the men by her interest in them and their families. She talked with them and inspected their billets and even their cookhouses. The evening was very pleasant. What a change it was to sit down in a civilized manner to a well-appointed and highly polished dinner table. The gleaming silver, the attractive dinner service, the candle-light and the flowers and plants produced an atmosphere of graciousness which had probably been habitual there for centuries, but which contrasted sharply with the mode to which we had been accustomed for a long, long time. Madame van der Gracht gave us her card with an invitation to call on her if ever we should be in Brussels. I was grateful for this invitation less than six months later.

Christmas Day was bitterly cold but bright and clear, enabling the Air Force to strike a decisive blow, a blow which marked the beginning of the end of Von Rundstedt's offensive with his Panzer Armies. I started out after an early service, taking with me a tin of bully-beef and some ration biscuits, and spent the entire day moving from post to post. The men were cheerful despite their disgust at the weather—we all like to have a good grumble, and if there are valid reasons, then so much the better! I left my driver behind because it was Christmas and my programme was intended to be a long one. He remained at the Château and had a restful time, enjoying such Christmas fare as the cooks were able to devise. The flying bombs were causing a great deal of irritation and considerable damage too in Liège at this time. One Troop had more than forty in or near their sector in twenty-four hours, and considered that they were receiving an unfair percentage of these German 'funnies'. I returned to Berlo in time for the party which had been organised for the local children. It was an uproarious affair, and was enjoyed equally by our men. Later that evening, the officers began the daily task of censoring letters. Imagine my surprise and anger too when I found in my pile one written by my driver in which he said something like this:

> Christmas Day has been awful. The Padré took me out very early, and we were out all day with only bully and biscuits for our Christmas dinner. We have only just come back, and I am tired out. You would have thought the Padré would have been more considerate for me—and on Christmas Day and all.

I showed the letter to the Squadron Commander, who was all for hauling him out of his bed for telling deliberate lies. In the end I cooled down and said:

"Let it go; he is as fed up as we all are, and it has probably done him good to let off some steam."

I spoke to him later, and he said that he had been upset at being miles from home on Christmas Day—it was his first Christmas away from home.

The 26th was another cold and clear day, and the R.A.F. were again swarming over the battlefield, wreaking havoc on the columns of German tanks and transport, some of which were stranded through lack of petrol. Despite this, the blessed 9 O'Clock News from London gave a gloomy account of the battle. Indeed, it was so bad that the Comtesse sent me a note at 9.30, asking me to come and see her. She and her friend had heard the bulletin, and were pretty depressed, understandably so because it stated that the Germans were only four miles from the river at one point. They felt that to be overrun a second time would signal the end for them, and for Belgium. I had to spend nearly half an hour trying to persuade them that all was well, and that May 1940 was not going to be repeated in 1944/45.

On December 27th, orders were received that the whole Division should return to the Roer front, where it would come under the command of the 12th Corps. When this became known, I had a distinct feeling that my assurances of the night before had become suspect, and that our imminent departure might be the abandonment of the sector, rather than a matter of redeployment. The Regiment concentrated that evening, and moved during the night to billets in Heerlen, a small mining town a few miles south of Heerleheide.

CHAPTER EIGHTEEN

Heerlen and the Roer

At Heerlen, as at Heerleheide, the Regiment were billeted in private houses. Its rôle, until the resumption of the weather-wrecked operation to liquidate the Roer-Geilenkirchen triangle, was that of a mobile anti-parachute force and a support unit for the Americans. Fortunately the Regiment was able to stage its deferred Christmas Dinner on December 31st and January 1st. A request at that time from the *Recce Corps Journal*, (via Div. H.Q.), for an account of the Regiment's operations and morale from June to 31st December took up valuable time. The closing summary of that long article, written as it was when the events and impressions were fresh in my mind, perhaps merits inclusion here:

> Those six months, in which the Regiment gained for itself a high reputation, are full of recollections both pleasant and unpleasant. Who could forget the wonderful welcome of the relieved villages and towns as we drove through? Men and women laughing and crying with joy and relief, children waving or climbing on the cars and asking for 'cigarettes for Papa'. But what sad tales some had to tell; the dust of Normandy, particularly the cinnamon dust of the valley leading up from Le Mesnil Auzouf to Duval, was something to be experienced to be believed.
>
> Finally, no-one will forget the eerie feeling of the strip of land between Nijmegen and Arnhem. When one of the bridges to Nijmegen was down, and our supply line had been cut near Venlo, and the German Air Force was out in some strength; that strip of land was not a place where one slept easily. It was indeed well-named 'that cursed island' by a Sergeant—that memory will remain when all else has been forgotten.
> *(J E Gethyn-Jones, Heerlen, January 3rd, 1945)*

John (the M.O.) and I were billeted with a Mr & Mrs Boer, as also were the medical orderly and truck driver. Mr Boer (who was known as Hank) was a retired mining official, quiet in manner but poor in health. His wife, who was considerably younger than he, had lived for some years in the States, and spoke English with a strong American accent. She was a kindly soul and made us most comfortable. The M.I. room was also in the house, and this led to the discovery of a saddening sidelight on the wartime privations that were the daily lot of many people in France, Belgium and Holland.

Corporal Pruitt, John's driver, made the eternal brew of 'char' for those reporting sick each morning. Mrs Boer always insisted on taking out the teapot to throw away the leaves when all had finished. We found out later that the leaves were not thrown away, but carefully strained off and dried, to be used once again by Mrs Boer and her husband. They were passed on to the lady next door who used them once before giving them to her neighbour on the other side; and so it continued down the street. There were fourteen houses in the row, so the leaves made, including the initial M.I. brew, no less than fifteen pots of tea before they were finally thrown away—I dread to think what the colour of the final beverage must have been when the last pot was made! The order changed each morning, so that each house in turn received the leaves direct from Mrs Boer.

At Heerlen we came for the first time face to face with the tragic results of the Germans' barbaric anti-Semitic policy. Directly we arrived, the local vicar approached me about the possibility of the evacuation to England of a Nurse Ruth Dobshenna, who had recently been brought over by the Dutch resistance from German-occupied Holland. The request for her removal to England was prompted by the fear which still lingered on that von Rundstedt's attack (which, at the time of our arrival in Heerlen, we did not know had been smashed) might change direction northward, embracing our thinly held district. The vicar was anxious that, should this happen, his people should not suffer through harbouring a Jewess. Miss Dobshenna's family had lived in northern Holland and were amongst the first of the early victims when the persecution of her race began. Except for Ruth, who was nursing in a hospital, imprisonment for the whole family was followed by the shooting of her mother and father. Here two brothers died of the brutal treatment they received, while her sister was deported and disappeared. Ruth, too, was imprisoned, and suffered great humiliation before her deportation was finally ordered. The train in which she and many others were heading for forced labour, and possibly the gas chambers, was strafed by the R.A.F., and in the confusion which ensued Miss Dobshenna managed to escape—several others who made the attempt were not so fortunate. For months Ruth lived the life of a hunted fugitive, knowing full well that capture could only result in possible torture and degradation, followed by certain extermination. She realised, too, that her capture might well involve those hiding her in dire consequences. Unlike her family, Ruth was a practising Christian, and she said that it was the power of prayer alone which gave her the strength and courage to go on and on when the prospects were so bleak. She gave me one of the text cards she had written out from memory, and which she read frequently, particularly when privations were at their worst and when capture, torture and death seemed inevitable and imminent. The welfare branch could not arrange for Miss Dobshenna's removal to England, nor did they deem it necessary. She was, however, taken care of and sent much further back into Holland for safety's sake.

A few days after our arrival it was planned to use the Regiment operationally, but such was the state of the ground that this proved impracticable, and instead we were given a purely infantry task of minor importance. The men, deprived of their armoured vehicles, and sitting huddled and frustrated in their frozen slit trenches, facing a bitter wind and heavy shelling, thought nothing of this unaccustomed rôle. It was necessary to give the hard-worked infantry (who, because of numerous earlier casualties, were under-strength) as much rest as possible before the final assault to clear the Reichswald and the flat country between it and the *Rhein*. This operation, twice postponed, was one which had to be carried through before any major crossing of that river could be attempted.

There in Gangelt I learned that the phrase 'stiff with fright' was an expression based upon a true human phenomenon. Years before, when returning from the New Theatre during my Oxford days, I had seen a Scottish piper, who had been playing at the University Caledonian Dinner and who had obviously taken too much of his national beverage, lying on the pavement. The undergraduate who had been charged with the task of seeing the piper to his digs said that directly they had come out of the hotel the cold had, metaphorically, pole-axed the Highland laddie. The poor chap was conscious (or at least, he appeared to be) and could roll his eyes, but when we helped lift him into a taxi, his body was rigid. I thought of that incident one morning when a jeep pulled up on the roadway above the cellar in which John and I were cooking sausages—the house above ground was too badly smashed, as were most of the houses in that village, to afford any protection against the snow, rain or cold. Two orderlies appeared at the head of the stairs, and shouted: "Stretcher down!" On it was a man whom I would have thought had little imagination and even less brain. He was unconscious and white as a sheet, but there was no visible injury. But directly Doc began to search for the wound, he realised that the patient was as stiff as a ram-rod. The degree of rigidity was such that, had his head and heels been rested upon confronted chairs, his body would have remained perfectly flat and probably capable of supporting a considerable weight. John examined him carefully (stripping him in fact) but found not a mark upon him, whereupon massage began in a big way, augmenting the warming up of the patient that the blankets and hot-water bottles had already begun. Slowly, after several minutes, the eyes began to flicker, the lips twitched, and slight sounds emerged which gradually became more articulate until, at last, two words could be distinguished:

"Smith! Blood! Smith! Blood! Smith! Blood!"

I turned to John and said;

"I'll bet Sergeant Smith (his Troop Sergeant) has bought it."

I grabbed a stretcher, called an orderly, and drove up in a handy P.U. to the back of the wood in which (on the forward edge) the Squadron's slit trenches were situated. We left the vehicle and hurried through the wood. To my utter amazement (and proving the folly of jumping to conclusions), the first head we saw sticking up out of the trench was that of Sergeant Smith. His account of the events that resulted in our patient becoming a casualty was simple; The two of them had been watching movement in the German sector across the frozen field, when an '88' shell (they were high velocity and, unlike mortar bombs, arrived before the sound) landed a few yards ahead of their position. Luckily, neither of them was hit, but a strand of barbed wire slightly ahead of the parapet was cut and whipped back, nicking Sergeant Smith very slightly on the cheek, drawing a few spots of blood. Our patient had apparently taken one look, shout "Blood!", and fallen unconscious to the ground. Smith understandably assumed his comrade had been hit, and wirelessed back for stretcher-bearers. The soldier had earlier had serious family trouble, and I believe that this, together with the cold weather and the unaccustomed rôle, had completely got him down, and that at last the old brain rang the bell and said *I've had enough*, and rigidity set in.

During this period I visited the large American cemetary of approximately 17,000 graves at Margaretan and, after much questioning, I was told of the graves of four unknown British soldiers. These were located and, although the printed captions on two of the crosses read '*An Unknown British Soldier of the Recce Corps*', a further search in the records showed that the grave cards in the 'unknown' file contained all information. In addition, they had the A.B.64 of both Taylor and Badman, and were thus in possession of the full details (i.e. name, rank, number etc.) of both soldiers. I was greatly relieved that the graves had been found, but furious at the inefficiency in documentation which had caused so much distress to the next of kin, and wasted so much of my time both in December and January.

Nobody was sorry when the Gangelt phase was over and the Regiment was pulled out of the line and, after a day or two to clean up and carry out essential maintenance at Heerlen moved on the night of 31st January and 1st February to Wielden. There we remained until the early hours of February 5th, and while in that area, I was informed that I was to go on a refresher course in the near future!

The move up from Wielden to the Nijmegen sector for the long-deferred 'Operation Veritable' to clear the west bank of the *Rhein* in the area of Kleve, Goch, Wasel and Xanten was a slow staged affair via Eindhoven, Helmond and (for a short distance) alongside the *Maas* at a point where it formed the front line. Several vivid memories remain of incidents that occurred during this move.

My decoration for the Normandy landing had just been gazetted and, as R.H.Q. were billeted overnight on the 6th/7th in a farmhouse, the C.O. invited me to dine with them. I arrived and enjoyed the pre-meal drinks and, later, the soup. When the main course arrived, however, I had a shock, for on a large plate were what looked for all the world like two small babies. They were of course suckling pigs, but they looked so human I was nearly sick and ate very, very little—and that only for politeness' sake. I know that I was foolish, but that first sight completely spoilt my evening.

The second incident occurred early on the morning of the 7th. The Doc and I were having our breakfast around our fire on the roadside when a party of French commandos passed, having been on a recce over the *Maas* to obtain information in preparation for the crossing. The French officer, seeing the Red Cross flag on the M.O.'s vehicle, stopped and, in excellent English, said:

"Good morning, gentlemen. Are you likely to be here for a short while?"

Hearing our reply to the effect that we might not move on for an hour, he replied:

"Good. I will see my men in, and return for some instructions from the Doctor."

On his return, he had a sad tale to tell: during the recce, one of his men had developed acute pains in the stomach and he, probably rightly, had diagnosed appendicitis. The man soon became incapable of movement and had to be left behind. This naturally distressed the officer, firstly because the man's life was endangered by lack of skilled medical attention, and secondly because on finding him, the Germans would know that a patrol had crossed the river.

The French officer's request was then made; would the M.O. please show him how to remove an appendix? the M.O. replied,

"Well, yes, of course I can tell you; but you will not have the instruments if ever another case occurs."

With a flourish, the officer pulled out a murderous looking sheath-knife and said,

"With this I chop up my food, I cut out bullets, and with it I have killed Germans. And with it, too, I could easily remove an appendix, provided I know exactly what to do!"

I had finished my breakfast by this time, so I left Doc and the Frenchman to their medical instruction and walked up the column to see the men before we moved off. The Doc and I were thankful we were not in that French commando unit, for the Doc said;

"I am certain the next poor chap in that unit who has a stomach-ache will loose his appendix without an option!"

Later that day I visited 2nd Army H.Q. and pleaded with the A.G.C. (John Steele) to let me off the refresher course so that I should not miss the opening of 'Operation Veritable'. He agreed to this, but ticked me off for not having my decoration ribbon up, saying that it was an insult to His Majesty. Before I left, he gave me a piece of ribbon and expressed the hope that he would not see me improperly dressed in future!

That night, we harboured near Nijmegen.

CHAPTER NINETEEN

The Reichswald to the Rhein

The battle which was about to begin was designed to be the first of three blows which, it was hoped, would crush German resistance. It was intended that the operation should be mounted with such force, along the whole front, that sheer speed and weight would quickly overwhelm the enemy. In our northern sector, the thirteen Divisions of the British 2nd Army and the Canadian 1st Army were to strike south of Nijmegen, while the twelve Divisions of the American 9th Army would form the other jaw of the pincer, to nip out the German forces west of Goch, Calcar, Uden and Xanten. Further south, other American armies were to make similar thrusts. The schedule of these coordinated assaults was badly upset by the Germans opening dam sluices and flooding the rivers *Roer* and *Rhein*. This resulted in the inundation of large tracts of land, making movement virtually impossible in some areas until the floodwater had drained away. The heavy rains, followed by the general thaw, added to the difficulties.

The Materborn Gap, between the formidable Reichswald forest and Kleve, was the key to success in the north. The opening chorus began (so we were told later) with 'the greatest artillery barrage in British history', while the British Tactical Air Force and Bomber Command each threw in up to a thousand planes to provide close support for our forces, and to obliterate (as they did) the bastions of German Defence in the north; e.g. Kleve and Goch.

The feature of this battle which impressed me most was the great part played by the units of the 79th Armoured Division. These tanks, generally known as the 'funnies', include *Crocodiles* (flame-throwers),

Flailes (which whirled heavy chains and swiples onto the road ahead of the tank to detonate buried mines), *Kangaroos* (troop carriers), *Buffaloes* (troop carriers fitted with inflatable skirts, enabling them to cross water) and *Beacons* (with searchlights mounted, to give artificial moonlight enabling operations to continue around the clock). Crocodiles, in action against pill-boxes and strongpoints, were a fearsome sight. They threw out a jet of flame, 60 to 100 yards long, which generated intense heat, consuming the oxygen in the target building and filling it with smoke and fumes. They were most lethal weapons and, with the sinister 'swoosh' of the thrown flames, were to my mind even more demoralizing than a rocket attack by Typhoons.

The Guards Armoured and 43rd Divisions took no part in the first phase, and had a steady move up behind the advancing forces, to be ready for the thrust through to Kleve. The restriction on movement on the route, caused by the rain, thaw and floods, produced conditions a little short of chaos; while the blanket bombing of Kleve by five hundred 'Heavies', though it temporarily stunned the enemy, virtually made the free play of vehicles impossible in that city until it had been physically occupied and the bull-dozers brought in. It was in Kleve that I buried my first and only high-ranking German officer, a victim of the bombing. General Essame, who had commanded 214 Brigade at the Kleve battles, said, writing of this period after the War:

> It is almost impossible to describe the sanguinary and confused fighting... amongst the huge bomb craters and ruins of Kleve.

My own diary entry for Sunday 11th February (when I attempted to take services or prayers as usual with most squadrons) records that:

> ... my L.A.C. (light armoured car) took two hours to cover a thousand yards—mud and traffic terrific—cup of tea with tank wallahs. Tried to go through Reichswald... tried four routes but failed... Afterwards walked back to R.H.Q.—much quicker and safer than car!

The 12th was a bad day. 'B' Squadron lost three cars and three supporting tanks in the first probe forward towards Goch. The two remaining cars managed to turn and withdraw, with several of the crew members of the 'brewed-up' L.A.C.s clinging to them. Later, a volunteer came with me and, under cover of a Red Cross flag, we brought in the bodies of Corporal Viggars and Trooper Ward without any interference or reaction from the Germans. There was no sign of the other missing members of the car crews.

After the burial of Corporal Viggars, Trooper Ward, and four others who had been killed that morning, had taken place, and while the documentation was in progress, an R.C. Padré from Division appeared, and enquired whether any of the men were Roman Catholics. I replied that I had not yet checked; two of them were reinforcements who had only arrived a few days earlier. We went through their A.B.64s, and found that Trooper Ward, one of the recent arrivals, was an R.C.. The Padré reported me to Divisional H.Q. for having taken prayers over a Roman Catholic. I was hauled up before the 'beaks' and received a large size in rockets for contravening King's Regulations in taking a C. of E. service over a Roman Catholic—the correct procedure was to bury the body, and then report the map reference to the nearest R.C. chaplain. This, to my mind (particularly when they were my men) seemed callous and unchristian, and I fear that I continued to take the normal burial service and commendation over my men, and later reported the map reference of the grave of any Roman Catholic to Divisional H.Q. for the information of the Divisional R.C. chaplains.

That same day, during a dive-bomb attack near R.H.Q., a gunner manning a nearby anti-aircraft gun had his nose, lips, chin and eyebrows removed by a bomb splinter—as cleanly as though he had passed through a bacon slicer. We carried him, fully conscious, to the M.O.. Years later, when visiting a Dymock man in a Gloucester hospital, a patient in the next bed, his head swathed in bandages, spoke and said:

"Weren't you in Kleve when we captured it, Padré?"

To the affirmative response he added:

"I thought I wasn't mistaken. I was the gunner who caught it in the face."

We had several talks over the next few weeks, and his story was amazing. He had had numerous skin and bone grafts to rebuild his face (I believe Mackendow had been one of the surgeons; incidentally, I never saw the patient's face). His lips, nose (the foundation of which he had been told was the breastbone of a blackbird, but whether this was a joke or not he didn't know!), chin and eyebrows had all been replaced. He said he believed that after a few more operations he would have an entirely new face, and one which he thought would be 'passable' and would enable him to meet his pals in the pub or at a football match, without too much embarrassment on either side. I have often thought of that cheerful gunner who never once during our talks grumbled or uttered a single word of self-pity. It was a humbling yet thrilling experience to talk with such a man.

On the 15th we heard that some more of our missing men, all badly wounded, had been recaptured by the 2nd Monmouthsires. I traced them back to the C.C.S., where I found that Sergeant Renvoize had just died and that Troopers Hallas and Hayward had been evacuated to the U.K.. The C.C.S. chaplain allowed me to bury Sergeant Renvoize. The ward sister told me that before his death, he had said that all had baled out of the cars when they had been hit. This was not quite correct, because I had found Trooper Ward's body *inside* his wrecked car. I wrote that same day to both Hallas and Hayward via their home addresses, asking for information about the three missing. Neither knew anything, but Hallas' reply gave an interesting account of their time in enemy hands. He wrote:

> Dear Padré
>
> Thank you for your kind letter to my wife. She is visiting me this week, and I have had the opportunity of reading it. I'm sorry I can't help the Regiment at all with regard to Binns, Hooper and Tipton. The only boys I know of are Hayward and Sergeant Renvoize. Corporal Viggers, God rest his soul, was killed by the same sniper who pipped me. The other two were picked up with me. The Sergeant was in pretty bad shape with a chest wound and leg paralysis. Hayward had half a foot off. I was lucky; I had two wounds in my left thigh, one a compound fracture. We were all pretty rough when picked up by the Monmouths having lain without food or water for nearly 48 hours in a cellar where the Boche had put us...

Later on the 15th we lost two of our most experienced men, Sergeant Darvell M.M., and Corporal Horsfall, together with a number wounded. Sergeant Darvell was one of the last of my Padré's Helpers. He was a great little man.

On the night of the 16th, I received a message from R.H.Q., asking me to examine a white half-track of the 12th K.R.R.C. (map reference given), and to make a note of any identifiable remains. I was warned that there were, or had been, boxes of live ammo and mills grenades aboard. A quick glance showed that it would be suicide to attempt the task in the dark, so I fixed it up to begin at 8 a.m. the next morning.

The K.R.R.C.'s M.O. and his staff met me at the vehicle at the set hour, and an orderly and I began the gruesome business (my diary records it as 'the worst sight and job of my life') while the rest remained at a distance. A mortar bomb had landed slap in the middle of the canvas roof of the truck. The explosion had been downwards, fragmenting everything except some of the bits and pieces under the seats. Mills grenades had added to the destruction. It was thought four or five men had been sitting in the back. We picked away the canvas tatters and then, slowly and with considerable care, we worked our way with hands and a small entrenching tool through the shambles. We established that there had been four men in the vehicle, and identified them by their discs. One of the damaged grenades exploded when we dumped them into a nearby bomb crater. We were profoundly thankful when the task was completed without further loss of life.

The Regiment was pulled out of operations on the evening of the 17th and told to concentrate in Bedburg, and for us (although we did not know it) the worst was over in this grim Reichswald-Kleve battle when the enemy '*fought generally with all the skill, experience and ferocity characteristic of the German Army at its best. It is not surprising, therefore, that our casualties were heavy. For the Division, the Reichswald was the greatest ordeal since Normandy...in almost unspeakable conditions of danger and exposure, the troops were almost continuously in action... facing the flower of the German Army fighting for their country with fatalistic courage...*' (from: the 43rd Wessex Division at War, 1944–1945; page 231)

At Bedburg, the Regiment took over an empty asylum. This was a collection of buildings clustering around a large central block four stories high, and containing several very large rooms on each floor. The whole made excellent barrack quarters. The main problems were lack of electricity and water. The next day (18th) was spent in general vehicle maintenance and preparation for the next move, so the lack of amenities was hardly noticed. Thirteen services were held that day with the Regiment and other units still operating.

On the 19th, the lack of water presented real problems and someone, having examined the pipes, said that the water had obviously been turned off at the main. The Doc overheard this discussion, and went over to investigate—he loved fiddling and tinkering, and was a better mechanic than most of the R.E.M.E. personnel. He reported that the mains had indeed been turned off, but so tightly that a large wrench was needed to restore the supply. This was produced, and John again sallied forth into the bowels of the building. He returned, triumphant with the news that the water was on—and so it was! Within three minutes, shouts echoed from almost every room, for jets of water were shooting out from small bursts in pipes in almost every room. Knowledgable people ran to the main stop-cocks to turn them off, but failed to budge them. They shouted for Doc, but John, satisfied with his earlier efforts, had wandered off. By the time he had been traced, and the heavy grip had again been collected, water was gushing down the stairs like a waterfall, and the ground floor, slightly below ground level, was awash with kit floating in eighteen inches of water. Water mains were a sore subject for some time after this episode!

While in Bedburg, I met Colonel de Pinto, a Gunner Officer seconded to Military Government. On my return to Dymock after demobilization, I was delighted to find that Colonel de Pinto had become a part-time parishioner, for his half-sister, and ex-F.A.N.Y. and the daughter of Sir Samuel Evans, had just bought a house in the parish. My diary records that on the 19th, I had with the Colonel 'the best meal ever; goose, chicken, fruit tart and cream, Welsh rarebit, and coffee.' I cannot recall the reason for this obvious celebration.

The *Luftwaffe* was still giving active support to the German ground forces, and bombs were 'two-a-penny'. On the 21st I learned that the Middlesex Battalion in the 15th Scottish Division was operating on our flank. That night I set out on foot and located them, and found Vivienne's cousin, Lieutenant Tony Gribble, in high dudgeon because the enemy had just destroyed some of his kit. We had a drink together and sent messages to our respective families. The volume of correspondence with the next of kin had, by this time, assumed daunting dimensions. Letters came not only from the families of my own boys, but from the R.A.F. personnel whom I had buried during the Nijmegen-Arnhem period, and from relations of soldiers in other units. Understandably, they wished to know all they could and frequently wrote several times. It was heart-rending to read those letters and to see how grateful the relations were for the smallest details—and how bravely most faced up to the death or mutilation of their loved ones. Letter writing was indeed a great problem. Scores, perhaps hundreds, of those letters have been depositied in the Regimental archives.

On February 22nd, with the floods receding, the Regiment began moving eastward from Kleve to Kellen, with the task of protecting the left flank of the Division, and at the same time rolling back the German delay forces.

One felt that the end was approaching, but feared that three periods of bitter fighting might still have to be faced before the final battle could be won. Firstly, with the flood-water still making movement difficult east of Kleve, it could be expected that determined pockets of resistance would be encountered. Secondly, it was realised that the assault crossing of the greatest river in north-western Europe, and the subsequent break-out, might be a stiff task, especially for troops who had already endured a grim and gruelling time for many months. Finally one envisaged a 'back-to-the-wall' finale, with Hitler compelling the German Army and people to commit national suicide. Fortunately, none of these happened.

From the Regiment's point of view, the first phase was much easier than anticipated. Kellen was our start line, and the following day (23rd February) the Squadrons probed forward and finally reached a major water obstacle in the form of a tributary of the *Rhein*, which barred our advance to Wissel. The Colonel sent for the Major commanding the R.E. Squadron, and instructed him to bridge the river to enable cars and carriers to cross. The C.O. specifically said, because the site was in full view of the enemy on the other side of the river and across the *Rhein*, that there must be no movement in the area during daylight, but that the task must be completed by midnight, or earlier if possible.

The C.O. went off to Corps and returned at 4.30 as darkness began to fall.

Both he and I were looking for a cup of tea when the R.E. commander came in, saluted smartly, and said:

"The bridge has been completed, sir."

This was the only occasion when I ever saw Colonel Kinnersley really shaken.

"Completed?" he said, "Are you mad? I gave orders that the work should not begin before dark. You have now told the Boche where we're crossing tonight. If our men run into serious trouble, I shall hold you entirely responsible!"

Poor man! Poor C.O.! Poor us! We had been committed by Corps to cross at 1 a.m., and the Doc and I were allotted to the leading squadron. Fortunately, very few knew of this bridging 'bog-up', so it was quite a cheerful party that prepared to move off soon after midnight.

Some of our assault troops crossed first and moved eastwards to the village of Greith on the *Rhein* bank, to prevent reinforcements being ferried over. Our men caught the enemy off their guard while we bowled merrily into Wissel without any opposition, and further west, 'C' Squadron 'bounced' the town of Calcar without a single casualty.

As the leading squadron drove in the moonlight along the road to Wissel, duck could be heard on the flooded meadows. Just after dawn, because there had been no opposition to our advance and the Germans had pulled out of the village, I borrowed the Adjutant's 16-bore shotgun (there were no cartridges for my 12-bore) and went off to bag a duck. Mad? Of course it was; stark, raving madness! Half a mile along the route in, I spotted some mallard and began to stalk them. Before I was within two hundred yards of the duck, a rifle cracked and a bullet ricocheted off the railway arch beneath which I had just passed. The shot seemed to have come from a farmstead some 500–600 yards away. I did not stop to investigate, but fled back towards the arch with all speed. There were two further shots before the embankment was happily between myself and the farm. The latter was searched some hours later, but by that time the place was empty. That evening I had a mallard; my first in Germany. It graced the mess table the following day.

From Wissel, a pleasant little place with a normal population of around eighteen hundred, we moved further south, handing over the empty village to a unit of the Division which was relieving the 43rd. Hitherto there had been almost no looting by the Regiment; an officer had 'nicked' some things in Kleve, but apart from that, the unit's record had been extremely good. Neither, incidentally, had there been many cases of womanizing in France, Belgium or Holland. Even while we were sitting in our cars, waiting for the convoy to move off, it became clear that the new unit had begun looting. A few days later, I and some others passed again through Wissel, and to our horror we found the place literally sacked, with stuff scattered all over the gardens and on the roads. Our unit was blamed for this at first. We were furious and told the Divisional staff to get on to the other Division and tell them to crack down heavily on the unit responsible. From then on, there was a feeling with a few of our men that if other units could loot in enemy country, then why could not they? We had to be very firm on this small minority. At this time, one of the new N.C.O.s even asked, now that the unit was in enemy country, whether the men might rape the women! He 'disappeared' quickly; our men *always* treated the women of *all* countries with complete respect. I am not saying that none of them ever went to bed with one of the locals, but I am certain that when this occasionally took place, it was with the full approval, and perhaps encouragement of the lady concerned.

From a café in Wissel, H.Q. Squadron moved to an empty farmhouse some miles south, where the final and very minor operation involving the Regiment took place. The Germans had been overwhelmed, and the divisions which withdrew over the *Rhein* were greatly depleted and not the efficent fighting machine that had been thrown into battle some weeks earlier.

In the farmhouse H.Q., the M.O. and I shared a room and lived very comfortably. Dead cattle lay everywhere, and the scene was in some respects reminiscent of the Normandy battle. A few cows still wandered around, some of them in obvious distress from lack of milking. The Doc and I milked several of the more docile animals, to the benefit of both man and beast.

One evening, when operations were finally over, I took a walk through the fields behind the farm, and came across two large ponds surrounded by thickets. On the water were numerous wild duck, while some pheasant were skulking through the bushes. This gave me ideas. The following evening, the Adjutant and I sallied forth to see whether duck and pheasant could be added to the mess menu. I was going on leave the next morning, so I stipulated that a percentage of the bag (if any) should also travel to England. It was a successful foray, and that evening a cock pheasant and a pair of mallard, wrapped in newspaper, reposed in my very large leave-bag. It had to be one of some size, for I was taking back with me the remnants of the two parachutes as well as much washing and clothes to be repaired, and I had every intention of purchasing several bottles of wine and liqueurs at the port of embarkation.

There was an amusing sequel to the packing of the birds, when I arrived home two days later. Our two spaniels, Duke and Duchess, became very excited when the unpacking began, thrusting their wet noses ever deeper into the haversack. Before the bag had been half emptied, a blood-stained shirt and surplice appeared. At this point, poor Vivienne gulped, believing that it was blood shed in battle. Duchess, unable to stand the strain any longer, thrust her head into the bag, sniffed, thrust deeper, and extracted the pheasant. The mystery of the blood was thus explained, and so began a good leave which, as always, passed far too quickly.

A Final Tribute

As this leave virtually marked the end of my close war-time association with the Regiment, it may be the moment when a brief tribute to the unit may rightly be added.

From a personal point of view, they were truly magnificent; no padré could have had such friendship and co-operation from all ranks. It was terrific and heartening, and one was made to feel that one 'belonged' as a member of a family. This, with the assistance from the Padré's Helpers, made a peace-time parish priest's normal life appear an uphill task! They taught me much, and helped me more than I can say. As fighting men too, they were first class. They had shown this as early as the Saar and Dunkirk periods, and after the catastrophic Normandy landing, they confirmed their stature in the grim campaign in the close 'bocage' country followed by the *Seine* crossing, the 'Island', and the Geilenkirchen engagements. All this led up to the Reichswald battles which were, perhaps, their greatest hour. Despite the appalling conditions, the fanatical fighting and heavy losses, the morale of the whole Regiment (as I believe was true of the entire Division) was amazing. The men of the 43rd Recce were, as experienced campaigners, realistic about the situation; they demurred at nothing, and fought with courage and determination at all times. They risked their lives for the wounded, showed consideration to prisoners (those fit, as well as those wounded), while their conduct toward the civil population, whether friend or foe, was exemplary. As Pericles said of the Athenian soldiers in the campaign of 404 B.C., so we in 1944–45 could truly say of our men in the 43rd Recce Regiment/5th Glosters that they were our country's finest ambassadors. In conclusion, all I can say is that I fully endorse what F.W. Harvey wrote of that earlier generation of 5th Glosters with whom he served:

> Lucky to live,
> Lucky again
> To have met and marched
> with the finest men...
> ...Earth ever bred.

CHAPTER TWENTY

Brussels

I returned from leave on March 26th to find that I had been promoted to take over the Chaplain's team with 21 Army Group Troops. A new chaplain, Rev. F.J.M. Hogarth, had been posted to my Regiment but had not yet reported. The Regiment was parked alongside the road, ready to move over the Rees bridge directly it had been completed by the R.E.s.

The posting created a turmoil of emotions. While the thought of promotion was naturally pleasant, I hated the thought of leaving my 'family' with whom I had been since 1938, especially so when it seemed that the end was so near. Time, obviously, was short, so I drove over to see the D.A.C.G. 30 Corps (Rev. Bill Gladstone) and asked that I might go over the *Rhein* with the unit and see them through the first three or four days, pointing out that it would not be fair to send a fresh chaplain into what might prove a sticky few days. However, the D.A.C.G. was adamant; I would hand over at once, and report to 21 Army Group in Brussels. I came back via 43rd Division H.Q., and found the S.C.F. (Rev. Ivan Neill) much more understanding and sympathetic. He sanctioned an extension for forty-eight hours, after which the new chaplain would join the Regiment.

The return journey was disastrous, for by this time all units appeared to be on the move. In a maze of troops, I found myself in a column of 15th Scottish, approaching a bridge north-east of Xanten, whereas the Recce were scheduled to be crossing near Rees. There was no turning back; the map showed a *bund* road and several lesser roads leading north from Xanten to Rees, so I picked one of these and set out. A mile or so from the bridge, Sappers were using mine-detectors on the road leading north, and said they did not know whether contact with the northern bridgehead had been established. They advised against going out into the blue. A couple of miles further on, an armoured car patrol from Rees reported that the road to Rees was clear and in return I suggested that as nothing had happened to me the road between us and the Sappers was clear of mines and enemy pockets.

Two hours later, I located the unit near Speldrop and remained with them rather longer than intended because, at first, return traffic over the bridge was restricted to essentials or casualties. Eventually, after a final visit to all sqaudrons, came the final break.

During these farewells, a certain sergeant thanked me for having saved him weeks earlier from cracking. When he spoke of the incident, I remembered the night well, but had had no idea at the time that he was near breaking point. 'C' Squadron had been holding a crossroad on the south side of Apeldoorn, and a troop post had been established to the south-east of the village. These were linked by the road running east from the crossroads and parallel with the village main street, which technically, as it proved in fact, was in enemy hands. There had been a nasty engagement near the troop post, and our people had suffered several casualties. After dark, I walked up to the crossroads and was told that I could go no further without an armed escort. I decided, after waiting half an hour, to go on my own, feeling that, having been a countryman all my life, and having been taught to poach at the age of twelve by the local blacksmith's son I could move along quietly enough, and in any case I would be less likely to be spotted on a dirty night than a party of three or four. All went well; I found the post, saw the wounded, and half an hour later set out on the return journey. I was relieved when I turned left at the crossroads and headed for R.H.Q., and, some distance down the road, a patrol under the said sergeant appeared. He said that he was on a patrol to the troop post, and when I reported that all had been quiet both ways, he simply said "Oh good!" Apparently, the thought that a fool of a parson had taken (as he imagined) a leisurely stroll there and back tickled him, and made him feel that it wasn't so bad after all—he had probably been very tired when ordered to undertake this near-midnight patrol, and fatigue can play tricks with one's nerves; as most people have experienced on at least one occasion.

I reported in Brussels to the Rev. Dick Yale. This very senior staff chaplain could not have been nicer. The post to which I had come was changing in character, and it was realised that when the battle ended, and static conditions were established, an entirely new set-up would evolve. It was in this vague period of planning for a future that was uncertain and for a policy which depended on so many contingencies that made life at that moment completely unreal.

On arrival, I was given a list of my chaplains and their possible locations. However, the situation was so fluid and uncertain that I was warned that much of the detail might be hopelessly out of date. I discovered to my horror that on my list was the one-time Principal of my Theological College. I had been ordained in 1934 and at that time the College had changed Principals. The earlier one had, of deliberate policy, introduced Medical and Dental undergraduates into the College, with whom we, the 'Theologs' shared all things except lectures; the idea being that embryonic parsons should not become 'pie' and far removed from the realities of life, and that the Medicos and Dentals (who were a pretty tough, but generally good, lot) should knock our corners off. I believed this to be a sound policy. But the new Principal reversed the policy, filling the secular places with additional theological students. On learning of this, I wrote to the local Provincial Daily a long letter deprecating this change of policy, and describing it as a retrograde move. I was then a raw deacon a few weeks old! Some days later, the Bishop, the great Dr. Headlam, sent for me. I arrived at the Palace with no misgivings and was ushered into the 'presence'. Headlam spoke little in private interviews. I knew this, so was not perturbed when, without a word, he motioned me to a seat and handing me a letter said:

"Read."

The letter, to which was clipped the cutting of my own correspondence to the Daily, was from the new Principal. He was annoyed, *very* annoyed, that his change of policy had been questioned, and that it had been done by one so newly ordained was the height of bad taste, and intolerable! (He was quite right.) The Principal flayed me in his letter to the Bishop. Having read the letter twice, I looked at his Lordship, who said,

"Well?"

"Well what, my Lord?" I replied.

"What do you mean by your letter?" he asked.

I mean what I have written. I feel very strongly on the matter."

There followed a long silence, typical of a Headlam interview, and then came the verdict:

"I am inclined to agree with you, but I would not, I think, have been foolish enough to write the letter. Good morning, Gethyn-Jones."

A rocket? Well, maybe. It was noticeable, however, that frequently, during my years in Gloucester, I was often called in to act as Bishop's Chaplain when his domestic chaplain was not available.

Luckily for me, two days after my arrival in Brussels, a posting order came through, stating that the Principal had been posted to another formation. He had obviously considered the position impossible, and had pulled wires—to my great relief!

The death of President Roosevelt on the 12th April brought problems for the American Chaplaincy Service. They were short of chaplains, and had not enough churches for the many Memorial Services which convention demanded; we might well have been in a similar plight, had the King or Prime Minister died at that time. Their Staff Chaplain telephoned and asked, *inter alia*, whether a Protestant church could be borrowed in Brussels. St George's Church was offered and gratefully accepted. Later came a request for a chaplain to take the Service at St George's. The Revd. Fred Bussby (who is now a Canon of Winchester Cathedral) consented, and was detailed for the task. On the day, the church was packed, and the Service was scheduled to begin with the National Anthems of both nations. Fred had obviously not been adequately briefed, and the silence which followed the musical preliminaries was rather longer than required. The large American negro organist, when he could stand it no longer, swivelled on his seat and, in a booming stage whisper across the choir-stalls, said:

"O.K. Boss, over to you!"

This tickled Fred, and it was with some difficulty that he was able to comply with the order and begin the Service.

With the approach of the end of hostilities, there was a rapid build-up of non-combatant and administrative personnel, and around about V.E. Day, the number of A.T.S. in Brussels, for example, had risen to nearly three thousand. None of my chaplains in the city were happy about the prospect. They were unit or ex-unit padrés, and the thought of having to cope with the female of the species in large numbers frankly frightened them—and me! Fortunately, the War Office came to the rescue. They telephoned, saying that they had two chaplain's assistants skulling around England with next to nothing to do. Could I employ them? Our combined prayers had been answered. 'Yes! Fly them over as soon as possible—today, if you wish. I will see to billets.' A day or two later, these very able ladies arrived and, very largely, the pastoral side of work among the girls was handed over to them.

V.E. Day was a time of general jubilation. For me, however, it was a day of great loneliness. I rejoiced, naturally, but I was desperately lonely. I knew very few in the H.Q., and had not a 'Staff' tradition or training. My thoughts had been with my Regiment the whole time, and every day I had visited the Situation Room to check progress and casualties. These last, I was relieved to find, had been light until the very last. Now, on V.E. Day, the day we had talked of and worked for together for nearly six years, I was not with them to join in their rejoicing. I felt thwarted, cheated of my rights to be with my 'family' to celebrate together as we had sweated, fought and played together for so many years.

When the day's routine work on V.E. Day was over I could not go out to celebrate and drink with men or women with whom I had, at that moment, little in common; nor would they have wanted a morose parson with them! So I went instead to *Madame Butterfly* at the Opera House, but even here my troubled spirit found no rest. The hilarity of the audience, and the gaiety of the opera ill suited my mood, and finally in sheer desperation, at the end of *Act 1* I left the theatre and went miserably to bed.

A few days later, I remembered the invitation of a Madame Simone van der Gracht, whom I had met at Château Bérlo during the Ardennes offensive. She had been cheerful and vivacious during those grim days of December 1944 (when a second over-running by the Germans was a distinct possibility) and belied middle age. She had chatted with the C.O. and the cooks, with the troopers, signallers and drivers. There, at least, I could talk of my boys with one who knew them, and had seen them at their best in action. I called, and found her entertaining Comtesse Nathalie in whose château, Schoonbeck, R.H.Q. had spent the first night on the move into the *Maas* gap, and who was a sister of Comtesse de Rénesse-Westerholt of Bérlo. For the first time in Brussels, I felt at home and at ease. Before I left, I had been invited to dinner at a later date. While they were telephoning another relation to invite someone nearer my age, an aside amused me; one had suggested a certain Minou should be invited.

"*Mais non! Mais non*!!' replied the other lady, "*Trés elégante, trés vive, mais une jeune flirte!*"

Another name, which I did not catch, was suggested, and the reply was;

"*Exactement*!"

Thus began a close friendship with a large family whose members were kind and hospitable and with whom, after Main H.Q. had moved up to Bad Oyenhousen, Herford, and Bad Salzuflen, I stayed frequently in my routine trips to those portions of H.Q. which remained in Brussels. One amusing incident resulted from this friendship. Years later, when the 5th Glosters were receiving the Freedom of the City of Gloucester, an ex-officer, Major Guilding, whom I had not seen for years, came up and said,

"How nice to see you, Padré. It is a long time since I saw you dining with that charming Belgian lady in Brussels."

Suddenly, he spotted Vivienne by my side, and it was clear from his expression that he wondered whether he had dropped a brick. To allay his anxiety, I replied:

"No black, Charles! Vivienne is fully in the picture, and we have stayed with the family, and she with us!"

It was felt in Brussels, now the fighting was over, that it was essential to move quickly as much as possible of our main H.Q. up to the selected area in Germany, so that the proposed administrative machinery could be established before local conditions deteriorated or even got out of hand. So began, before May had ended, the transfer of personnel and material two hundred and fifty miles into the heart of Germany.

CHAPTER TWENTY ONE

Days of Occupation

Very soon after the hostilities ceased, plans were formulated for the moving up of H.Q. 21st Army Group from Brussels to Western Germany, and by mid-June, Main H.Q. was occupying Herford and Bad Oyenhousen, while G.H.Q. Troops H.Q. (the unit which carried me on strength) was at Bad Salzuflen.

The settling-in period was an interesting time, although in some ways extremely disappointing. The response to the work of the chaplain, which in the Recce days had been almost phenomenal, was now poor. This can perhaps be attributed to two main reasons; firstly, the stress of the battle was over, and the presence of God was not so deeply desired. He can in fact become embarrassing at times, demanding what might appear to be an undesired self-control or positive effort. Secondly, I was a 'new-boy' in a strange set up, and it is generally felt that a chaplain needs six months before he can make any impression on his unit.

The Commander sent for me the day after we arrived in Salzuflen, and expressed anxiety lest the period of comparative inactivity and the leisure hours following upon peace should result in boredom, perhaps the most dangerous problem facing occupational troops. We discussed field sports, fishing competitions, bathing parties, concerts (both impromptu and E.N.S.A. when they could be brought up), historical excursions and, for the future when the A.T.S. arrived, dances.

The following evening, there was organised the first fishing competition in the lakes and pools of the Spa Gardens and park. It was a most primitive and hilarious affair, with bent pins (literally) and stout wire, produced by R.E.M.E., doing duty for hooks. The quarry was the golden carp, which ran to considerable size. Within a week, proper hooks and kit were flown in from the U.K., or came up by lorry from Brussels, and the experts settled down to serious fishing. The prizes for these nightly competitions were nominal, a bottle of beer or a few cigarettes, paid for by the Commander's discretionary fund. The fish were soon discovered to be really inedible so, after the first evening or two, it was customary for them to be returned to the water, having first been weighed. Many competitors swore that, not infrequently, the same fish was pulled out more than once during the same evening! Fishing was my responsibility, and I enjoyed those quiet forays. A small stream ran through the grounds of the Mess, and occasionally I slipped out before Reveille or in the moonlight, and caught the odd trout for breakfast. The largest just topped the two-pounds mark. Major Brian Valentine (the Kent and England cricket captain) and the Revd. Middleton-Brumwell, an ex-Deputy Chaplain-General working with Welfare, ran the cricket, and Captain Tummy? (the Channel swimmer) organised the swimming. And so the catalogue could go on.

Directly the immediate chaplaincy problems had been settled, the Commander asked me to plan three-or-four-day or half-day excursions to places of historical interest or scenic attraction. These included visits to the Möhne Dam (breached by Guy Gibson V.C. in the dramatic raid by 617 Squadron, Bomber Command, but rapidly repaired by the Germans), the Bielefeld Viaduct where the first experimental 10-ton 'earthquake' bomb was exploded, Hameln (Hamelin) of Pied Piper fame, the gigantic monument to Arminius or Herman in the Teutoburger Wald (Arminius was the German leader who, in A.D. 9, roused the tribes between the *Rhein* and the *Waser* and drove out the Romans, annihilating three legions under Varus; hence Caesar's cry: '*Varus! Varus! Give me back my legions*!'), and the renowned Extern Rocks near Horn. These last, a site of sun worship, were later occupied by a monastic community whose magnificent carving of the Descent from the Cross (dating from the 12th century) is one of the finest examples of Romanesque work surviving in the open air. I wrote a brief hand-out for each of those set tours, which formed a précis of the talks given by those in charge of the parties. Today, Cook's and similar companies charge large sums to take people to these places, but in 1945 our men (and later, women too) were visiting them as part of their organised recreational activities, and with erudite lecturers.

Local and E.N.S.A. parties supplied excellent entertainments and sometimes surprises. Yvonne Arnaud came on one occasion, appearing in a Ben Travers farce. The house was packed when, a short time before the curtain was due to rise, the lights failed. Miss Arnaud asked for a match and by its flickering light found the piano, a baby grand. There followed, at first in total darkness, then by the light of a few candles and lamps, an astonishing example of a single-handed impromptu show. Miss Arnaud catered for all tastes; classical pieces, Gilbert and Sullivan, and community songs flowed out, and I believe that most of the audience were truly sorry when, after some forty minutes, the lights came on again and the play replaced the piano recital. Miss Arnaud received what must have been one of the greatest ovations of her career, and she well deserved it.

Despite all these recreational facilities, welfare problems continued to increase. Our problems, in an essentially agricultural district where food was not really scarce, were minor compared with those arising among units stationed in the rubble-ized industrial areas; there, civilians were sometimes near famine level, and there, in consequence, even a slice of bread was a powerful corruptor.

The barbed-wire fence which surrounded our cantonment, supposedly segregating the Forces from the civilians, was a challenge which was accepted, and so was not fully effective. We had a large Lutheran church within the perimeter. It was a plain, stark building, but it had a good two-manual organ. The Royal Engineers quickly built the smaller pieces of furniture to which we in the Anglican community had been accustomed (i.e. Cross, candlesticks, lectern etc.). We were fortunate in having at the H.Q. an organist from St John's Church, Cardiff, who soon had an enthusiastic mixed choir (mainly from the Principality) which produced an anthem almost every weak.

Soon after our arrival permission was granted to our men to purchase watches and clocks from a small shop in Salzuflen. The prices were remarkably low and within a day or two the entire stock had been sold. The proprietor then approached the Commander for a permit to travel down to Bavaria to obtain fresh supplies. This was granted and a lorry with armed escort was sent to ensure that adequate supplies could be brought safely back for the benefit of British troops. This happened more than once, and it was interesting to observe the steady rise in prices after each trip.

My chaplains were attached to units stationed as far east as Hanover and as far west as Brussels. In this latter city remained very large numbers of troops, mainly administrative, and several chaplains were retained there during the whole of my time. One of the Padrés, Canon H.A.V. Moreton, Chancellor of Hereford Cathedral and a D. Litt. of Besançon University, had a peculiar assignment. He was required to interview every Belgian or French girl who became engaged to any British soldier. He had to explain to them the very great differences they would find if they married and settled in England. He spoke to both parties about the glamour of the uniform, and the change which could follow its abandonment on return to civilian life, and discussed with them the many problems which would face them after demobilization.

Routine visits to Brussels were necessary at regular intervals. Occasionally, urgent welfare cases compelled additional journeys; I was once telephoned at 2 a.m. because of an emergency, and had to leave within half-an-hour. These trips, 247 miles each way, could take anything from six to ten hours, depending on the weather and traffic congestion, especially at river crossings, where the bridges were still of the Bailey or pontoon type, and often single-tracked. In this respect, however, I was fortunate. My driver, Smissen, was a Lance-Corporal of the C.M.P.s from my old Division. He had been wounded in Normandy and forbidden to ride a motor-cycle, and so had been drafted to G.H.Q. Troops H.Q. where he 'took me over'. He was always cheerful, had a quick brain, and was a magnificent driver. His first remark, when he found he had become the Senior Chaplain's driver, was:

"Well sir, we'll make a good pair. What with your clerical collar and my Military Police hat, we'll get anywhere!"

He worked miracles at river crossings; if the queue was long, Smissen would lean out of the car and speak to the C.M.P. on duty, and we were passed through with minimum delay.

On my trips to Brussels, after main H.Q. had moved up to Herford, I often stayed with the Van der Burchs. They were a charming family, and treated me as one of them. I owe them a great debt of gratitude. I came and went to my work in Brussels as normally as from the Leave Centre when I stayed there, and above all, I felt free from embarrassment. Since the War, their eldest daughter, Françoise, visited us at Dymock, and my wife and I stayed with them in Belgium.

The Mess at Salzuflen contained some interesting members, including the Major Valentine already mentioned. The Commander, Colonel

Humphries (who took over when we first moved in), was a shrewd Lancastrian who surprised me when I sat next to him the first night the Mess was operational. He asked me where I came from, and when I told him Gloucestershire, he said:

"Where?"

"A little place of which you have probably never heard;" I replied, "Dymock."

Dymock!" he laughed, "where they buried the man without a shirt!"

I was staggered that he, a Lancastrian, should know of this cause célèbre which so tarnished the good name of Dymock in the 19th Century.[1] He said that a group of officers, waiting for an attack in North Africa, were exchanging stories of their own districts and one of them, whose name he could not remember, had told the story of poor old Bob Meredith.

Another member of the Mess was a Major Squires of the Education Corps. He was an able but strange man.

My chaplains, C. of E. and Free Chruch were, with one exception, an excellent team who pulled well together. They had to cover, as I did, considerable distances to minister to the numerous units of G.H.Q. Troops stationed in Belgium, Holland and Germany. We were greatly under strength, but were fortunate in being able to call upon certain members of the Army Welfare Organisation, who were either ordained ministers or lay readers. These good gentlemen gave freely of their time and were a great help.

On June 24th, my old Division held its Victory Celebration in Celle. I was invited to stay with the Recce Regiment and take part in the Thanksgiving Service the following morning. In the afternoon, the festivities included sports, which were opened by General G.I. Thomas, who arrived in the arena in the State Coach of King George I, which had been loaned by the local museum for the occasion.

Leave came in August, and the R.A.F. at Buckeburg kindly found me a seat on one of their routine flights to the U.K., saving me a long train journey. The day was fine, and it was interesting to see the country over which we had fought unfolding beneath me—I had taken with me two 1/4 inch maps, covering much of the Kleve and Nijmegen area. The return trip was via Brussels, where we were grounded for several hours by fog. After the long wait, the pilot came into the hangar where we were sitting on our packs, and said;

"Come on, you chaps, I think we'll risk it now!"—a remark not too encouraging to most passengers!

We took off in what seemed to me to be thick fog, and almost at once entered a thunder-storm where visibility appeared to be nil. What with the lightning flashes, passengers were apprehensive. A second storm was encountered near the Teutoburger Wald, and someone said to the co-pilot, who had just come into our compartment;

"I hope you know the passes through these mountains." The airman replied,

"Oh I think so, but we reckon to lose one plane a week on these flights."—a jocular remark that did not go down too well with a senior officer!

The Recce Regiment wrote to me in May, saying that Tommy Zwollo, who had not been heard of since the fateful patrol at Druemel in October 1944, was in a British Military Hospital in Brussels. It was wonderful news that he was still alive. I found him outwardly cheerful, but at heart he was anxious about the future. He had been a P.T. instructor in a school, and realised that his shattered knee would make it impossible to continue his profession.

Negotiations began at once with the view to commissioning Tommy into the Netherlands' Army so that pension rights could be established. These went on fruitlessly between the Recce Regiment, the 43rd Division, and the Netherlands Mission at the 21st Army Group H.Q.. In June, Colonel Kinnersley, C.O. of the Recce Regiment, asked me to take up Zwollo's case personally with the Mission. On 24th August, when I returned from leave and found that no progress had been made (due, I felt certain, to indifference on the Mission's part), I drove down to Apeldoorn with the intention of seeking an audience with Prince Bernhard on the matter. The Prince was in England for the day, but after several hours of waiting, discussion and argument, I finally left late that evening with the assurance that Zwollo's commission would be authorised at once. Four more weeks went by without result, so on the 27th September I wrote the following letter to the Prince:

Rev. J.E. Gethyn-Jones
Headquarters G.H.Q. Troops
B.A.O.R. (late 43 Recce Regt)

H.M. Prince Bernhard
H.Q. Netherlands Forces
APELDOORN
27th September 1945

Your Highness,

On the night of 22/23 Sept. 1944, T. Pl Zwollo of Hengelo joined the 43 Recce Regt. as a guide and an interpreter—3 other Dutchmen also were sent to us in the same way. In October, when things were more quiet, steps were taken by the B.L.A. to legalise the position of these attached Dutchmen.

Before negotiations had been completed, Zwollo went out on patrol with a party of our men and was taken prisoner—11 of our men also failed to return from this patrol.

On 23 Apr. of this year Zwollo, still in hospital in Apeldoorn, was recaptured by the Canadians.

Zwollo is likely to remain in hospital for some time.

In mid-June, at the request of the C.O. of the Recce Regiment (Lt. Col. C.H. Kinnersley), I took up his case with the Netherland's Military Mission, 21 Army Group, and also with the Interpreters' Pool there.

They promised to do all they could to get him taken on officially by your Army as an interpreter with Officer's rank. Zwollo is an officer type and was always ranked by us as a Lieut., e.g., pips on his battledress blouse and living in the Officers' Mess.

The C.O. is extremely concerned about this matter. It was requested too that Zwollo's commission should be retrospective, i.e., with effect from 23 Sep. 44.

I have called many times both at the Mission and the Pool and could get no reply beyond they were doing all they could.

Finally, in despair, I came down to Apeldoorn to see Your Highness on 24 Aug. to ask you personally to take up the matter.

Your Highness was not there, but was expected soon.

I saw a lady secretary, and a Major took my papers with full details of the case to a G.2. This Major returned after half an hour and assured me that a letter would be sent out that same evening sanctioning Zwollo's commission with effect from 23 Sep. 45. He assured me that there was no need to worry you, and promised that both the C.O. and I would be fully informed. Two telephone calls to Apeldoorn from Netherlands Mission in H.Q. B.A.O.R. last week failed to obtain any information.

I saw Zwollo in hospital on 26 Sept. and he too was still without news.

I feel that the case is now one that Your Highness should take up personally, as other people here cannot or will not see the matter through.

I would be most grateful if Your Highness would do this.
I remain,

Your Highness' respectful Ally,

J.E. Gethyn-Jones

(Copy to: O.C. 43 Recce Regt.)

The reaction was immediate. On 3rd October, a letter from Tommy arrived in Dymock saying that his commission had just come through and was back-dated to September 1944. I at once sent a letter of thanks to the Prince:

Rev. J.E. Gethyn-Jones
Dymock Vicarage
Gloucestershire
late of 43 Recce Regt.

H.M. Prince Bernhard
H.Q. Netherlands Forces
Apeldoorn

3rd October 1945

Your Highness,

Today I heard from Lt. Zwollo that he has been notified that he is commissioned into the Dutch Army.

I feel that after my visit to Apeldoorn in late August or early September Your Highness must have taken a hand in the matter and I am most grateful. I was very anxious to see this settled before my demobilization should come into force. Had it not been for the near approach of my release I would not have written that rather desperate letter last Thursday.

Once again I must thank Your Highness for putting the matter through—Zwollow was a first class lad when with us, and his case is not a happy one.

I remain,

Your respectful Ally,

J.E. Gethyn-Jones

I became worried when the time for my age and service group release drew near. Others had been notified of the dates for their demobilization weeks before, but I had heard nothing. With only ten days to go, I appealed to the Chaplains' H.Q. at Herford. They replied that they were awaiting the date and authorisation. This reply was given on three consecutive days. I became desperate because of the uncertainty and the inability to plan, and so wrote a letter to Chaplains' H.Q. at Herford, saying that the Rev. J.E. Gethyn-Jones, C.F. 3rd Class, would be released on September 19th, and signed the letter in the normal way...

J.E. Gethyn-Jones
S.C.F. G.H.Q. Tps.

...with copies to the War Office and the Paymaster. The letter was received by D.R. that day, and on the following morning, an order arrived stating that I would be released on September 19th, quoting my own letter as authority!

The chaplains of G.H.Q. Troops were attached to units which were dotted about in an area 280 miles by 60, and the hierarchy suggested that at least a week would be needed for the introduction of a new Senior Chaplain to the major units and their chaplains. However, because my successor (Revd. John Fawcett) had been my deputy for four months, two days only were needed for the handover.

In view of this, I asked Chaplains' H.Q. whether I might be allowed to visit Berlin. Restrictions were tight but they arranged it splendidly. Despatches were carried up almost every day from Herford and Oyenhousen to Berlin. I merely became a temporary courier and was given leave to stay an extra day before returning.

Good use was made of the free day in Berlin; I went into the Russian Sector, seeing and photographing the *Reichstag*, the Old Royal Palace, the Anti-aircraft towers in the park, some churches, and the *Unter den Linden*. That evening, I was told that I had been somewhat foolish in photographing to the extent that I had done, but as far as I could see the Russians took no notice of me, nor anyone else for that matter.

I was greatly impressed by the gigantic anti-aircraft towers; they simply dwarfed everything, and their strength was testified to by the little impression made on them by direct hits from heavy-calibre guns.

I enjoyed my trip to Berlin in many ways, and in the few hours available, I had seen much more than I expected to see. I had, however, probed too deeply for my peace of mind into matters of welfare and human relationships.

It was on the forecourt of a ruined but still impressive church that I began a series of glimpses of the horrifying physical and mental aftermaths of a long war and final defeat. An elderly person passed me and stopped. In his hands, behind his back, he displayed a *Leica* camera. While still facing forwards, he said in a low, but cultured, voice:

"Leica camera; two hundred cigarettes."

Here was an elderly, educated man, in odd garments which had seen better days, attempting to sell his top-grade camera not for money (for that was valueless) but for cigarettes which, along with food, were the most desired commodities for barter. The mental picture of the possible personal privation behind that heart-rending incident was devastating—and I had not a single cigarette to give him in his obvious distress.

During that morning, afternoon and evening, I learned a great deal about the demoralization that can follow surrender and occupation, especially when one of the occupying powers appeared indifferent to the basic dictates of humanitarianism. Enquiry revealed that the civilian mortality rate through malnutrition and downright starvation (though this varied between national sectors), especially amongst children, was high. It was said, and clearly this suggestion was related to the above, that in one unit within the British Sector, a considerable percentage[2] of its personnel slept out from time to time, taking with them food to alleviate the suffering. There was a façade of respectability which deceived few. I was glad, on balance, when I left for Salzuflen.

I wrote to the Chaplain General prior to my release, asking that I might be considered for re-employment in the T.A., if and when that body should be reformed. I had enjoyed the work amongst the men, especially in the days as a Regimental Chaplain, and felt that, should the T.A. or some comparable organisation be created in the foreseeable future, membership of it would give me in some measure the cameraderie which I would certainly miss after six years.

During the Salzuflen period, I had opportunities to stop and inspect the graves of many of the men whom I had buried in Belgium, Holland, and Germany west of the *Rhein*. I had been impressed by the care taken of these graves in Holland and Belgium, especially the road-side ones, and also the speed and care with which the Imperial War Graves Commission were bringing in the bodies of our men to large War Cemetaries similar to those created and well-maintained after the 1914–18 war. It seemed reasonable to assume that next of kin would wish to know what was happening to the graves of their loved ones. One felt too that not a few would be planning a pilgrimage to a particular grave or graves. Consequently I sent a letter to the next of kin of my Recce boys, giving them my impressions and telling them of the War Graves Commission photograph which they would be receiving in due course:

GHQT/608/SCF
19 Sep 45.

Subject: Graves

Dear...

Please excuse this typewritten letter, but time is short and there are many photographs to be sent.

In the course of my official trips during the last few weeks, I have passed a number of graves of 43 Recce, and in each instance a photograph was taken.

When I saw Graves Registration they told me I could not send prints to relatives unless I pointed out that;

(1) they were unofficial photographs and
(2) the graves photographed might *not* be the final resting place, i.e. the single graves and small groups would one day be moved to a large Military Cemetary in some other place.

In every case I found the graves were well cared for and tidy, and even in the one instance where the tide of battle had swept back over the area, the single Recce grave was being cared for, although surrounded by wreckage, and a pot of flowers had been placed there by some civilian.

I am sorry that I have not been able to visit every grave, but seeing that I am more than 400 miles from some, it is just not possible.

You will all, in due course, be receiving the official War Graves photograph, and in the meanwhile, the enclosed photograph will assure you that the graves over here are being cared for.

I am shortly leaving the Army, and my address, if I can answer any further questions, will be (as from 1st November): Dymock Vicarage, Gloucestershire

I left the Recce for G.H.Q. Troops on the 29th March, so any question (of events) after that day had better be addressed to the new Padré.

God bless you all,
Yours very sincerely,
H.Q. G.H.Q. Troops B.A.O.R.
J.E. Gethyn-Jones
S.C.F. G.H.Q. Troops

I left Salzuflen on the 29th of September, and drove down to Ostend, where documentation began. The officer i/c demobilization asked my address, and on being told Dymock, Gloucestershire, announced that the demob centre for me would be Taunton. I explained that Taunton was some ninety miles from home, while Hereford, another demobilization centre, was only seventeen miles away. He replied:

"I am sorry, Padré, but all Gloucestershire personnel have to go to Taunton."

On being asked what would happen if my address was entered on the sheet as 'Dymock, Herefordshire', he laughed and said;

"In that case, you would be compelled to go to Hereford!" To Hereford I went!

I made a telephone call to Dymock at 2.30 p.m. from Folkestone, giving my estimated time of arrival at Hereford, and the possible time needed for the final fitting-out and documentation, thus ensuring that I would be met and be home before midnight.

An amusing incident occurred at Hereford when the demob outfits were being issued; I watched with interest while two very tall men immediately ahead in the queue were being carefully measured for their suits. This courtesy was in sharp contrast to the treatment extended when my turn came. The gentleman with the tape did not waste time measuring me, but simply shouted to the Private at the top of the bales of suits:

"Short and podgy."... and the suit that was thrown down fitted as though made for me!

Thus ended my embodied service, and I became once more a country parish priest.

Notes

1. J.E. Gethyn-Jones, Dymock Down the Ages, 2nd Edition, 1966, pp 141–2
2. 50% was the figure quoted. This was, no doubt, an exaggeration.

CHAPTER TWENTY TWO

A Padré's Pilgrimage

This chapter was written years ago for a specific event. It forms, however, an integral part of these memoirs; consequently the occasional references to incidents narrated earlier in the text are inevitable, and must be accepted.

And there was war in Heaven, Michael and his angels going forth to War with the dragon...

(*Revelations 12:7*)

From the dawn of earth's history too, there have been clashes between opposing forces. Sometimes these conflicts have been of a wordy nature, but often the outcome has meant a life and death struggle of armed men.

The battle, campaign or war over, the survivors of the armies return to their native lands, or else carve out a new kingdom for themselves.

Behind, they left much death, devastation and dejection; or liberty and high hopes—depending on the accidents of events, or on the viewpoint of the individual. Behind, too, they left something of themselves, the impression on the minds of friend or foe. Yes, important that; but important also the bodies of their comrades now resting in foreign soil.

The returned warrior told his tale of success or failure, while those at home sought by means of many searching questions to know some little of the final fleeting moments of their loved ones and of their resting places in foreign fields. This has been particularly the case since that fateful 4th of August 1914, when the modern world, the world of the aeroplane, submarine and high-explosive, began to mature.

The million and more British Empire dead of that struggle lie mostly in large military cemeteries sited in many parts of the world; and in the years closely following 1914–18, these became centres of pilgrimage for many a heartbroken, but proud, parent or wife.

1939 marked the commencement of Part II of the Anglo-German contest. After six long years, hundreds of thousands more British and Allied graves lay grouped upon the distant battlefields, while the sad sea waves formed the shroud of many of our best.

As in the 1920s, so in the late 1940s those isolated corners are being relieved of their precious burden, and the resultant military cemeteries are closely following those of the earlier generation.

The Imperial War Graves Commission have done a splendid work, and the photographs of individual graves sent by them have brought a modicum of comfort to many a saddened soul who could not visit those sacred spots. The British Legion, and other bodies, organised visits for parties of the next-of-kin and ex-servicemen. Since 1945 the Dutch people have kept the 17th of September as Arnhem Day in a manner not easily forgotten by those who have been their guests.

Early in 1947, perhaps because the T.A. was shortly to be re-born, the urge came to visit once again a few of those places whose names and memories have been indelibly written, nay seared, upon hearts and minds.

On St. George's Day (an appropriate date) my wife and I set out, and by the following evening we were in Brussels. Here the pilgrimage began.

Nearly seven years earlier a green Territorial Battalion had milled about in the the *Bois de Soignes* and had seen in the distance the famous field of Waterloo, where another band of Gloucester lads had come to oppose a tyrant's might. In one's mind the scene changes, and one sees the city as in the September of 1944; gay and happy in its liberation, swift though it came to this pleasant capital, it had not been bought without price. One thought of the hospital wards where men from further east came back to die. One of my men, Trooper A.D. Martin, died there. In the large cemetery, close to the uniform headstones of the earlier war, I found a number of wooden crosses of airmen, British and American, buried while the city was still in German hands, and of the soldiers who had lived a little longer. Each grave was neat and tidy, and spring flowers blossomed on every hand; Belgium honoured her dead liberators as she had fêted the living.

The following day, with a Belgian Red Cross and ex-resistance worker as interpreter, we came to Bruyelle where, in mid-May 1940, 144 Brigade had had its first engagement since the 5th Glosters had fought the skirmishes at Grindorff, and in the *Grossenwald* a month before. The village was much as it had been seven years earlier, except that now people moved about freely, and even the backfire of a lorry did not clear the street as a similar sound would have done in 1940. The hundred or so graves in the small military cemetery appeared dishevelled at first sight, but on examination one realised that a huge change-over was taking place. The German crosses (or were they the Red Cross crosses?) were being replaced by the official I.W.G.C. temporary crosses, and in many cases, the two (they were of different lengths) were cheek-by-jowl on the same grave. In addition, I noticed two ladies—one a girl whose brother had died soon after the day (May 20/21) that the Glosters and Worcesters had suffered heavily in that village, and the other a woman whose husband had survived the war—cleaning some of the crosses and weeding the graves. The three-cornered plot was almost bare of grass, but flowers were blossoming on most of the graves. One felt that the locals were doing their best to help forward the formation of this Garden of Remembrance.

On the next day, we headed for Deventer. The run was broken on several occasions to visit scenes I remembered well. At Dièst, we took the road to Zéal and looked at the Burgermeister's house where, early in September 1944, I shared a billet with 'C' Squadron, who were acting as Defence Troop for T.A.C. H.Q. 2nd Army, and personal bodyguard to General Dempsey. The Germans were on the run then, and the talk had been of 'how many days until the end?' Little did we think, in those pleasant surroundings and with the euphoria of the rapid advance, that the grim struggle on 'the Island', the eerie month near Geilenkirchen and the fierce fighting of Kleve, Goch and the *Reichswald* and in the flooded area eastward to the *Rhein*, lay ahead.

On the road to Eindhoven we saw the twisted wreckage of some '88's which, well placed and camouflaged, had knocked out the leading troop of tanks of the Guards' Armoured Division who, with the

43rd Division were the force briefed to link us with the First (British) Airborne Division at Arnhem. My wife's cousin had been lucky at that spot; his tank had brewed up when hit, but three of the crew, all badly wounded and burned, had crawled out and lain in a ditch for twenty-four hours before they were found, more dead than alive. We saw the graves of their troop comrades in a little break in the pine trees a short distance away. This was a temporary resting place and soon, no doubt, their mortal remains would be placed in some nearby British Military Cemetery.

At Uden Cemetery, we found the grave of Lance-Corporal E. Hawes, whom I had buried in September 1944 at Opheusden. I pictured that morning burial; Lance-Corporal Hawe's armoured car had been hit. Lieutenant Davies and Trooper L.G. Scott, under fire, brought Hawes back to the town centre. Opheusden was one of the prettiest large villages, or small towns, I have seen in any country. I asked permission to dig a grave in a plot of ground in the churchyard nearby, but I was told 'Our Liberator' must be placed in the garden in the town centre, 'where our people can tend his grave and pray for his soul and for his family'. Perhaps I might tell the sequel. Some days later, the town, then held by the 101st American Airborne Division, was bombed flat. Opheusden was no more. In September 1945, on my way back to Ostend and demobilization, I called to see the grave. In horror, I viewed the piles of rubble that had been the picturesque town of Opheusden. A patient search failed to locate the object of my search. Then, as if in answer to an unuttered prayer, a woman, the left sleeve of her blouse empty, emerged from a cellar, saying;

"English, comrade?"

We clambered over a huge pile of masonry—all that was left of the Church, the *Mairie*, and the houses in the centre of the town—and there in the centre of that chaos stood a battered, but repaired, wooden cross. It was obvious that many tons of débris had been cleared to expose the grave and its damaged symbol. Fresh flowers were on the grave. 'Our Liberator' was still remembered by people who had suffered as few have suffered. Unashamedly, I wept.

At Nijmegen bridge, I thought of the gallant action of the American Airborne and the tanks of the Grenadiers which had secured this vital river crossing, and of the splinters which hit my car when a shell burst nearby. The engine was still working, the wheels were still intact, but the driver had stopped and said:

"What shall we do now, sir?"

He was unhurt, and all I had was a scratch on the face and knee. My reply had suggested that we drive off that obvious target, to the comparative safety of the Island!

In Deventer, we met Tommy Zwollo, the Dutch Resistance man who had joined us on the night of 22nd/23rd of September, when the Regiment crossed the bridge.

The following day, with Tommy as interpreter, we passed through Nijmegen to Warmel and Dreumel where, on the 26th of October 1944, a patrol of nineteen, including Tommy and another Dutchman, were ambushed. Only four, all wounded, had returned that day. Five of our men and the second Dutchman had been killed, and the rest taken prisoner. Tommy took me over the fort, and explained what had happened. 'A' Squadron H.Q. looked much as it had done in 1944, but the church tower at Dreumel had fallen.

That afternoon, we drove rapidly to Jennep, and approached the German frontier road leading to the Reichswald and Kleve. The Chaplain General (Canon F. Ll. Hughes) and other bodies such as the I.W.G.C. had tried to obtain permission for me to cross into Germany to photograph the graves of my men in the Reichswald Cemetery. They failed; Control Commission would have nothing to do with the project. A few cigarettes, however, produced from the frontier guard, by way of the interpreter, the information that the C.C.G. patrol was not expected before 6 p.m., and that the C.M.P.s and the German patrol had made their daily inspection. More cigarettes changed hands and my wife (who would not be left; she had said, "If you go to jug, I will come with you!"—what a wife!) and I were through for a quick visit—Tommy, naturally, remained behind. To this new military cemetery were being brought the remains of those killed in the bitter fighting in the Kleve, Reichswald, Goch and Zanten area. The task of centralisation was at that time incomplete, and conditions were such that I felt that the photographing of individual graves was inadvisable. We found the graves of several of my lads including Sergeant J.F. Darvel M.M., Corporal B. Viggars and Sergeant C.F. Cawthorne. Looking at those rough wooden crosses, which I had myself placed on the pathetic little mounds at the roadsides and in the fields between Kleve and Zanten, my mind conjured up the events of two years earlier, and especially of those black days of February 12th to 15th; black, because so many of our ablest and best became casualties; black, not only for the 43rd

Recce, but also for the Wiltshire, Somerset and Worcester Battalions of our Division in the attack from Kleve, down the eastern side of the forest to Goch; black also for the 53rd Welch, who were blasting their way throught the *Reichswald* itself, alongside the 15th and 51st Scottish Divisions. Great glory had been won by these four Divisions in that pincer movement to clear the western bank of the *Rhein*. They had forced a fanatical German defence, set in ideal defensive country, first to bend and finally to break; but the cost had been heavy—the serried ranks of crosses in the *Reichswald* told, partially, the tally.

On our way back to Deventer, we called to see the new cemetery at Nijmegen, which was only just beginning to take shape. We found the grave of Lieutenant Lindsay Baker M.C.. Lindsay had been one of our best Troop Officers and had won a fine Military Cross at the *Seine* bridgehead in August '44. Later, he had been given leave when coming out of hospital. But he refused this and returned to the Regiment 'so as not to miss the final party'. At 5.00 a.m. the very next morning, a sniper's bullet closed a chapter. A Dutch family tended the little roadside grave, and when I visited it a few months later, meshed wire protected the plot from any stray animals, the grave was paved with stone slabs, and flowers grew between them.

The next day, we visited the communal cemetery at Utrecht, where Trooper R. Merritt of the ill-fated Dreumel patrol was buried. On our way to Nijmegen, where we were to spend the night, we made enquiries in the area opposite the fort across the *Waal*, whether any English soldiers had been buried in the locality. Several blanks were followed by a gleam of hope that at least one of our missing dead from the patrol might be located. A Dutchman took us to a schoolmaster who understood a little French. These two conferred, then the latter said he knew of the grave of an unknown Englishman. A short trip along twisty riverside roads, and we came to a rough cross, bearing on it the letters J.W. WALKER—one of our patrol. The I.W.G.C. were very grateful. With the sun lowering, we passed again the fort, and on through Dreumel and Maasbommel (where a certain doctor had been 'impervious' to heavy rain) to Nijmegen.

The following day, we travelled to Brunnsum where, in November 1944, a small Divisional cemetery had been sited in an orchard. Even before we left the area in January 1945, it had begun to take shape and form. On that May day, with the fruit trees in full blossom, the tiny cemetery looked a picture; every single grave seemed to have been adopted by families from Brunnsum, Heerleheide, Heerlen and other villages or towns where the 43rd and 52nd Divisions, who had taken over from us in December had had their 'out-of-line' billets. In Heerlen that night, we discussed old times. Mrs Boer and Hank, her husband, in whose house Doc and I shared a room off and on for three weeks, spoke of the weekly pilgrimage that many people made on Sundays to Brunnsum and the huge American cemetery at Margratten. Mrs Boer had adopted the grave of an American who had stayed at 23 Station Straße just before we arrived, and I am certain that had Doc Ellis or I 'bought it' during that period, she and Hank would have visited our graves at Brunnsum.

The following day we left early for Margratten, where Lance-Corporal N. Taylor and Trooper O.G. Bademan, who had died of wounds in an American Field Dressing Station at Geilenkirchen, had been buried. The Americans had begun the gigantic task of transferring the entire American Section (something over twenty thousand) back to the states. The British dead were scheduled to be moved to the British Cemetry at Venry in Holland.

From Margratten we drove to Château Schoonbeck where R.H.Q. had bivouacked for a night, on the way down to the *Mass* when Von Rundstedt began his Ardennes offensive in December '44. That night after dinner we went to the woodland grave of an unidentified British airman, and the following day we were taken to another lonely R.A.F. grave. Once more, the tulips *en masse* showed the care and consideration for those whose lives had been given for a cause.

At Schoonbeck we rested for a few days; we needed it after the strenuous days of travel and, in my case at least, a great deal of emotional tension. The Châteleine, Comtesse Natalie de Rénesse, was most kind to us, as indeed she had been to our Regiment in the days of war; and when we left on the road for Bérlo, we felt we had known Madame for many years.

At Bérlo, where H.Q. Squadron and part of R.H.Q. had been based over Christmas '44, we spent a further two days before returning to Brussels. Madame la Comtesse was a great (and imperious) lady. During the days of occupation, she had terrified the local German troops, and flayed a wretched Major when he had suggested billeting himself and his staff at the Château. She was, too, a woman of cold courage, who aided a number of soldiers and airmen to freedom. The Gestapo suspected the Comtesse and her three nieces, but were outwitted in the dangerous game of hide and seek. The second night at Bérlo we had an unusual experience; we were taken out to dinner in a chauffeur-driven ex-American wartime 'Champ'.

At 10.00 p.m. on May the 8th, having picked up the eldest niece of the Comtesse in Brussels earlier in the day, we landed in England and our 1947 pilgrimage was over.

A few days later, the photographs of the graves were developed and, through the kindness of the *Gloucester Citizen*, a contact print and a 6x4 enlargement were sent to the next of kin, together with the following letter:

The Vicarage
Dymock
Glos

June 1947

Dear...,

A little over two years ago the War in Europe ended, but unfortunately many thousands, who left their homes to fight for the safety of their loved ones, did not return. They, the real person, began the Greater Life to which one day you and I will be called. Their earthly shell, the body, was laid to rest in many distant parts of the world. Those graves and Cemeteries will become places of pilgrimage in the days to come, and indeed in some cases have already become such centres.

During late April and early May, I visited most of the graves of the men of our Regiment (5th Glosters, later 43rd Recce Regiment) in Belgium, Holland and Germany west of the Rhine—I hope to visit France (Saar, Dunkirk and Normandy areas) next year.

Belgium: The graves of 1940 were now, of course, all in Military Cemeteries, and were very well kept.

The Imperial War Graves Commission have replaced all the old crosses with more permanent ones, and have corrected slight errors that may have existed on the original crosses—often erected by Belgians civilian or Germans. Oftentimes the two crosses are there, and presumably will remain until the final Regimental stone or cross has been erected.

The graves of 1944, too, are now mainly in Military Cemeteries and well cared for.

In the Military Cemetery at Bruyelle two ladies were 'spring cleaning' and in consequence some of the photographs will show crosses lying on their sides or at an angle, to enable the second cross behind to be cleaned.

Holland: In Holland the task of bringing in the graves to large central Military Cemeteries was progressing—in fact all 43rd Recce

Regiment, except two, had been removed to their final resting place. Because work was progressing in some of these cemeteries it was not possible to photograph all graves.

Germany: In Germany, West of the Rhine, too, this difficult task was being carried out with great reverence and care, and here too photography was not yet allowed.

The Imperial War Graves Commission will, when their task is completed, be sending you an official photograph of the permanent grave. In the meanwhile, I am sending you an unofficial photograph, or if I have not been able to photograph the grave you wish to see, for the reasons stated above, then I am sending you a photograph which will give you some idea of how well the graves and cemeteries are maintained.

Many civilians make a weekly pilgrimage to our cemeteries to bring flowers and to say a short prayer for 'their liberators'.

I visited many villages and districts where our Boys either fought or were billeted while on rest, and everywhere I found that the Regiment had left a wonderful name—a name second to none in the whole British 2nd Army. If our Boys were 'their liberators', they were at the same time Britain's finest ambassadors.

You will be anxious to visit these 'corners of a foreign land that are forever England,' but I would like to advise you *very strongly* to defer this until a little later date, say 1948/9 so that when you make your pilgrimage you will see the whole picture in its more or less final setting. It would have been a gigantic task to write all these letters by hand, so the 'Citizen' of Gloucester very kindly offered to print them, and also to print the photographs I have taken, and I should like to thank them for their kind co-operation and help.

Yours very sincerely,

J.E. Gethyn-Jones
(One time Padre to 5th Gloster 43rd Recce Regt.)

CHAPTER TWENTY THREE

Reformation

In January 1947, it was announced that the Territorial Army would shortly be reformed. All holding T.A. Commissions were notified that if they wished to maintain unbroken service, they would need to apply for re-employment before 1st November 1947. I sent in my request immediately but, apart from an acknowledgement that my communication had been received, nothing happened for six months.

One day in July, the telephone bell in my study rang. On lifting the receiver I heard a voice saying,

"Is that the Bishop of Dymock?"

It was the Revd. Lloyd-Evans, who had been instrumental in the cancellation at the fifty-ninth minute of the eleventh hour of the posting order which would have severed my connection with the 5th Glosters in 1941. He was now D.A.C.G. of South-West District, again stationed in Taunton, and had, *inter alia*, the task of supervising the building up of the chaplains team for the newly reformed 43rd (Wessex) Infantry Division of the Territorial Army.

Over a cup of coffee in the Bell at Gloucester on the following day, he asked me whether I would, if selected by the War Office and approved by the Divisional Commander, take on the duties of Senior Chaplain of the Division. I accepted this provisional invitation with delight.

Some weeks later, my wife and I were summoned to dine with General Sims, the Divisional Commander. I was also requested to bring with me any of my photographs of the 43rd Division which might be in my collection. The invitation was very formal, and gave full instructions in regard to dress. All this put myself and my dear wife into a bit of a flap—could she find a suitable evening frock, and could I get into my pre-war dinner jacket? New outfits were out of the question financially, and in any case, clothes rationing was still in operation.

I well remember the preparations and the subsequent 'vetting'. On the Saturday before the dinner party, Vivienne, who had been digging out a suitable creation for herself, and pressing my old dinner jacket suit, suddenly announced that she must have two rabbits at once. Duke and Duchess, our two spaniels, were delighted at this unexpected outing. It was at the dinner party the following Tuesday that the reason for this urgent request for rabbits revealed itself. While drinking a glass of sherry before dinner, I became conscious of what felt like a penny on my knee, underneath my trouser leg. It proved to be a patch stuck on the trouser from inside, filling a large moth hole. A closer inspection revealed a number of other puncture patches on both legs of the trousers! Luckily for my peace of mind, dinner was announced at this moment of truth. Afterwards, when showing the General the wartime photographs of the Division, the album firmly placed on my knees to cover the patch-holes, I suddenly noticed a large, unpatched moth hole in the cuff of my left sleeve. The Commander, spotting that I had seen the hole, laughed and said,

"That is one your wife missed, Padré!"

The party then went with a swing, and on December 1st, I was posted to the 43rd Division as its new S.C.F..

One chaplain had already been accepted for a T.A. commission within the Division, but the remaining fourteen vacancies had few possible candidates. The aforementioned chaplain was a gentleman with a good war record and many excellent qualities. He was an able man, and was rarely at a loss, while his interests in civilian life were numerous and varied. Did the Mess require a side of bacon or smoked ham when rationing was still rigid? Was the N.A.A.F.I. short of cigarettes or beer? Did Private 'X' need petrol to return from camp to see his daughter who had been rushed to hospital? This padré was equal to each and every crisis. On one occasion he invited me to shoot with him. Fortunately, it was an impossible date. I say fortunate, because the day had been selected in view of the absence of the local land-owner, a man who reared many pheasants; but I only learned this later! Although we did not always see eye to eye on certain matters, I was nevertheless very sorry when he left the Division.

During the winter of 1947-48, and well on into the summer, I interviewed some twenty-five or thirty clerics in connection with possible commissions into the T.A., and slowly but surely the team began to take shape. I had been advised by the D.A.C.G. to hasten slowly, to see personally every candidate, and to be somewhat choosy in the selection of chaplains; for he rightly pointed out that it was easy enough to bring them in, but it would be ducedly hard to get them out if they proved to be below the required standard. This was sound advice. I may have lost one or two good chaplains through this policy, but it saved me on several occasions from bringing in men with whom the units would undoubtedly have been disatisfied.

The first Divisional chaplain's conference was held at Bagshot in April 1948. The Chaplain-General and the D.C.G. came down and took part. We were delighted with their attitude towards the T.A. and the civilian parson, which contrasted markedly with the pre-1939 outlook. We now felt we were wanted and were part and parcel of the Department. Conditions of service, too, were greatly changed. No longer was it required or possible to visit every company each month, as had been expected before the war. The reasons for this change were many; for example, the units had much larger areas of recruitment, petrol rationing was still in force and, last but not least, parochial clergy were fewer on the ground and could not spare the time which their predecessors had been able to set aside for work in the T.A.. Camp was now the main obligatory duty, and everything over and above this—and many chaplains did a great deal more—was looked upon by the unit with considerable pleasure.

In those early days of 1948-49, we had the nucleus of a first class team; the Rev. George Hailes M.C., a wartime D.A.C.G. of the Airborne Corps, the Rev. David Wild M.B.E. M.C. T.D., who had been such a tower of strength in the P.O.W. camps after being captured in 1940 near Dunkirk, the Rev. Barry Wainwright, and the Rev. Dick Cullington. They came from widely separated areas; Hailes from Wiltshire, Wild from Oxford, Wainwright from Devon and Cullington from Cornwall, all of which were within the Divisional boundary. These were men of vision, men of experience and above all, men of God. The 43rd Division was fortunate that clergy of this calibre offered themselves for work in the Territorial Army.

CHAPTER TWENTY FOUR

Peacetime Activities – a Brief Survey

The work of the Senior Chaplain in a T.A. Division in peacetime was more remote and less personal than that of his colleague in embodied days. During the war all around one, day by day, were the personnel of H.Q., and the chaplains too were usually within easy striking distance. We were together as a corporate body with no outside obligations.

In the peacetime T.A., the personnel of the 43rd Division and, so too the chaplains were scattered over the seven counties of the South West and, excepting the small number of Regulars, we all had our civilian occupations which had to be our first concern. Consequently, the Senior Chaplain rarely saw the members of H.Q. Staff all together, except during a Divisional Camp. Thus it was obvious that he had to concentrate most of his time throughout the year on his chaplains, who were the persons on whom the spiritual work within the Division largely depended. This entailed seeing them at every opportunity, listening to them, and getting to know their Commanding Officers upon whose good will so much of the unit chaplain's work depended. In other words, it meant trying to be available to each chaplain (perhaps fourteen) by post or in person, to help, support and, very very occasionally, defend him. Fortunately, in the 43rd Division the relationship between chaplains and their C.O.s, especially in the early days, was excellent. This was due in no small measure to the fact that in most cases the chaplains and C.O.s had seen war service, and each knew the value of the other. And indeed those early chaplains of the 43rd team contained men of great distinction, such as David Wilde, who had been a tower of strength for five years in prison camps, and George Hailes, who had become a D.A.C.G. in the Paras. That tradition of co-operation was generally maintained when new blood was injected into the system. The Senior Chaplain did, however, ensure that his concern for his chaplains did not prevent him from trying to get to know the Divisional H.Q. Staff, for they were his family, and it was they who could advise him, and assist the work and life of the unit chaplains.

I began my *Apologia* by saying that the basic daily work beyond his own personal devotions of the unit chaplain in war—pastoral visiting, welfare work, prayers, services and so on—would bore with repetition, but must always be remembered; so too, the pastoral life of the T.A. Senior Chaplin must be recognised and accepted, though rarely recorded. In the case of the T.A. D.A.C.G., life became even more remote because of one's civilian commitments, which had to be the primary obligation. Consequently, in this final chapter, covering almost fourteen years, and because this work is a type of autobiography, it will only be possible to select certain events which exemplify not the more important pastoral work, but the more unusual, infrequent duties or incidents which left a deep impression.

The Annual Camp was in many ways the most important event in the calendar of the T.A. units at all levels. We met together, usually for two weeks, in Brigade groups or as a complete Division. Life for the Senior Chaplain was much easier, and probably more fruitful, when the entire Division was in the field at the same time and in the same area. Thetford (Norfolk), Castle Martin (Pembrokeshire), Dartmoor and Cornwall, as well as Salisbury Plain, became well-known camp-sites for the troops of Southern Command and the 43rd Division.

Perhaps the most important of these annual camps was the Divisional Atomic War Exercise (code-named Ethen Down) which took place in September 1955 on Salisbury Plain. It brought home the fact that war as we had known it, horrifying as it had been at times, had irrevocably changed. We realised two things; firstly that atomic war on a general scale would produce such devastation that even Hiroshima and Nagasaki would appear trivial. At the same time, it became clear that, given training preparation and thought, a percentage of the forces and civilians could hope to survive.

The camp which lives most vividly in my memory, however, took place in Castle Martin in 1959. It was a Brigade grouping, but as they had only one chaplain able to attend camp, I went down for the last few days, which covered the drum-head Service and the final considerable exercise. Perhaps the fact that the Glosters were in that Brigade was an additional attraction. The Drum-head Service was shared with Padré Crofts. Later came a day-and-night exercise involving a long and tough approach march (in full battle kit) over rough and often boggy ground, which was, as intended, merely a preparation for the formidable night attack on the Mynydd Preseli (highest point 1760 feet) and, at dawn, the drive through the marsh on the far side, after which we ate our breakfast. Directly the meal ended, units were lorried back to camp to be ready for a formal inspection. All this ended around mid-day. At two o'clock, I started out for home, nearly 150 miles away. I was dog-tired, the afternoon was hot, and twice I dozed off and hit the kerb. A little later, near Llandeilo, I must have dropped off completely, for I awoke suddenly to find myself driving up a bank, luckily a gentle one with no fences. On returning to the road, I paused, and suddenly remembered a quarry a few miles away. There I pulled in and slept for three hours before continuing the drive—so nearly had a serious accident been avoided.

In the cause of closer co-operation between the T.A. and the Regular Army, T.A. chaplains occasionally did their annual camp with Regular units in B.A.O.R. (Germany) while the Regular chaplains took their places in T.A. camps. This scheme was warmly welcomed by all chaplains, but ended (probably because of the costs involved) after a short while. My turn came in 1950, when I had a week with the King's Liverpools, and the second week with the Enniskillen Dragoon Guards.

On another occasion, major units of the T.A. exercised with the British Army of the Rhine. The 43rd Division, in skeleton form, took part in such an exercise in the late fifties. During these manoeuvres, I met several wartime personnel of the 43rd, such as Aubrey Coad, by then a Major-General.

Special parades added welcome variety and interest to the work of all T.A. chaplains. Often these parades were occasioned by the laying up of old Colours and the receiving of the new ones. Normally, the unit chaplain, the Senior Chaplain, and often the D.A.C.G., would be on parade and usually took some part, while the Chaplain General or one of the Assistant Chaplains General normally consecrated the new Colours.

In addition, the 43rd Division held three services of great poignancy when most chaplains were present. These were the unveiling of the Divisional Memorials at strategically placed sites in the area. The first, at Mere in Hampshire, was preceded by a service in Salisbury Cathedral, when the Book of Remembrance was laid up.[1] This took place on 21st May 1949. The unveiling was performed by General Sir Ivor Thomas, our wartime Commander. Indeed, he carried out this ceremony on all three occasions. The second memorial, at Wynyards Gap in Dorset, was unveiled on 20th September 1952. The Dorset Regiment have held several anniversary services at intervals at that memorial, and have most kindly invited me to take the service and preach. The final memorial was at Rough Tor on Bodmin Moor on 4th September 1954.

Promotion to D.A.C.G. Southern Command came in 1956. This increased responsibility, for the Corps troops were numerous, and located over the whole of the Command area. The policy of allocation of time had to be the same, with chaplains receiving priority. We in Southern Command were extremely fortunate in that, by and large, the T.A. chaplain was fully recognised and appreciated. This attitude was largely due, I believe, to the presence and influence of the Rev. D.D. Lloyd-Evans in his various capacities when in Southern Command. Later too, when he became D.C.G., he fought our battles. It was at the highest levels that the T.A. chaplain was occasionally forgotten, and necessitated action on the part of the D.A.C.G., T.A.. On one occasion, Her Majesty was presenting new Colours to eight cavalry units, three of whom were T.A., including one from Southern Command. Despite this, no T.A. chaplain was selected to be on that important ceremonial parade. It was pointed out in no uncertain terms that at least one chaplain from the three T.A. units receiving Colours should be on the parade.

Pay and allowances, too, occasionally necessitated vigorous protests by the T.A. S.C.F. or the D.A.C.G..

Personally, I felt that promotion was where the T.A. chaplains really had a raw deal. I was able to stress this defect in the system because I came in to the reformed T.A. as a 3rd class chaplain, and became 2nd class (D.A.C.G.) at the one and only promotion to that rank between 1947 and 1961. All commissioned combatant

T.A. personnel received some promotion by seniority or length of service. Because there was only one D.A.C.G. and two S.C.F. per Command, many able chaplains could expect no promotion even after ten or fifteen years. The chaplains accepted the situation loyally, but I felt that it was iniquitous. I fought this policy for years, suggesting *inter alia* that promotion to Brevet rank of C.F. class 3 should be granted to chaplains after a certain number of years. After a long struggle, a compromise was accepted by the Chaplain General's office. There would be a limitation of tenure of the office of D.A.C.G., thus ensuring at least one promotion to D.A.C.G. and S.C.F. every three or four years. This was not a great concession, but it was something. The most amusing result, of which naturally I was aware, was that I was the first to be retired to the T.A.R.O., though on the old ruling I still had three and a half years to run!

1958 marked a milestone in the history of the T.A., for it was in April 1908, under Lord Haldane (Secretary of state for War, 1905–1912), that this new force was born of the old Yeomanry and Volunteers.

To mark this Golden Jubilee, on the 22nd June in Hyde Park, Her Majesty reviewed some eight thousand Territorials, representing all branches of the Service. In other parts of the country, parades, services and other gatherings were held with this theme in mind.

Here in the West, one of these functions was a Thanksgiving Service in Bristol Cathedral, at which I was invited to preach.

It was probably with the Jubilee in mind that I was selected to consecrate a *guidon* which Her Majesty was presenting to the Warwick and Worcestershire Yeomanry at Pembroke Castle on the 8th June. The Consecration of Colours were normally performed by the Chaplain General, the D.C.G., or one of the Assistant Chaplains General. It was a very rare distinction for a T.A. chaplain to be called upon. When he read of the Pembroke ceremony, my Bishop spoke to me, and said,

"My dear Gethyn-Jones, you cannot consecrate a *guidon* or anything else, for you are not a bishop."

"My Lord," I replied, "Her Majesty is Head of the Church of England, and if Her Majesty orders me, as she has done, to consecrate the *guidon* then consecrate it I will, and I am sure the Almighty will accept the offering." After quite a pause, His Lordship replied,

"Well, perhaps so."

And that was that! It was one of those days which will always be remembered.

The third distinction which came my way that year was the privilege of being one of Her Majesty's chaplains at the unveiling of the Memorial to the Land Forces of the Commonwealth. This took place on the 25th of October at Brookwood.

In 1959, Her Majesty most graciously appointed me one of her Honorary Chaplains. This, of course, was the climax of my Army career and, I consider, the greatest honour I could ever receive. Perhaps 1958 had been a leading-up to this appointment. Vivienne too shared in this distinction in that we were invited to attend certain Garden Parties at Buckingham Palace.

It was in 1959 too (on the 29th of October) that the Chaplain General entrusted me with the task of taking Colonel Fred Carne's stone cross, carved in a prisoner of war camp in Korea, from Gloucester to Chichester, where it was to be a major centre-piece at a Services Exhibition.

Notes

1. On examining the Book, I found that the names of three chaplains who had been killed in Normandy in August 1944 had been omitted. This mistake was quickly corrected.

CHAPTER TWENTY-FIVE

Reflections

By comparison with the years 1958–9, 1960 was quiet, and in 1961 came my transfer to the Territorial Army Reserve (T.A.R.O.). This enabled Ettrick Eynon to receive the promotion he had fully earned, thereby making it possible for an able and experienced 4th class chaplain to be upgraded to 3rd class as Senior Chaplain of the 43rd Division. On the old system of age retirement, I would have served on for a further three and a half years as D.A.C.G., T.A.—the highest rank permitted to a T.A. chaplain in peacetime. The new Chaplain General, my old friend Ivan D. Neill, who had been Senior Chaplain of the 43rd Division during the latter part of the war, had seen and endorsed my earlier recommendation, advocated soon after becoming D.A.C.G..

Thus ended almost twenty-three years of service with the T.A., in peace and in war. From those years, and especially the war years, I learned much which later undoubtedly helped me in my civilian ministry. I can never fully express my gratitude for the guidance, help, support and, above all, the friendship extended by all ranks and, of course, especially from those of the 5th Glosters/43rd Recce Regiment. This unbelievable support is fully exemplified in the fact that, as recorded earlier, over fifty men openly volunteered to become Padre's Helpers in operations, and were fully prepared to have their names published in regimental orders. One of the few survivors of that brave band, ex-Sergeant Stanley Midgley, is now a sidesman at Berkeley Church, and we meet most Sunday evenings.

During those long war years, there were times when I was extremely frightened (who wasn't?), and others when I almost cursed the day I had joined the T.A., usually when red tape caused great frustration. Those moments, however, quickly passed and I realised how lucky (or fortunate; call it what you will) I was and had been. Today, in the twilight of my ministry, I am even more conscious of what I owe to the members of the Glosters and Recce units, and certain members of the R.A.Ch.D., notably D.D. Lloyd-Evans and Ivan D. Neill.

At the same time, when looking back over my T.A. and embodied service, I realise that at times I must have been a very difficult chaplain, from the point of view of the R.A.Ch.D. hierarchy. In addition, I occasionally refused to accept certain Army regulations which I felt were totally wrong. This applied mainly to burial procedure. In April 1940, I took an Anglican burial service over six German soldiers killed that morning by our men in the Grossenwald battle ahead of the Maginôt Line; this should not have been done. Similarly, a non-Roman Catholic chaplain was forbidden by King's Regulations to take a service when burying a Roman Catholic soldier. I always took a service, because I considered that King's Regulations, on this point, were callous and un-Christian.

Again, at times I crossed swords with my Senior Chaplain or D.A.C.G., usually when I thought he was being too officious. The only two 'serious' confrontations took place in the Dover days, when perhaps my rather violent reactions, even if understandable, were culpable. The first flare-up took place when the D.A.C.G. Dover Area, at a weekly Chaplain's Meeting, attempted to cross-examine me about my wife's visit to a local vicarage. The Vicar was a godson of my maternal grandfather. I replied that this was a personal matter and that it was no concern of his, for technically I was not under his command. Finally, exasperated by his persistence, I said,

"Sir, inordinate curiosity killed the cat. I will continue to take services for your unit near me, but I will attend no more of your meetings."...and stormed out.

The dust only settled weeks later after the D.A.C.G. apologized for the unwarranted intrusion into personal affairs, and I for being rude to a senior officer.

On the other occasion, I deliberately kept a brand-new, very officious (and objectionable) S.C.F. waiting for twenty minutes, which I spent reading the daily newspaper in a convenient 'loo'. On my final arrival at the office, the S.C.F. flew into a rage.

When he had finished his tirade, during which I had not said a word, I told him that if his officious new-broom attitude continued, he would receive little or no co-operation from his chaplains. And I reminded him that I, too, was a priest, and that the crowns on his shoulder signified nothing to me when it came to priestly work in my unit and in the division.

I felt that I did other things that were reprehensible, but only one which I believe in retrospect was utterly wrong. It was, as narrated earlier, going on patrol with the Worcesters during the Saar operations. This, I later realised, was extremely culpable. I did not put anyone in physical danger, because I knew that I could handle a revolver as well as anyone else on the patrol, and had proved it on the ranges before we came to the Saar. But (and it was a big 'but') had anything gone wrong that morning, the poor wretched subaltern leading the patrol might well have been court-martialled, and the R.A.Ch.D. would have been badly disgraced.

My fracas with Colonel Buxton, also in the Saar, was caused by lack of diplomacy on my part. That I was correct in my intentions was obvious, but my method of approach to the situation was badly at fault. That the Colonel later recognised this was patent when, in 1941, he appealed to the War Office for my retention with the unit when I had been posted to another Division. Further, after the war, he left a request in his Will, that I should be traced and asked to take his funeral. This I did.

The two very senior chaplains to whom I owe most for guidance and support during my Army career were, as mentioned earlier, Revd. D.D. Lloyd-Evans and Revd. Ivan D. Neill, who became Deputy Chaplain General and Chaplain General respectively. I blew my top with them on several occasions, but in true Christian spirit, they turned the other cheek. I still have a letter from the former, after I had let off steam in a letter to him when he was D.C.G.. An extract shows his forgiving nature and his wise counsel:

> I know you are not getting at me—I'm glad you've blown up to me and not to anyone else. I think we've got that arrangement that when you are brewing up for a bloody row, you open up on me. I then take it and inwardly digest it—and tear up the letter... Your next step, Quite clear. Say Nowt. I will summon you up here

> early in Jan. By that time we shall know something of the fight on point I...

Random Recollections:

Of the numerous Regimental, Divisional and Command ceremonies, in which I was involved, several stand out in my recollections.

The first was the most difficult and mentally exhausting commission of my service career.[1] The 1st Glosters, just before they sailed for Korea, held a parade service at Dymock Church at which Colonel Fred Carne and Captain Pat Angier had read the lessons. It will be remembered that in late April 1951 the Glosters fought that epic battle of the Imjin River and disappeared—but by their resolution they had saved the Allied Forces. A few days later, at a Drill Hall Conference in Gloucester, it was decided to hold a Service of Intercession and Commemoration for the 'Lost Battalion' on 17th June at Gloucester Cathedral. The meeting insisted that I should give the Address, because of my close association with so many of the missing Battalion. I had strongly pressed that the Bishop, Dr. Woodward, whose nephew was in the 1st Battalion, should preach. Emotionally, this was frightening. To add to my worries, because the service was national news, there came many hostile letters and telephone calls from the anti-war lobby and peace campaigners, who even attacked me as I entered the Cathedral. I survived as, thank God, did so many of the missing Battalion. The following year, I dedicated a Memorial Garden to Pat Angier and his brother.

Most of the other well remembered extra-Regimental ceremonies had humourous moments which probably account for their retention in the memory.

The Coronation of Queen Elizabeth II took place on 2nd June 1953, but for many thousands the preparations for that great day began weeks, indeed months, before that date. One of the most vivid memories of 1952–3 is centred on the Coronation.

In January 1953, a letter arrived stating that I had been selected as one of the four Territorial chaplains and eight Regulars who would represent the Royal Army Chaplains' Department on the Coronation march. It was pointed out in no uncertain terms that considerable training must be undertaken to ensure that we would stay the 13½ mile course and be firmly on our feet for approximately twelve hours.

A manual of personal preparation was drawn up.

Stage One was purely parochial. The car and bicycle were virtually 'stalled', and visiting was carried out almost entirely on foot. The parish of Dymock was some four miles by three, which entailed a great deal of walking.

After a month of parochial perambulations, Phase Two of the schedule began. This consisted of walking twice a week to Ledbury, a small market town four miles away, where the hospital was visited and minor shopping undertaken before returning on foot.

In March, the switch was made to the Gloucester route. That city was thirteen miles from the parsonage.

At first, I walked in, visited the hospitals, and then came back by bus. After a fortnight, the return journey also was made on foot, after a light meal, giving a round trip of some twenty-six miles. This final stage caused no problems. Indeed, the only embarrassing episodes during the whole five months of preparation came during phases Two and Three, when parishioners driving past stopped and kindly offered a lift to their poor parson whose car they assumed had broken down. Later they tooted their horns and waved a friendly greeting to the padding padré.

Finally came the military-imposed period of drill and ceremonial manoeuvres, preparing the fourteen chaplains (twelve, plus two reserves in case casualties occurred during these exacting sessions) for the great day. Most of these exercises took place at Bagshot Park, the R.A.Ch.D. Depot, when a senior Drill Instructor from the Scots Guards called the tune, and new suits of Blues and peaked caps were issued.

The party, in single line, marched, wheeled and halted, repeating the movements, and others, almost from dawn to dusk, and gradually acquired the art of keeping our dress reasonably well (though the instructor did not always agree!).

Before the week ended, I was profoundly thankful for the stamina built up by the Ledbury and Gloucester route-marches during the preceding five months. The move from Bagshot to Olympia took place on Saturday, May 30th, and on the Sunday we were taken round the course, preparatory to a rehearsal on the Monday.

Coronation Day began early, with the magnificent news that Everest had at last been conquered by two members of the British expedition, E.P. Hilary and Sherpa Tenzing; led by Sir John Hunt.

Movement of marching columns began around 6.00 a.m., and a long halt took place in the Green Park, at the bottom of Constitution Hill near the Palace. Here, final refreshments were available, and other vital necessities were at hand. Slowly, the day moved on with alternating rain and sunshine.

After the Coronation Service had ended, the Sovereign, and the vast escorting body of troops of all arms and peoples, began the return journey from the Abbey to the Palace, via Whitehall, Piccadilly, Hyde Park, Oxford Street, Regent Street and the Mall.

As far as I was concerned, all went well until we came to Oxford Street, when I became conscious of a splitting headache which grew rapidly worse. In Regent Street, the buildings on either side of the route began to sway drunkenly. Mercifully, I realised that the brand new hat, sodden in the earlier stages of the march, had dried out and shrunk, constricting the blood flow to my head. So, contrary to the manual of military training, my right had ceased its rhythmic swing and, mounting higher, removed the offending item of dress (with some difficulty), and placed it lightly back on top again before resuming its metronomic movement.

Slowly, the buildings ceased their gyrations and stood rigidly to attention; a crisis had so narrowly been avoided. Had I fainted, I would probably not have received the Coronation Medal!

After Her Majesty had been returned safely to the Palace, the columns marched back to their respective temporary barracks. Half way up Constitution Hill, another chaplain ran into difficulties. His new trousers had shrunk badly: the braces had presumably been drawn too tightly. This had resulted in severe chafing of the legs and crutch. Fortunately, with support from his companions on either side, he completed the course, but was ill for some days afterwards.

Thus ended a day I can never forget.

Vivienne became involved in an incident which took place at Bagshot Park on the 10th of May, 1957, when H.R.H. The Princess Royal came down to unveil the Chaplains' Memorial Window in the Chapel. All went well during the service. The pre-lunch gathering, too, was going with a swing when suddenly a rather worried-looking D.C.G. (Lloyd Evans) came up and whispered,

"Vivienne, a major crisis has blown up in the kitchen, and the lunch will be twenty minutes to half an hour late. For God's sake come and cope with the Princess Royal. Tell her fairy stories, or do a song and dance, or anything else you like, but for Heaven's sake, keep her happy for the next half hour!''

Poor Vivienne! But, resourceful as ever, she went into the 'Royal Presence' and found the task surprisingly easy, with china and gardens amongst the subjects of interest to Her Royal Highness.

Another 'occasion' took place on St. John's Day (27th December) 1960, when the recently-retired Chaplain General (Victor Pike) was to be consecrated in Southwark Cathedral as Bishop of Sherborne. Eighteen chaplains, six from each of the three Services, were detailed to robe. We were all in the Canons' Vestry, fully apparelled, when the Provost (George Reindorf, later Bishop of Guildford) came in and having wished us good morning said,

''And now, gentlemen, we are ready to start; so please sort yourselves out for the procession, in your correct order of precedence, known only to God and yourselves!''

Most of us were greatly amused, but certain of the 'top brass' disapproved of what they felt was unseemly levity.

Envoy

Despite being fully occupied, both as Rector of Donnington and Dymock, and Rural Dean of the large North Forest Rural Deanery, the break with the T.A. and Army life, after twenty-three years, was quite an experience, and one which even Vivienne could not fully appreciate. Thus it was with very great pleasure (and astonishment) that some time later, a letter and card arrived from the Headquarters of the Gloucestershire Regiment saying that I had been made an Honorary Life Member of the Gloucestershire Regimental Association, with membership Number 0/1187. This was a most generous gesture, and has resulted in my being in touch, from time to time, with men with whom I had spent many happy as well as difficult and dangerous days. The regimental padré had become, in a way that had not been in the past, a Regimental Member. It was to me a very great honour.

At one of our meetings, I thought of King Henry's speech before Agincourt, and on the back of an envelope updated it ('doggerelised it' would, perhaps, be a better description) thus:

> Old men forget; yet all shall be forgot,
> But he'll remember with advantages

What feats he did of yore. Then shall those names,
Familiar in his mouth as household words,—
George and Elizabeth, Wavell and Gort,
Horrocks and Thomas, Montgomery and Gloucester
Be in their cups freely remembered;

Henry V, act IV, Scene III
(with apologies to William Shakespeare.)

Notes

1. I do not include the memorial service in the Normandy orchard after our tragic landing, because the D.C.G. (Freddie Hughes) preached and the A.C.G. (John Steele) took most of the service. To a considerable degree, and in a very real sense, I was one of the 'mourners'.

ADDENDUM

Normandy '84

On the 20th September, 1952, at Wynyards Gap in Dorset, I dedicated the second of the three 43rd (Wessex) Divisional War Memorials. The Dorset Regimental Asociation, thence forward at set intervals, held a service at that monument, and invited me to take many, if not all of them, with the assistance of the local clergy.

In 1982, the service was of special importance, for the Dorsets had invited over on a friendship visit the Mayors of several of the towns and villages with whom they had an intimate relationship, such as Bayeux, the first French city to be freed, and with whom Dorchester had been twinned. Thus the Mayor of Bayeux, M. Charpontier, was the Guest of Honour in 1982.

It was at this time, I suppose, that the Dorset Regimental Association decided to take an official part in the proposed '*Normandy '84*' commemoration. I was delighted to receive in August 1982 an invitation from Brigadier A.E.C. Bredin, D.S.O., M.C., D.L., to join their party as their unit padré.

On Sunday, June 3rd 1984, the Regimental party of perhaps a hundred crossed to France. The Brigadier, however, remained in Portsmouth on duty with H.M. The Queen Mother at the Cathedral, and later, with the Mayor of Bayeux, attended a reception on board the Royal Yacht Brittania.

Monday and Tuesday (4th/5th) were mostly spent settling in and making preliminary recess for the events on our official programme which began on the 6th, 'D-Day'.

'D-Day' dawned fine, and the 1st Dorsets were early on parade at the beaches where they had come ashore forty years previously. At 11 a.m., all members of our Association, including wives, attended a reception given for the Dorsets by the Mayor of Bayeux at the Town Hall. It was a memorable—and moving—occasion. After speeches by local dignitaries, the Mayor presented the Brigadier with the large, specially-struck Bayeux Liberation Medallion, and all veterans of the early campaign (I had never previously thought of myself as a 'veteran'!) received a smaller replica. It is a memento that I greatly treasure. The *Vin D'Honneur*, which followed, was a convivial occasion. The French had invited some members of the French and Dutch resistance groups who had worked with us. This was a greatly appreciated gesture.

After lunch, many attended the ceremony at the British Cemetery.

The Queen's visit was blessed with magnificent weather. The only chaplains taking part were the Chaplain General of the British Army, his deputy (both resplendent in their scarlet cassocks) and the Senior Roman Catholic Chaplain. It interested and pleased me to see Her Majesty receive the French President and invite him to inspect the Guard of Honour—the cemetery is, technically, British soil, so Her Majesty was the hostess on this occasion.

That evening, some eight hundred British Veterans marched past Her Majesty at Arromanches, and an A.D.C. was heard to say, as the Dorsets passed, "Well done, Speedy!"—the Brigadier's nick-name.

The 7th began with a commemorative service at the Monument of Liberation at Bayeux. The massed bands of the Ontario Teen Marching Band (Canada) and the U.S. Air Force in Europe Band—perhaps 250 to 275 instruments in all—provided the music. Wreaths were laid by the Mayor, Brigadier Bredin, and an American officer (because of the Bands' presence, maybe) and various high military and political figures. The four Colours of the Dorsets and eight French Colours were lowered and raised scores of times while the wreaths were laid, and the Last Post and Réveille (British and French) sounded, and following also, the playing of nine or ten National Anthems. These last ended with the Polish Anthem.

We then went directly to the British Military Cemetery, led by the marching bands who were to provide the music.

The Mayor of Bayeux led the participants and, as at the Monument of Liberation, a vast concourse of many nationalities poured into the cemetery. The Brigadier was accompanied by three French Generals and the Mayor by several politicians, while the clergy party included the Bishop of Bayeux, the Bishop of Plymouth, and myself. A Canon of Bayeux Cathedral acted as *Major Domo*. When I was called forward for the main prayers, I had been on my feet in blistering heat for more than two hours. This physical strain, added to the considerable mental reaction (in front of me in the distance was the monument on which were inscribed the names of 168 of my men who had died in the landing, but who have no known graves) resulted in a shaking of the muscles in my thighs and calves which was most disconcerting. However, all went well. The City gave a *Vin d'Honneur* and lunch for the Dorset party.

That evening, a Mass of Reconciliation took place in the Cathedral. This was a massive gathering headed by four French Bishops, one German, and the Bishop of London. It was a moving ceremony, and lasted for two hours and ten minutes.

Friday saw the beginning of what might be termed the commemoration of the build-up and struggle for Hill 112, in which the Dorsets and the 43rd Wessex Division (which had included the 4th and 5th Dorsets) had played a major and costly rôle. This part of the programme had also as an important aspect the fraternisation with the local people, many of whom were old friends.

After the initial landings and lodgement areas had been established, and Caen had been more or less neutralised, the next, and indeed the most vital, feature which had to be taken before any break-out by the 21 Army Group could be attempted, was Hill 112, of which the Germans said, '*He who holds 112, holds Normandy*'. Their vast expenditure of men and materials thrown into its defence and retention, demonstrated their conviction of its supreme importance.

The battle for 112 had begun in earnest on 10th July, and ended in final British victory on the 24th. There were three phases: July 10th/11th, the first and very costly British attack and equally furious German counter-attack, followed by the period of consolidation and building up, and the second all-out assault and hoped-for capture of Hill 112. This latter took place between the 19th and 24th. All these phases were covered in our programme for the 8th and 9th of June, 1984.

Early on the 10th of July 1944, the Dorsets had fought their way into Eterville on the lower slopes of Hill 112. Their losses were heavy but they had held their ground. On this 8th of June, a plaque was unveiled in the village square, commemorating the liberation of the village, and expressing the deep gratitude of its people to the Dorsets. The Mayor, at some length and with deep feeling, spoke of their suffering under occupation, the unforgettable joy of liberation, and the profound gratitude and admiration they felt for Britain 'who had stood alone' when France capitulated (and he did not mince his words) and fulfilled the promise to return and free France, and in doing so, had accepted appalling sacrifices. Their special gratitude, of course, was extended to the Dorsets who, at great cost, had given them back their freedom and, equally important, their self-respect. The schoolchildren were on parade, and placed flowers beneath the plaque. One child, who had obviously been told of the horrifying slaughter of our men, on seeing so many veterans on parade, said;

"Oh, so they were not *all* killed?"

A local band, who had been allotted to us for the day and had their own transport, were both enthusiastic and excellent, while an appointed *Major Domo* efficiently ran this and the other engagements. A great tribute must also be paid to the police. Their police van and several *gendarmes* escorted our convoy of buses and private cars on both days, diverting or holding up traffic when necessary. They were magnificent, and cheerful.

During those long speeches at Eterville, when they dwelt upon our appalling losses, I thought back to another sector not very far distant when, at a forward dressing station, to which I had been attached for this operation, eighteen hundred wounded had passed through our hands in forty-eight hours—at dawn on the 11th, I buried nearly fifty, including several of our own staff, and when the German counter-attack was at its height, we were told to be prepared to be over-run in the next hour.

I have expanded upon this first commemoration on Hill 112 because it set the pattern for much which followed; long speeches, National Anthems, Last Post, Réveille, and the Brigadier having to respond in French very frequently.

At 12.45, there was a municipal reception and a *Vin d'Honneur* at Château Maltôt, when the local villages clubbed together to say an official 'thank you' to the Dorsets.

At 3.00, a combined ceremony was held at Cheux British Military Cemetery; there are over forty British Military Cemeteries in Normandy alone. The local Resistance and French Forces paraded, and the local parish priest, fully apparelled, welcomed us, while the Major Domo kept everything moving and in order.

The next ceremony (which was intended to be brief) was at the 43rd Divisional Memorial on the crest of that battle-torn feature, Hill 112. Here, the French pulled out all the stops, for they knew well its vital importance and the devastating carnage which had taken place there in July 1944. High-powered parliamentary, military and local dignitaries were present, and each felt entitled to a voice. For over an hour, speech followed speech, while we stood bare-headed in ranks, again in blistering sunshine and with no shade, and the hundreds of relations and spectators also suffered. After each speech the band played the British and French National Anthems, and frequently the Last Post and Réveille. These preliminaries completed, the Major Domo led me, an ex-chaplain of the 43rd Division, to the rostrum and handed me a microphone for the main prayers. Halfway through, my thoughts flew back to July 1944, and I suddenly realised that the granite block behind me symbolised the sacrifice of men with whom I had prayed, to whom I had given Communion, with whom (in some cases) I had lived for nearly five years before that holocaust, men whom I had buried, friends of mine in the fullest sense, and to whose wives I had written. The horror of it all, and the stark tragedy, almost broke me when I turned and commended my comarades to God's care and keeping. The two French priests followed.

A two-kilometre march, led by the band, brought us to Fontaîne-Etoupefour, where the monument to the 5th Dorsets had been erected. This ceremony completed, our large party had time to pause and ponder, and this was necessary, and especially for the Brigadier who had to respond in French to almost every speech.

During this interval, Vivienne and I discussed these many long and largely repetitive speeches and occasionally their translation. We came to the conclusion (a correct one, I feel sure) that these Normans wished us to appreciate fully their tremendous gratitude to the British forces who had liberated them and given them back not only their freedom, but their dignity. To this end they had told us of the numbness following capitulation and the horrors, degradation and suppressions of occupation. They did this to try and make us understand some little of their sufferings, not to curry sympathy, but to help us understand the true depth of the gratitude, both for their restored freedom and dignity and for the fact that they had lived in peace for the last forty years. There was no trace of passivism, nor of militarism, but a firm determination to work, shoulder to shoulder with other nations, for permanent world peace. This may well have been behind the parading of the children at every ceremony, and the placing of their flowers at each grave, monument or plaque.

That evening, the 'region' gave a dinner in honour of the Dorsets, their liberators, when the locals, the Résistance and our party ate, drank and danced together.

The second 'Dorset Villages' day followed the pattern of the first. It began with a short, but impressive and symbolic service at Norrey Church. Again, a band was with us for the whole day. M. le Curé of the previous day, who must have been the Rural Dean, took charge. From Norrey, we moved to Loucelles, where a plaque to the 1st Dorsets was unveiled by the Mayor, and a civic reception followed. A French War Memorial was honoured at Lingevres, and the Dorsets' memorial at Hottôt-les-Bagues, and the British Military Cemetery there, were visited. There I found the grave of the Revd. Francis Musgrave who joined the 43rd Division on the 25th July 1944 as a replacement, and who was killed on August the 2nd—one of the three Divisional chaplains killed within ten days during the advance from Jerusalem crossroads to the last Normandy strong point, Mont Pinçon.

The Dorsets' final engagements were centred on Tilly-sûr-Seulles on the 9th of June. The cemetery attracted a very large gathering of French and British, and this final service of the Dorsets' pilgrimage (1st, 4th and 5th Battalions) was a fitting conclusion of Remembrance.

After the service, the Battle of Tilly War Museum was visited, a *Vin d'Honneur* attended, and at about 9.30 p.m. we sat down to a fine buffet—our farewell meal together.

In conclusion, I will make several points.

Firstly, I am most grateful to the Dorsets for inviting me to be their unit padré for that memorable week, a week which began for the 1st Battalion on the beach code named 'Jig' near Arromanches; also for the privilege of taking part in the many ceremonies which followed on the 6th to the 9th in Bayeux and on or around Hill 112. During those last four days, one began to appreciate the feelings of the stubborn Norman people who had suffered more than most during the periods of occupation and liberation.

Secondly, I was profoundly thankful that Britain had not been occupied, and that our families had not suffered the indignities, privations and humiliations that the people of Calvados, and other areas of Normandy too, had experienced.

Thirdly, the tragic loss of friends and relations was felt by all, and I was almost ashamedly grateful that, by the grace of God, I had survived, hopefully to have done some little good during the forty years which had been given me.

I would also like to thank not only Brigadier Bredin who invited me, but the whole Dorset Regimental Association membership and their wives, who accepted me and my wife, though not a Dorset, but as one who experienced with them that bitter struggle for Hill 112 from 10th/11th July and again in the long final phase which ended on the 24th.

Please God such slaughter will never happen again.

Finally, I wish to express my sincere thanks to the people of Normandy, and especially the Mayor, Bishop and Citizens of Bayeux – a city to which (because of an event in June 1944) I make a pilgrimage almost every year—who planned our programme and showered upon us such friendship and hospitality.

My grateful thanks go out equally to all people of the area on and around Hill 112—indeed to all mentioned in this personal record of the 3rd to the 10th of June 1984. They were kind and generous, and their friendship was greatly appreciated.

Grand Merci!

J.E. Gethyn-Jones
former Padré to the 43rd Recce Regiment
(the Gloucestershire Regiment)

Glossary of Abbreviations

2.I.C.	Second in Command
A.B.64	Army Book 64: Soldier's service and pay record
A.D.M.S.	Assistant Director of Medical Services
A.D.C.	Aide de Camp
A.Q.	Adjutant & Quartermaster (General's Department)
A.S.R.	Air Sea Rescue
A.T.S.	Auxiliary Territorial Service
B.G.S.	Brigadier, General Staff
C.C.S.	Casualty Clearing Station
C.M.P.	Corps of Military Police
C.O.	Commanding Officer
D.A.C.G.	Deputy Assistant Chaplain-General
D.C.G.	Deputy Chaplain-General
D.C.L.I.	Duke of Cornwall's Light Infantry
D.M.S.	Director of Medical Services
D.O.	Direct Order
Don R, or D.R.	Despatch Rider
E.N.S.A.	Entertainment National Services Association
F.A.N.Y.	Female Auxiliary Nursing Yeomanry
G.1098	Standard issue of equipment to all soldiers
G.H.Q.	General Headquarters
H.Q.	Headquarters
I.W.G.C.	Imperial War Graves Commission
K.R.R.C.	King's Royal Rifle Corps
L.A.C.	Light Armoured Car
L.D.V.	Local Defence Volunteers
M.G.B.	Motor Gun Boat
M.I.Room	Medical Inspection Room
M.M.	Military Medal
M.O.	Medical Officer

M.T.B.	Motor Torpedo Boat
M.T.O.	Motor Transport Officer
N.C.O.	Non-commissioned Officer
O.C.	Officer Commanding
O.C.F.	Officiating Chaplain to the Forces
O.R.	Other Ranks
P.S.I.	Physical Sergeant Instructor
P.T.	Physical Training
P.U.	Public Utility
Q.M.	Quartermaster
R.A.Ch.D.	Royal Army Chaplains' Department
R.E.M.E.	Royal Electrical and Mechanical Engineers
R.H.Q.	Regimental Headquarters
R.H.U.	Regimental Holding Unit
R.Q.M.S.	Regimental Quartermaster-Sergeant
R.M.O.	Regimental Medical Officer
R.S.M.	Regimental Sergeant Major
R.T.O.	Regimental Transport Officer
S.C.F.	Senior Chaplain of the Forces
S.L.I.	Somerset Light Infantry
S.S.M.	Squadron Sergeant-Major
T.A.	Territorial Army
T.A.R.O.	Territorial Army Reserve of Officers
V.E. Day	Victory in Europe Day